D0733577

A WOMAN'S
JOURNEY
TO GOD

A WOMAN'S JOURNEY TO GOD

Finding the Feminine Path

JOAN BORYSENKO

Riverhead Books

a member of Penguin Putnam Inc.

New York

1999

Riverhead Books
a member of
Penguin Putnam Inc.
375 Hudson Street
New York, NY 10014

"Together" by Kuan Yin, from *Kuan Yin*
by Palmer, Ramsay, Kwok. Reprinted by permission
of HarperCollins Publishers Ltd.

Library of Congress Cataloging-in-Publication Data

Borysenko, Joan.
A woman's journey to God : finding the feminine path /
Joan Borysenko.
p.   cm.
ISBN 1-57322-144-9
1. Women—Religious life.   2. Spiritual life.   I. Title.
BL625.7.B67   1999   99-40416 CIP
291.4'4'082—dc21

Printed in the United States of America

1   3   5   7   9   10   8   6   4   2

This book is printed on acid-free paper. ∞

Book design by Chris Welch

To my retreat partners:

Elizabeth Lawrence, priestess and healer
Jan Maier, mystical weaver of song
Janet Quinn, patron saint of relationship

CONTENTS

THE POWER OF BEAR

Reflections on a Path of Our Own

Caroline, Beth, and I walked through the lush, expansive meadows in back of Caroline's house, a massive-timbered log home set high on the mountain in our little town of Gold Hill. We could see ranges of purple peaks, snowcapped and majestic in the distance. A mountain spring bubbled at our feet, just to the side of the small, rocky footpath that people and animals share. The earth beneath our feet was dry and sandy, arid high desert. Yet a carpet of wildflowers rioted around us—columbine and Indian paintbrush, chamomile and purple loosestrife—taking advantage of a short but potent summer season. And as the locals will tell you, there are only two seasons in these mountains, July and winter.

It was early in the afternoon of a perfect summer day, the sky that heartbreaking shade of azure characteristic of the Rockies. The nearness of the endless blue expanse made us want to cry with the unexpected beauty of it all. The warm sun heated beds of sage and released the clean scent of earth to the sky. We each tucked a sprig of sage behind one ear, washed our faces with it, smelled our scented hands. The wind caressed us with a gentle breeze. Earth time seemed to stop and eternal time to begin. Our conversation was deep and wise, slow and steady. Cradled in the arms of the earth mother, we shared the changes in our lives and the longings in our hearts. The paths we take home to our deepest selves—to love, to work, to God—opened before us as we spoke.

THE POWER OF BEAR

We were just a tiny bit afraid of bears, Caroline and I. We knew they were here, lurking just out of sight. My husband, Kurt, and his son, Christian, had met up with one on this same trail just the week before. And a bear had recently broken into my assistant, Judy's, car to savor a jar of Coffee-mate. The meal complete, she sat on the roof of the car, licking her chops. Will the insurance pay for the bear dents in the roof? For the broken window and paw prints on the upholstery? Is this an act of God or an act of vandalism? Can the bear be sent to jail?

We told these stories to our friend Beth who lives in the suburbs of Maryland where bears are rare. She was not worried. She expected that our three large dogs would protect us. I did, too. And although I knew that bears could be dangerous, I felt disappointed that we probably would not see one rising up on her hind legs to shield the cubs she had borne during the winter's hibernation.

How clever the she-bear. She goes into winter retreat and has a long, restful Sabbath. She sleeps through the really uncomfortable, cumbersome part of her pregnancy. She comes out renewed with her cubs, who have found their way into the world at winter's end. The bear is mythologically feminine. The name of the Greek goddess Artemis, the huntress, means "bear." She embodies the wisdom of the wild. She symbolizes the intuitive that relies on its own inner experience rather than patterning itself on the experience of others. The bear walks on a path of her own. She dares to question. And she dares to believe. She fights for her children. She is brave and strong, maternal and defiant. She is a wily survivor. She is also a strong genuine archetype for me.

I once had a dream about the feminine. I am riding in a truck with a man who has twin toddlers, a boy and a girl. He tells me that the boy is a joy, he does everything according to the books. But the girl is a little terror. She has a mind of her own and is temperamental and unmanageable. As we speak, the little girl climbs onto the back of the truck and begins to dance. We hit a bump and she flies off, falling into a hole in the ground. We stop the truck and the father comments that she has gotten what she deserves. I look down into the hole, which opens into a large cavern. She is inside, unhurt. It takes me a full day to dig down to her. When I reach her she is exuberant and unafraid. Still dancing.

Women's spirituality is as wild and free as that little girl. It is natural, earthy, relational, mystical, embodied, intuitive, sensuous, and compassionate. Slowly but surely, women's poems, psalms, songs, and liturgy are being written and prayed, sung and danced in a way of our own, suitable to a path of our own. We are digging back down to ourselves.

Like the she-bear, we need Sabbath. Most religions include one—Jews on Friday evening to Saturday evening, Christians on Sunday, Hindus on Tuesday, Muslims on Friday. Some American Indian tribes celebrate Sabbath on the day of the week that follows winter solstice, the New Year. Whether our Sabbath is a day or an hour, a prayer, a breath, or a meditation, we relax for a time and listen in the stillness for the inner voice. In the quiet our intuition rises, sniffing the winds like a curious cat. These are the times when we are awake enough, alert enough, present enough to see the path as it opens before us, as Caroline, Beth, and I did on a sage-soaked summer day. For the truth is, no one has ever walked our path before.

The spirituality that we three shared as friends was essentially feminine, if unspoken. The intimacy of our conversation, the deep rest provided by nature, and the oldest women's ritual of all—sharing our stories—reminded us that God is everywhere. The Divine shone in every bush and tree, in the sounds of birds and the sound of silence, and especially within one another. The ease of our connection to God during that walk, and to the certainty that we are cocreators whose choices affect the natural order, was so simple that it easily could have been missed. The most important things tend to be invisible, after all, like oxygen to a land creature or water to a fish.

The invisible ease and steadiness of the feminine path stand in sharp contrast to the angst that many women have over the journey to God. Many of us are religious dropouts. Others are loyal to our religion of origin but get little in the way of spirituality from it. Some of us are so angry at religious institutions, or at an image of God that cannot possibly reflect who we are, that we have shut our eyes to the feast that is always laid before us.

Imagine a woman standing in the back of a church. She is so thirsty to drink the waters of Spirit that her legs can hardly support her. God speaks in her heart, yet she cannot identify the sweetness of that inner voice over the cacophony of her own inner dialogue. She grasps the back of an old wooden pew, crafted in the days before women were welcome in any pulpit. Her sadness and anger at religions that judge, that demean women or any other group, weaken her. It seems impossible to move forward, to walk down the aisle to reach the nave.

It is my hope that this thirsty woman will drink deeply as she reads this book. That she will celebrate and heal and that, like the she-bear, she will stand on her own strong legs. As she finds her balance, she can reclaim Spirit in whatever way suits her, whether within a church or temple, or outside institutional religion. Perhaps she will even reinvent religion. The cubs we protect are so precious. They are faith born of experience, the right to worship as we please, the natural order of a fragile planet where everything is interconnected, the future of our children, and the ability to create nourishing rituals that provide strength and hope, healing and love.

You are at my side, dear friends, and God is everywhere. Yet ultimately we are alone, making our way home by the candle of the heart. The light is steady and sure but extends only far enough to see the next step. That there are steps beyond is a matter of faith. That we have the faith to endure and walk our own journey—even when we think that we are lost—is a gift of grace, and of friendship. Many times our light seems to go out. But another light, one held by a stranger or a friend, a book or a song, a blackbird or a wildflower, comes close enough so that we can see our path by its light. And in time we realize that the light we have borrowed was always also our own.

A WOMAN'S
JOURNEY
TO GOD

WE ARE ALL RELATIONS

The Household of God Is Big Enough for All

What is holy?
    That which is received.
What is holy?
    That to which we are present.

Looking into the dreamy eyes of my newborn child
    lifted from the salty ocean of the Great Mother,
    blood still pulsing in the cord that joins two hearts.

Sunning myself on a warm rock, carefree as a cloud
    snowcapped mountains reflected in the
    deep blue-black waters of a crystal lake.

Listening to a lover's lament, tears over a gentle man
    with roots as yet too shallow to drink in the
    full sun of her being without wilting in the light.

Praying at the Wailing Wall, the ghosts of ancient women
    whispering their stories into the ears of stones
    worn smooth by the slender fingers of their longing.
                                                    Joan Borysenko

A quiet awakening is under way across America as women are coming together to worship, to tell their stories and to find their place spiritually, if not always religiously, in the household of God. Women's spiritual groups are cropping up everywhere like mushrooms after a nourishing rain. Far from being some kind of New Age phenomenon, they involve women of every Christian and Jewish sect including Catholics, Mormons, Mennonites, evangelicals, and others. Buddhist, Hindu, and Muslim women also discuss the woman's way. Women of color and Hispanic women are likewise exploring their spirituality and roles in organized religion. Gay women and straight, those who consider themselves feminists and others who abhor the word, are nonetheless searching for authentic spiritual expression.

We do so organically, through the medium of sharing our stories, writing and performing songs and poems, celebrating the Divine with our bodies through dance and movement, creating rituals that celebrate the important passages of life and heal its inevitable wounds, creating egalitarian and participatory models for worship and by reaching out to others to heal social injustice, racism, and discrimination. God as a jealous, punitive white Anglo-Saxon male with a long beard and a longer arm lacks appeal for many contemporary women. This has led some to run into the arms of the Goddess and find meaning in earth-centered or neopagan rituals. It has led others to join Buddhist sanghas where there is no personified God. And it has led many more to question the relevance of their religious beliefs to the homely realities of everyday life.

For eons women have been viewed as second-class citizens by the three "religions of the Book," Judaism, Christianity, and Islam, because of Eve's act of disobedience in the Garden of Eden. It is written in Ecclesiasticus 25:24, "From a woman sin had its beginning, and because of her we all die." Many women are tired of repenting for Eve's imagined sins and are ready to reclaim the energy that has been lost to religious traditions in which the framers were singularly unconcerned either with women's spirituality or with their basic rights and gifts as human beings. Nineteenth-century women like Elizabeth Cady Stanton, editor of the controversial *Woman's Bible* that appeared at the turn of the century, fought for women's suffrage in part by stating that we would never be truly free until the theological errors underlying the discrimination against women were corrected.

Many contemporary feminist theologians are attempting to do just that. Elisabeth Schussler Fiorenza of the Harvard Divinity School has written fifteen books of scriptural exegesis and commentary from a woman's viewpoint. In a 1978 essay she wrote that "feminist spirituality proclaims wholeness, healing, love, and spiritual power not as hierarchical, as *power over*, but as power *for*, as enabling power." In the twenty years since she wrote those words, the wave of the baby boom has crested, washing up an enormous number of midlife women on the shores of wisdom with the power and motivation to create change. Women are, in fact, the backbone of a rapidly growing social movement called Cultural Creatives, 44 million strong, who are committed to healing, community, social justice, spirituality and to creating a sustainable environment. This emerging group is fascinated by other cultures and religions that can enrich our lives spiritually, increase our understanding, and help bring a new world of tolerance, respect, and care into being.

Baby boomers, now grown to the age where we wield economic clout and are in key positions of decision making, are redefining religion. An impressive survey by Wade Clark Roof, a professor of religion at the University of California, found that 42 percent of the 76 million baby boomers, one-third of the population of the United States, are religious dropouts. Another 25 percent are returnees who left their religion of origin but returned to some form of worship that felt more inclusive, more spiritual than their original church or synagogue. But many of the dropouts are also on a spiritual quest that may have led them to women's groups, yoga, depth psychology, twelve-step programs, or Eastern philosophy. Feminist theologian Mary Daly of Boston College predicted this trend in 1971, in an article written for *Commonweal* magazine in which she said, "The women's movement will present a growing threat to patriarchal religion less by attacking it than by simply leaving it behind."

Hartford Seminary professor Miriam Therese Winter is a Catholic sister, theologian, songwriter, and developer of women's liturgy. She is the coauthor of *Defecting in Place: Women Claiming Responsibility for Their Own Spiritual Lives,* along with her colleagues Adair Lummis and Allison Stokes. These women designed a study of how and why women defect from traditional religion by remaining in it and reclaiming it, developing their own more personal forms of ritual, understanding, and worship. Rather than seeking God from the outside in, which is the old religious model, women are reinventing religion by seeking God from the inside out.

A variety of women's worship circles have sprouted both within and beyond the walls of traditional religion, honoring the ritual spontaneity spoken of in *Defecting in Place.* Jewish women may celebrate together in Rosh Hodesh groups, a monthly celebration of the new moon, which many link to their menstrual cycles. Books like Rabbi Lynn Gottlieb's *She Who Dwells Within* plumb the depths of the feminine face of God in Judaism, the Shekhina, and give elegant and moving advice for celebrating the Sabbath, Rosh Hodesh, and other women-centered rituals. In *Four Centuries of Jewish Women's Spirituality,* there are many stories of women's ritual relevant to the emotional concerns of daily living, created by friends for other friends outside the bounds of the synagogue.

E. M. Broner writes of sitting shivah for a lost love, shivah being

a week of ritual mourning for the dead. But even though this ritual is called a shivah, Broner describes a practical, heartfelt outpouring of friendship and healing that women of any faith can
relate to. She tells of a friend with a broken heart, whose coloring
has changed to "boiled red," because she cannot stop weeping. Her
sixty-three-year-old lover of nine years has taken up with a young
woman of twenty-three. On the day of his marriage to this young
woman, a circle of friends gather, bringing only a tape recorder and
a cooked chicken.

Taking turns talking into the machine, they "correct" their
friend's memory and remind her of her own intrinsic wholeness. It
is a holy circle, a sacred circle. They "acknowledge amputation, separation as part of life." They cook and eat together, talking of everyday things. Life goes on. They toast the wholeness of the friend.
They embrace her and let their tears wash her clean. Finally they
cut a black armband for the friend to wear while she grieves, stipulating a period of mourning, and a time to end it. Women from all
religious traditions crave person-to-person ritual relevant to the
problems and celebrations of everyday life. One of the difficulties
with organized religions is that there is so little of this kind of
connecting.

Women are intrinsically mystical, that is, we tend to experience
direct connection with the Divine. This may occur not only during
formal worship, prayer, or meditation but any time. Women often
report a deep sense of connection to God as part of friendship, or
mothering. We see the God in others. Finding God by adhering to
specific rules and regulations, plans and paths, priests and mediators is not a necessary component of the woman's journey. For
women there really is no journey. Life and spirituality are one and
the same.

Another problem that women experience with traditional worship is the lack of inclusive language when referring to God. If you are not white and male, God cannot be an adequate mirror of who you are, of who your ancestors are, of the diversity of creation. Nelle Morton gave a lecture at Harvard Divinity School in 1973 in which she set up a "thought experiment" to raise male consciousness of how women feel in a world where language reflects only one gender. She asked the audience to imagine that they were a lone male divinity student in a classroom of women in a completely feminine institution where you are expected to understand that feminine words are meant to apply equally to both women and men.

How would you feel if, "every time a professor says 'womankind' she means, of course, 'all humanity'? When one enrolls in a seminar on 'The Doctrine of Woman' the professor intends at least to deal with men also. When one sings of the Motherhood of God and the Sisterhood of Woman, one breathes a prayer that all men as well as women will come to experience true sisterhood."

I do admit to enjoying referring to God as Her, or the Mother sometimes, though, simply to make the point that this terminology is just as reasonable as viewing God as male and a Father, and that at times Motherhood is what speaks most deeply to my soul and provides needed comfort and familiarity. But as true mystics of any religion experience, God is beyond gender, a strange and paradoxical mystery that is big enough to contain the world in all its beauty and ugliness, cruelty and grace.

In Sara Maitland's beautifully written spiritual odyssey, *A Big Enough God*, she writes of her journey as a feminist who grew up in a lukewarm Presbyterian upbringing that "simply slipped off" without any anger or angst. She became an Anglican (Episcopalian) and finally a Roman Catholic who moves with remarkable ease in that patriarchal structure because of her respect for the ultimate mystery of God.

She writes, "The self, myself, while wrestling with these issues was also—in my own writing, in my own praying, in my own loving—more and more encountering a strange and enormous God. A God who reflected back to me always a tension between beauty and suffering; between joy and sinfulness; between past and future; between the individual and the community. . . . More and more I found that I do not base such frail faith as I have on the feeling of 'what a friend I have in Jesus' but rather on the continual inescapable sense of the power and the mystery and the danger and the profligacy of it all. I mean *all*, from the bizarre goings-on inside each atom, right through to the social complexity of history and class and gender and race and individual experience." This Christian feminist writer is able to balance her radical nature with orthodox religious structure because she feels that it gives her ballast, prevents her from collapsing into chaos.

Going through menarche, infertility, stillbirth, cesarean sections, normal births, the decision not to bear children, the loss of a child, menopause—these are women's mysteries and passages that are intimately related to our spiritual lives, and for which we seek meaningful ritual to celebrate, to find strength, and to mourn. Rituals such as these are exactly what are missing in biblical Scripture, written by men for men. Scripture, moreover, is concerned largely with public life rather than the details of private life, so little is known about the role of women. Only 151 of 1,400 people who are referred to by name in the Hebrew Bible, and proportionately about twice that number named in the New Testament, are women. These numbers testify to the small attention paid to us, to our daily lives, forms of worship, hopes, and dreams.

Theological scholarship is one face of the women's spiritual movement. Contemporary women's personal experiences of God are another. One of the problems that many women report is that they are just too busy to have much of a spiritual life. The daily tasks of living, particularly for those women who are working mothers, are exhausting. At the end of a long day there just isn't time left for the soul. One of the 3,746 respondents to a survey on Christian women's spirituality reported on in *Defecting in Place* said, "This survey made me realize how little time I have devoted in the past year to my spiritual growth. But that is because I have a ten-month-old daughter, and I tend to believe that God the Mother regards the care of babies as an act of worship in itself."

For many years I have been intimately involved in facilitating or cofacilitating women's spiritual retreats for dropouts, returnees, and loyalists who have managed to find nurture in whatever their religious orientation of childhood might have been. Protestant, Catholic, Jewish, Unitarian, Christian Scientist, Wiccan, and Muslim women have come together at these retreats to celebrate commonalities in women's spiritual experience. The retreats have had formats as different as the creation of ritual, celebratory liturgy, and occasions of deep healing, to an exploration of spirituality as it evolves through the feminine life cycle, to weekends of silent, centering prayer and humor. Central to each has been the act of women sharing their stories, not in any contrived way but as women do when the occasion presents itself. We talk over breakfast, in pajamas, in the bathroom, out on walks. The stories unfold, often surprising the speaker as well as the listener. The hidden reaches of the heart become accessible as words are received by a compassionate listener. Where there once were two, there is a wiser one.

Rabbi Nachman, the grandson of the Baal Shem Tov who founded mystical Judaism, said that if you wanted to find the Shekhina, the Divine Feminine, then you should go to the place where the women tell stories. Women's spirituality, after all, is less about the hereafter than the here and now. It is embodied and earthy, relying on personal experience versus abstract theology and the validation of that experience by sharing our stories. Women's spirituality can be summarized as relational, active, emotional, mystical, imaginative, creative, practical, positively concerned with the healing of the world, body centered, sensuous, given to spontaneous acts of ritual and worship, based on a sense of inner divine authority, composed of a diversity of images of God, tolerant of other religious traditions, and rooted in the everyday practicalities of living.

Women who love God as Father, those who love God as Mother, and others who couldn't give a hoot about God's theoretical gender or existence, find themselves sisters on the journey. Beyond our religion or lack of it, beyond the warm fuzzies or cold scars that ideas about God have planted in our minds, the unmistakable perfume of divine belonging envelops us as we come together as friends.

Coming together as friends in religious contexts requires respect for forms of worship different than our own. These differences keep heart and mind open. They are soul food. If we are to find a path of our own, it helps to know and appreciate the paths of others. To realize that the household of God is indeed big enough for all gives everyone room to live and grow. The idea that there is only one right way home, one path for all, creates judgment and separation. Women's spirituality is about connectedness.

My former housekeeper, "Rebecca," became a born-again Christian. I watched her faith bloom. She looked wonderful, suffused by Spirit and the excitement of the journey. I loved reading Scripture with her. Unfortunately, our conversations soon became strained. While I respected her path, she was sure that Jews like me would burn in hell. From her strong faith she tried to save me, convert me. She prayed for my soul. But we couldn't find common ground. We couldn't pray together. After a while I made sure to be out when Rebecca came to our home. The house of her God was not large enough to contain me as I was.

In the chapters that follow we will take a journey together that stretches the mind and heart. One hopes the journey will make us big enough to appreciate God as Mother or Father, Divine Beloved or Infinite Mystery, Friend or Guide, personified or as consciousness itself rather than deity. We will begin by exploring the nature of faith. While I have many fortunate friends who don't need miracles to have faith, the same has not been true for me. I'm like the doubting Thomas who had to thrust my hand into the wound on Jesus' side to believe that He had returned from the dead. Perhaps you will be able to relate to my own miracle story of finding faith.

We will go on to explore the ways in which religion and spirituality are different, and how we can find our spiritual path even if we have left the religion of our childhood behind. In Chapter Three intuition is explored as the inner voice of the Divine, and contrasted with reason to differentiate the masculine and feminine paths to God. Regardless of gender, all of us have both a male and a female aspect. Both intuition and reason are part of every person's journey to God. But, for women, the intuitive is almost always a reliable guide along the way. Chapter Four invites you to appreciate the way that you image God, whether as Father, Mother, Mother-Father, or Other.

In Chapter Five we'll explore and celebrate intimacy, sensuality, and sexuality. Our warm, soft bodies, alive with sensate awareness, beckon us into a world of deep empathy and attentiveness. While long a taboo in most religions, both sensuality and sexuality are an important part of the woman's way. Even the thirteenth-century celibate Christian mystic Mechtild of Magdeburg related to God as a lover. Her writing is quintessentially sensual as well as sexual, bringing God into the most personal sphere of life.

After we've explored the psychological intimacy of friendship, we will turn our attention to the heroine's journey. The hero's journey is a solo adventure of becoming oneself by separating from the community, slaying the dragon, and returning with new wisdom.

But the heroine is different. Just as women mature psychologically by developing a sense of self in relation to others, we develop spiritually in relation as well. The ancient myth of the descent of Inanna to the Underworld is the archetype we will study to find the thread of the relational feminine path that lies hidden in myth and Scripture. We will continue to search for the hidden thread in Chapter Nine, reclaiming Eve from her role of ultimate sinner and appreciating the seminal role of Mary Magdalene in the life of Jesus.

As we continue to follow the thread of feminine spirituality through ancient labyrinths, we will come face-to-face with our power, the power of the she-bear. The energy that may have been tied up in old religious wounds will become freed to speed us on our way. That accomplished, the question remains, "How can we find our own path within the feminine way?" Considering ritual and prayer, as well as the conflicts and synergies between doing and being, what we do versus who we are, our authentic soul voice can emerge. Appreciating both the hero's and the heroine's journey, the balance of female and male in ourselves, our religions and the world, women can come home to themselves, to communities of worship, and to God.

A SPIRITUAL PILGRIMAGE

The Renewal of Faith

There is little use talking about a journey home to God if one is an atheist. Rare creatures these. Gallup polls indicate that only 5 percent of the United States population lacks a belief in God. Yet even for believers, faith is a complex palette. We may believe in a personified deity or one that is more abstract. Our faith may reside in a God somewhere out there, a transcendent force. Or we may orient to a God who dwells within, immanent in all creation. Our God may be omniscient and omnipotent, the Creator of a divine plan to which our duty is to surrender. May Thy will be my will. Or perhaps our duty, what Eastern religions call our dharma, or path, is more cocreative.

As we grow and change, tasting the bittersweet realities of life, our faith is likely to change as well. Faith in the God of childhood ripens with the challenges of life. Both victory and defeat temper faith, as do wisdom and love. Along the way it is healthy to undergo periods of questioning and reevaluation. Have we arrived at our own faith and our own path or simply internalized the beliefs of parents, clergy, spouse, or friends? Do our beliefs nourish us and give us the strength and guidance to be better people? Does our faith inspire us to serve life and to make a difference in the world, or is it based on the narcissistic hope that a Santa Claus God will fulfill our wish list if we are good?

Like the moon, faith can wax and wane as the events of life call our theology into question. A friend of mine named "Angela," who is a Methodist minister, underwent a crisis of faith when her four-year-old daughter, Jennifer, died of meningitis. She wondered how a loving God could allow such a beautiful child to die. It took several years for Angela to work through some of the vexing spiritual riddles that the death of a child can pose. How can a beneficent deity allow tragedy? Is it true that the sins of the parents are visited on the children? Was her daughter's death Angela's fault? Is there some larger divine plan in which Jennifer's death might make sense? If so, are we pawns of an omnipotent deity, or is there free will? What about karma and reincarnation?

Angela took a year off from the ministry to grieve and to live along into these questions—questions that we often puzzled about together, questions that are impossible to answer. When Angela returned to the pulpit, she began,

"I'm angry at God for Jennifer's death. But at least I still think there is a God, although I understand less than ever what God is. In a way you could say that I've lost faith. But what I've really lost is a simple, childish, black-and-white faith. I've always known that the guys in the white hats don't always win. But I'd never experienced that fact so personally before.

"There's more room for mystery in my life since Jennifer passed over. I have faith that some greater Mystery exists. I have faith that, as St. Paul wrote, now we see but through a glass darkly. Someday we'll see face-to-face. I believe that someday I'll see Jennifer face-to-face again. Hold her and hug her and hear all about her life in the Spirit World. I have faith that then I'll understand why she died. Now I don't understand. Maybe my anger at God is not just about taking my beautiful child but also about being so mute and opaque. I want to know things that we mortals cannot know. And I have to renew my faith and go on with my life in spite of the not knowing. Perhaps that is the only true definition of faith. The belief in a fair and loving Universe despite the overwhelming evidence to the contrary."

Emily Dickinson wrote about faith as a fragile thing, a winged thing. Like a thin diaphanous membrane, it changes the color of the world. Under the spell of faith the ordinary shimmers. The mundane becomes miraculous. The daily sunrise and sunset are a call to celebration. The seasons in their majestic turning, a succession of holy days. Every face holds the possibility of love, and strangers are just friends whom we don't yet know.

With faith, even pain like Angela's can hold the promise of new possibility. Grief and heartbreak can become challenges for the soul to grow, imbued with meaning and even nobility. But when faith flies away, its rosy wings gathering the morning light before it, the world turns pallid and sullen. When God moves out of center stage, we move into the spotlight. And we are jealous actors, imagining that the world revolves around our wants and don't-wants. The pettiness of desire turns even triumph into dust in our mouths, because whatever we have is never enough.

Periodically coming to grips with our faithlessness, and the strength of our ego, is part of the journey to God. We don't have to face a crisis like Angela's to find that we are in a questioning period. Whenever we realize that God has moved off center stage, and that we are world-weary, we have reached another crossroads on the journey. Where does the true path lie? What is the real art of happiness? When we are jaded and discontented there is a precious opportunity to deepen faith.

When faith is scarce and the color drains from the world, some people tend toward beer and pretzels. I personally prefer chocolate, movies, and mystery novels that occupy the mind and keep it from dwelling on the dryness of the heart. Through the years I have found that these dry spells, while trying, often lead to renewal and a deepening of faith that requires some course correction in the journey. When all else fails, I often go on a spiritual pilgrimage, hoping that the fragile bird of faith found roosting in some holy place can be induced to nest once again in the deserted rafters of my heart.

I reached such a spiritual crossroads, yearning for a renewal of faith, in 1998. Like one-third of the American population who are religious dropouts, I am nonetheless a spiritual seeker. But I found myself oddly dissipated. Respecting all religious traditions, and enjoying prayers and practices from several, I was feeling a lack of focus. "Waring blender spirituality," composed of a little of this and a little of that, was no longer meeting my needs. I yearned for a community of worship, for the company of like-minded others. I yearned for some stability and focus in my spiritual practice.

The little bird of my faith has multicolored tail feathers. I have been introduced as a Jewish, mystical Christian, Hindu, Buddhist, Native American psychoneuroimmunologist. Responding to the call of pilgrimage I have traveled through Eibingen and Bingen in Germany, tracing the life of the twelfth-century mystic, scientist, composer, artist, and physician Hildegard of Bingen. Praying at the Western Wall in Jerusalem, I sought a link to my ancestors and to the ancient God who was forced to dwell in the human heart when the Holy Temple was razed. Living in an ashram in India for several weeks, I tried to deepen the practice of meditation. My husband, Kurt's, Native American roots have led us to sweat lodges and sacred yuwipi ceremonies. During the native journey we encountered the living presence of White Buffalo Calf Woman, who appeared to the Lakota people many hundreds of years ago, and who, like the Virgin Mary, is a form of the ancient Goddess who emerges in every age and culture.

Years of intense traveling for business had interrupted the quiet rhythm of home and family. Holy days and ordinary days filled with the quiet sustenance of friendship and community were too rare. Even the dogs became strangers. Holiday Inns had the queer feel of home. I began to fret and worry, compare and complain. God was nowhere to be found, and as sole director of the play of my life, I became a master of the maudlin. So I declared a time out and, hosting an ecumenical group of forty-nine spiritual seekers, returned to India for the third time in twelve years. My prayer and intention was for a renewal of faith.

January was unseasonably cold in New Delhi, even under sunny skies. I was swaddled in a red fleece sweatshirt borrowed from my husband, wishing fervently for my luggage that had been lost for the two days since our arrival. A wizened old man in a soiled white dhoti and bare feet, topped with a brown wool pullover, was intent on selling me a miniature chess set and a four-foot-long wooden cobra. I couldn't get him to leave me alone. The playful Kurt succeeded by reaching into his pocket and pulling out a piece of string, chanting, "A hundred rupees, just a hundred rupees for this bee-eautiful string."

He kept smiling at the vendor and offering the string, repeating his sales pitch, trying to put the string in the man's hand. The vendor finally smiled back, shook his head, and disappeared into the crowd. Strange Americans.

A hundred Tibetan Buddhist monks filed by, dressed in robes of crimson and yellow, some fingering their prayer beads. They were sent around the world by the Dalai Lama on a pilgrimage for peace.

We were all barefoot, in socks or in big, blue paper booties that the tour bus driver provided. Appropriately shoeless, we ascended the immaculate white marble steps of the lotus-shaped Bahai temple. Gleaming in the midafternoon sun, high on a hill, it stood like a shining white icon of religious tolerance. One of the monks turned around and flashed a beatific grin at our group of forty-two women and seven men. He wanted to know if we would like to take a picture of him. Many of us snapped away at that young Buddhist fellow, hoping to carry some of his peaceful joy home with us.

We, too, were on a spiritual pilgrimage for peace. We hoped both for inner peace and the inspiration to do more outwardly to bring peace to the world. The group was predominantly women, a salient characteristic of most of the seminars, workshops, and trips that I lead. It was also largely Catholic, some observant loyalists who gained succor from their faith, most religious dropouts. Two of us, myself included, were Jewish although we were both interested in a variety of religious traditions and spiritual practices. Kurt was the sole Indian, part Native American by blood, full-blood at heart. There were several Protestants of various denominations, and one devotee of the Hindu miracle man Satya Sai Baba, believed by his millions of followers to be an avatar, or divine incarnation, just as some believe Jesus to have been. After visiting a variety of Hindu, Sikh, Muslim, Christian, and Jain sites, our group would go to the village of Puttaparthi in southern India and spend five days in Sai Baba's ashram.

First we flew to southern India, to the town of Chennai, which was once called Madras. No one was wearing the plaid cloth that I associate with that name, and which we wore in our teens until our skin was thoroughly saturated with the blue, green, red, and purple dyes. I remember sitting in a bathtub while my mother scrubbed those stains away with Lestoil and Brillo, so that I could wear a strapless dress to a bar mitzvah party over a body that looked parboiled. The women in India wear either saris or Punjabis, long dresses over voluminous pants. The point is to hide the ankles, which are considered the sexiest part of the body. The tour guide explained tactfully that only prepubescent girls wear skirts and blouses. I looked down at the long skirt and blouse I had bought in Delhi and realized why I had been getting the hairy eyeball from the locals. Resolving to do better, I bought an inexpensive Punjabi, which decayed into threads by nightfall.

The next morning we visited a Catholic church, where the apostle Thomas's bones are supposed to be buried. I love Catholic churches, and I miss the mystery of the Latin mass. Candles, holy water, and incense are among my earliest memories. My live-in nanny from childhood was French Canadian and Catholic. She often took me to church with her on Sundays, which my Jewish mother must have dismissed as developmentally unimportant. It wasn't. I can, and sometimes do, genuflect in my sleep. I have always loved the Virgin Mary, who I think of as a dark-haired Semitic Jewish sister who had some fast talking to do when she got pregnant out of wedlock. And I love the rebel Rabbi Jesus who, if you know anything about Judaism, preached its highest truths. Catholic convents seem like home since I spend so many weekends in them every year, offering women's retreats. They provide inexpensive sacred space, although not without discomfort to some Jews and lapsed Catholics. That's good. It becomes grist for the mill of healing.

We got to the old stone church just as mass started. The music was exquisite, a blend of Hindu call-and-response chanting and Latin. Ordinarily I would have queued up in the center aisle and taken communion. It reminds me of the Hebrew blessings over the bread and wine, and of the growth of Christianity out of Judaism. An odd part of my spiritual work is that, while I'm a neophyte Jew, even after ten years of twice-a-week Hebrew school and eight years of spending the summer at a Jewish camp, I've become a de facto rabbi at our women's retreats. Christian women, whether loyalists or dropouts, are generally fascinated with the Jewish roots of Jesus, Mary, and Joseph.

But in this ancient church my heart was heavy. On the plane to India, I had read about the Portuguese Inquisition in Goa on India's west coast. The inquisitors forced perfectly happy, God-centered Hindus to renounce their religion and become Christian. If the converted "Christians" were caught worshipping their own gods, they were tortured and killed. One image in particular was seared onto my brain. The inquisitors cut off the eyelids of parents so that they could not shut out the sight of their children being slowly dismembered in front of them. The Inquisition in India lasted into the late 1800s. It was too close for comfort.

I couldn't shake the feeling that the church in which we stood contained more bones than those of the apostle Thomas. I am sensitized to such images of religious evil because, when editing Kurt's book, *American Indian Prophecies*, I encountered similar scenarios played over and over again as one hundred thousand indigenous peoples were killed in the Americas in the name of Christianity. The spirituality of these people was considered pagan, and the people themselves less than human. Perhaps as a Jew I feel some special kinship with those persecuted for their religious beliefs.

I was in no mood for communion. My friend and colleague Beth, the priest, smiled and beckoned me to join her in line. I shook my head and sneaked out the back door where I wept with long, wracking sobs.

MODERN MIRACLES

Our flight out of Chennai to the town of Puttaparthi, where Sai Baba's ashram is located, was delayed. One of the women in our group struck up a conversation with a young Indian woman sitting next to her in the departure lounge, who turned out to be a niece of Sai Baba. We were desperate to pick her brain but managed to restrain ourselves. We did get the message that even his relatives get no special treatment in the ashram, and that if we were expecting a private audience, it would be best to let go of the thought.

The Puttaparthi airport was like a Sai Baba Disneyworld. "Sai Ram, Sai Ram," we were greeted. Ram is the name of a previous male divine avatar, one of the many faces of God worshipped by Hindus. *Sa* means "Divine." *Ai* or *ayi* means "mother." So Sai Ram means Divine Mother and Father. This Baba-referential phrase is a vocabulary unto itself. It is not only praise to God, it also means "good-bye," "hello," "I recognize the God in you," "excuse me," "I'm grateful," and, in summation, "ain't life grand." I wished I had the faith these people did, but jadedness was still the order of the day. I had followed a Hindu guru for several years and ended that part of the journey disillusioned and hurt by the bad behavior of the guru and the organization. My ashram days were long gone. Despite all the valuable things I had learned, I still had festering wounds. I had no idea how deep they ran, or how they had undermined my faith, until I faced the prospect of entering another ashram.

We loaded the luggage into taxis and vans. I was fortunate. All I had was a small handbag. My luggage had still not arrived. Our motley caravan pulled into the ashram, Prashanti Nilayam—the Abode of Pristine Peace—through an arched gate painted in the traditional Indian shades of gaudy pink and blue. It looked like a child's giant birthday cake with the middle nibbled out.

Immediately, our thoughts of transcendent peace and quiet evaporated. Thousands of other pilgrims plied the quiet pathways between the main gathering hall or *mandap*, the cafeterias, shops, and dormitories. It was a festival day. Sports Day for the children. Sai Baba has founded many free schools and universities, based on

spiritual principles of love, tolerance, and service. There was an ath-
letics meet in the stadium at one of these schools, adjacent to the
ashram. Devotees from all over India, and from many other coun-
tries, were in attendance. We sat on the concrete steps of a dormi-
tory for foreigners, waiting for our room assignments. The ashram
map indicated that we were just steps away from the coconut
stand, but it would take another day to be initiated into the joys of
drinking coconut juice.

The day was warm and cloudless. We were hot and thirsty but
managed to find a stand that sold water and apple juice. We went
there in shifts, so that if our room assignments came through, someone could alert us. As the hours dragged by, we were beckoned into
the mysteries of Indian time. Things happen when they happen.
There is no rush. Nothing to do, no place to go better than where
you are. This is a great clinical exercise for type A personalities. You
either learn to go with the flow here or resign yourself to dropping
dead from a heart attack.

As the "spiritual leader" of this pilgrimage, I was feeling responsible for the well-being of the group, the fabric of which was
beginning to fray around the edges somewhere into the third hour
of the waiting-for-a-room vigil. Kurt and I decided to check out
some of the local hotels. There were rooms available, and several
pilgrims opted to stay in these sparse establishments. They were
not much better appointed than the austere concrete rooms at the
ashram, but at least we could check in. The rest of the group
braved the wait for their rooms, complete with Western-style toi-
lets, cold showers, giant cockroaches, and more roommates than
they might have signed on for. Each person had a new foam mat-
tress to sleep on, a part of a service project that our wonderful trip
coordinator thought up. The foam pads would be left with a poor
family who could become middle class by running a mattress-
rental business.

The check-in was finally complete at dinnertime, and we were about to lose our identity as a group, absorbed into an ever-changing river of thousands of devotees. We agreed to post notes on the door of one member's room and to meet once a day for those who wanted to. Some didn't. They elected to be in silence, to experience Prashanti Nilayam as it unfolded.

We were, by and large, a game and loving group. One of the women's father died the second day of the trip. Since it was not possible to get home in time for his funeral, the family thought that she might as well stay in India. The group reached out to her. They held a memorial service in her room, and Catholic ritual held sway for an evening in the land of the Hindus. We outlanders, the hotel crew, did not attend since the ashram gates are locked at 9:00 P.M. and we didn't want to interrupt the ritual by leaving early. The gates open in the wee hours of the morning as people begin to line up for darshan—the grace of seeing the holy person—before 5:00 A.M. Even the glance of a holy person is said to have the power to raise one's vibrations and eliminate past negative karma.

My precious progesterone oil, which prevents this nearly menopausal body from experiencing migraines as its circuits are being rewired for wisdom, was in my lost luggage. I entertained a migraine every afternoon and most evenings. So I generally slept in, mobilizing only twice during the five days for darshan. We walked to the ashram in the gentle darkness those mornings, the dusty narrow streets already teeming with people and bullock carts, mangy dogs and enterprising young boys selling postcards and Baba souvenirs. They can spot new people instantly and are among the world's most engaging entrepreneurs.

"But lady"—there was hurt in those big brown eyes—"you promise Angelo yesterday you buy postcards."

I protested that I'd never seen him before. I would have remembered an Indian with a name as improbable as Angelo. We bantered for a while. He wanted sixty rupees for the postcards, about a dollar and a half. You are expected to bargain here. It is the polite thing to do. I offered the eight-year-old supersalesman forty-five rupees. The look of hurt on his face deepened.

"Mama," he cajoled. "Wholesale price to me is fifty-five rupees. I make only five rupees. Come on, please."

I paid up and we became fast friends. Whenever Angelo saw me he introduced me to his buddies, protecting me from having to buy things I might not want.

The four pounds of Starbucks coffee, pot, filters, and voltage adapter I had carefully packed were also in the lost luggage. It was hard enough to mobilize at 4:30 A.M. for darshan. We needed something hot and caffeinated before sitting in the *mandap*, or outdoor assembly hall, for the next four hours. So Kurt and I took our chances drinking spiced milk tea at a crowded *chai* stand. It was five rupees a cup, about twelve cents. They probably inflated the price a little for us Westerners. The crusty little metal cups were a microbiologist's dream. But we were desperate. Our hotel coffee shop didn't open until 7:30 A.M. or so. Water buffalo milk is not half bad in tea, it turns out, although the cardamom is a good disguise. We hoped that it was also an antibacterial.

Thus fortified, we entered the ashram gates by the statue of Ganesh, the popular Hindu elephant-faced god and subduer of obstacles. He is eight or ten feet tall, a garish Ganesh, painted the omnipresent pink and blue. Faithful pilgrims had covered him with fragrant strings of marigolds and jasmine. The air was filled with incense, and dawn was still a promise of things to come. A Brahmin priest had just led a service here, and the collective intent and prayers of the people had rendered the place holy ground. We could feel it like a living thing, settling like a mantle of peace around us as we passed by to line up with the thousands of other people waiting for darshan in the nearby *mandap*.

It is hot in Puttaparthi, even in January, and we were grateful for the open-air hall. Men sit on one side. Women on the other. *Seva dahls*—volunteers doing service—passed us through a metal detector and then patted us down. Purses are not permitted, and most of our group wore neck pouches with passports and travelers checks inside. There was once an attempted assassination here, and no chances are taken with Baba's life.

The *seva dahls* are efficient—brusque, but clear and kind. I was told that my inexpensive Indian skirt was too sheer, and that the slit in the front of the blue silk blouse immodest, even though I was clutching a thick silk shawl around myself. I could come in but must cover myself better next time. This, I realized, would require a shopping trip since my luggage was still on a pilgrimage of its own. They crammed us into the *mandap* knee to back, shoulder to shoulder, like sardines.

People wait patiently like this for hours, hoping that an early arrival will get them a better seat from which to watch Baba make his brief appearance each morning and afternoon. The devotees believe that no one comes to see Baba unless he calls them psychically. Many relate stories of his appearance to them in dreams. Some of our group did dream of him back in the States, or had strong synchronous events involving him. They felt called. Others were just open to the experience or to watching how faithful people from another culture worship. A few came grudgingly, viewing the ashram stop as a necessary delay in an otherwise interesting itinerary.

I was interested, had specifically chosen to come to Prashanti Nilayam, but my old guru wounds made me a reluctant pilgrim at best. They also contributed to a certain cynical irreverence. You say Baba is omniscient? Show me. I wondered why we arrived so early to sit all cramped up for hours in the hopes of getting a better seat. I figured that if Baba was really omniscient and wanted to see or talk to you, he could find you even in the worst seat. My portable back rest was also in the lost luggage, and after an hour or so every bone in my body was issuing loud complaints.

At long last the assembly began to chant a Sanskrit hymn of praise, meditation, and prayer called the Gayatri mantra. This ancient, twenty-four-syllable mantra invokes the goddess Gayatri, praying for illumination in body, mind, and spirit. Baba has said that the essence of the chant is a prayer to the Divine Mother to dispel the darkness in our hearts by nurturing the light within us. I could relate to that prayer, especially since a dark and heavy heart had been the prime motivator for the pilgrimage. The beginning of the Gayatri chant is equivalent to the fanfare that announces the arrival of royalty. A red carpet is unrolled down the aisle and Baba glides in, as graceful as a swallow riding invisible air currents. He is a tiny man in a thin, straight orange robe. You recognize him instantly because of his amazing, ultrabushy Afro. This is an oddity in a country where straight hair is the norm.

He cruised down the aisles, stopping here and there to talk or to take letters. His tiny hands are amazingly graceful and well formed. Several of our group saw him circle a hand in the air, producing sacred ash to give away. He is known for this kind of manifestation of objects. But the ash comes not only from his hands but also spontaneously appears on pictures of him in private homes around the world. He selects a few people during the darshan for private audiences. They walk up to a platform at the front of the hall and wait to be called into his private quarters when the rest of us have gone. If one member of a group is called, the rest get up and follow. Private interviews are hard to come by and cannot be begged, borrowed, or connived through connections. Even Indira Gandhi couldn't get one.

For a dyed-in-the-wool seeker who will go to any darshan of any apparently legitimate holy person, from the pope to the Dalai Lama, I was curiously sluggish in my response to Baba. I fidgeted through the darshans, unable to meditate, feeling peevish. The floor was hard and my behind was sore. Part of me would rather have been at the Sai Towers Hotel drinking coffee and eating breakfast. I watched the inspired, blissful people sitting so still, in reverence of this sweet holy man in his early seventies. Little children sat with more poise and patience than I, occasionally laying their heads in the laps of mothers and grandmothers, then jumping and straining to see Baba when he appeared.

The grandmothers were particularly beautiful. Such love and gratitude shone in their faces. They lived to see a man whom they believe is God incarnate and the fulfillment of their holy Scriptures, the Mahabharata. According to its ancient prophecies, the Lord Vishnu—the part of the Hindu Trinity that sustains the world—will incarnate in the Dark Age, the Kali Yuga, the time of godlessness, greed, and violence. We are in Kali Yuga now, and through the incarnation of Vishnu in Sai Baba they believe that people will once again find the divinity within themselves and others. Their faith was brilliant. Like a bank of thousand-watt bulbs, the grandmothers radiated a pure intensity of joy. Some might have doubted Jesus, but at Prashanti Nilayam there is rock-solid faith in the godman Sai Baba.

I was in awe of Sai Baba's service projects, which include bringing water to thousands of rural villages, building numerous schools and free hospitals, feeding the poor, encouraging people to follow their own religious traditions, and carefully tending to the spoken and unspoken needs of his devotees. The greatest form of worship, he says again and again, is service. It is the highest form of prayer. I agree. Yet on pilgrimage to India, halfway around the world, he didn't seem to inspire any sense of devotion in me. It was beautiful to witness the faith of others, but, as I often joked, I seemed to be lacking in Baba receptors.

At our first darshan he spent nearly all his time on the men's side. I wondered if this was random or whether it was the usual pattern. His name might mean Divine Mother and Father, but I was wary of the men being accorded more respect and attention than the women. As this thought arose, I realized that another old wound, the religious devaluation of women, was surfacing and preventing me from enjoying the moment. I asked a devotee whether he usually spent more time with the men. She informed me that since Baba is omniscient, the men must have been thinking better thoughts than the ladies this morning. I tried valiantly to keep my features from twisting into a mask of despair. Had I come all the way to India only to encounter the old archetype of God as Santa Claus who rewards the good and punishes the bad?

"That's no way for an avatar to act, I was thinking. Jesus didn't act that way. The lost and suffering are the ones who need help. Not the contented, inspired ones."

I spent a few seconds puffing up with spiritual self-righteousness, then I deflated. She was entitled to her own opinion. God is an endless screen on which we project our deepest fears and greatest hopes. I thanked her and walked to the ashram shopping area where sacred ash is sold in plastic bags that look like miniatures from a cement company. Everything is unspeakably cheap in Prashanti Nilayam, and a bag of *vibhuti*, this sacred ash, is only two and a half rupees, about six cents. One is supposed to eat a little *vibhuti* and place some in the center of the forehead to promote healing and spirituality. Stories of *vibhuti*-induced miracle cures abound. I bought ten sacks of ash, thinking they could mortar a small wall. Friends at home had requested the *vibhuti*, which, according to legend and my own experience with a ten-year-old container of this ash, has the peculiar property of regenerating itself. It is hard to use up.

Next I went to breakfast in the south Indian cafeteria, eating on the women's side, naturally. The separation of men and women in the ashram is to avoid sexual preoccupation, which might get in the way of worship, service, prayer, and meditation. A hearty breakfast of hot cereal bursting with mouth-destroying chilies, a spicy soup called sambar, two bland white dumplings called idli, and a cup of milk tea cost four or five rupees. This is a lot of food for a dime. They are certainly not raking in the bucks here.

The shopkeepers in Puttaparthi are a friendly lot, and I got daily lessons in Islam from a man in his midthirties, a refugee from the violence in Kashmir that erupted as India tried to claim it. When the daily migraine abated, I visited Abdul, who sells Kashmiri rugs, shawls, bric-a-brac, and better dresses. We struck up a friendship when I dutifully went to buy a more demure outfit for the next darshan. It was a long white Punjabi, with red embroidery and little square mirrors at the neck. It came with drawstring pants roomy enough for Killer Kowalski, or four or five of the petite Indian women for whom it was designed. They like roomy pants here. A funky green shawl edged with white cowrie-type shells completed the outfit, which doubled as a sauna in Puttaparthi's tropical winter. It certainly was modest, though. I brought my lady friends to buy clothes from Abdul, and soon we were talking about religion—a major topic for even casual acquaintances in India.

It was near the end of Ramadan, the holiest month in the year for Muslims. It turns out that our religions—Judaism and Islam—have a great deal in common. Sitting on the floor together, each of us leaning on a low glass display case, we debated, exchanged, taught, and learned. Jews and Muslims have a common root in the patriarch Abraham. Both of us believe in the One God. We recite, "Hear, O Israel, the Lord our God, the Lord is One." They recite, "There is no God but Allah." This is the same thing really. God is everything, everyone, everywhere. There is no place and no thing that God is not.

Hospitality to strangers, gratitude, praise, and prayer are common threads to Judaism and Islam. We should be friends, not enemies. Each time a customer walked into the shop I hoped they would buy something from Abdul. His family at home needed the money. And I also hoped they would leave promptly, so that we could return to our conversation. While Abdul talked of not being strict, he still fasted all day during Ramadan, gave up his smokes for the month, and remained awake all night on the final Friday when the angels are said to come to earth, and the veil between their world and ours thins.

He offered me tea each day, which I drank while he fasted. We deduced that I am about as Jewish as he is Muslim. Neither one of us is truly observant, but both find succor and meaning in our rituals. I asked him what Muslims think of Sai Baba, since the belief in any God but Allah is the only unforgivable sin in their religion. "He is a great Hindu saint who does good works," allowed Abdul, "a lot like Mother Teresa." Climbing up the stairs from his quiet shop into the busy street, I put my shoes back on and went for a walk so that the conversation could settle. The time in Puttaparthi was well spent even though I wasn't getting much out of the proximity to Baba.

I dreamed of Baba on the third night in Puttaparthi. "We are at a small darshan, maybe a hundred people in a simple little room. He walks down a center aisle between the rows and stops beside me. We look into one another's eyes. I feel nothing. He tells me that my group is invited to a private audience. I still feel nothing, other than a certain weariness. One more audience, one more holy person. What difference does it really make?"

I woke up confused, slightly anxious. The greatest dream of almost everyone on the pilgrimage was to have an audience with Baba. The majority of the group had been hoping and praying for such an encounter. With a few exceptions, I was about the surliest holdout. Now I have dreamed of a private darshan and felt nothing but my own emptiness. Not only was I resigned to not having an audience, I was relieved. In my state of guerrilla faithlessness I couldn't imagine what I would say. My fantasy darshan revealed the depth of the emptiness I was feeling.

"Are you really God, Baba? No kidding? What are all these miracles about? And if we are here by your invitation, whatever happened to free will? Are we just puppets in a cosmic drama or are we cocreators? The Buddhists believe that meditation and self-inquiry are required to attain the awareness of the Ground of our Being. We are to practice diligently out of compassion for the suffering of others, that we may become Buddhas—awakened ones—and help set other beings free from the endless wheel of karmic existence. Yet you say that faith and service are more important than meditation. And furthermore, Baba, I have to tell you that as a Jew, avatars are strictly nonkosher. God is Ein Sof, the Endless Mystery. There is no God but God. You may not remember how much trouble it caused the last time we tried to worship an idol, but I sure do. That golden calf kept us out of the promised land for forty years, and even when we found our way to Israel, there were constant wars. For the most part we are a people in perpetual exile. So where does that leave you and me, Baba? The nonobservant Jew and the avatar?"

I wondered whether the dream was pointing to a spaciousness, a realization that spirituality is beyond any person or form, or to the spiritual depression, confusion, and lack of faith I was feeling. Seen 'em all, done 'em all from Judaism, to mystical Christianity, to sweat lodges, to meditation, to prayer, devotion, supplication, and rituals galore. With sadness, I opted for the latter interpretation. It was this very dryness of heart, this absence of faith, after all, that had led me to India. And now I was afraid that my heart would not be watered during this pilgrimage, that it would continue to shrivel up like a grape in the sun. It was all I could do to get up and face the day.

I dream of Tibetan Buddhist monks from time to time. Dreams with a numinous quality, yet I have not delved seriously into those practices. During the pilgrimage I began to think that maybe I'm just not serious, only a dilettante. On the other hand, perhaps I am an explorer. The Tibetan Buddhists speak of three kinds of mind. The dull mind with no spiritual interest. The average mind content with dogma and blind faith. The inquiring mind that is curious and filled with doubt. It is comforting to think of doubt as an elevated state of mind since it leads to research into the nature of reality, and ultimately to the knowledge that can come only through experience. Holding on to this thread of hope, I managed to brave a cold shower and a breakfast of cheese toast that tasted like cardboard boxes au gratin.

None of the spiritual angst that had come into focus got resolved in our remaining days in Puttaparthi. My "inquiring mind" was little more than a nitpicking pest that gave me no rest at all. I was tempted to buy pictures of Baba to bring home, but could not figure out why I would want them. I already had a drawer overflowing with pictures of holy people. Enough was enough. I did buy a candle holder that looks like a little metal grotto—or half of a tin can with a canopy over the top. As the candle heats the back of the enclosure, a picture of Baba slowly appears, developing from bottom to top. They called this a Godlight at the souvenir shop. It was mine for only eighty rupees, and I was thinking of it as a piece of prime religious kitsch. But I was secretly happy to have it. I put it on my altar when I got home along with the Virgin Mary, Kuan Yin, Jesus, the Dalai Lama, and an antique medallion that once hung from a Torah. I suppose I'm into idols after all.

On the final morning in Puttaparthi, we outlanders piled our bags into taxis. I was now the proud owner of a suitcase that, like most gear bought in this ashram town, displayed the seal of Baba's organization. I looked like a serious devotee, toting my worldly goods in an Om Ram, Sai Ram suitcase. Baba's logo incorporates the symbols of many of the world's religions. The Jewish Star, however, is conspicuously absent on the Indian logo, although I later found out that it is included in the American version. I was chewing on this as we drove in through the ashram gates for the last time, to await departure with the rest of the group. Our gear was loaded onto one of the big white tour buses we had hired. A short three hours later we pulled up at the West End Hotel in Bangalore. It felt like we'd arrived in Hawaii, complete with waterfalls and palm trees. Five stars and good food were a profound relief after a hotel that could have won the "dirtiest place in the universe" award. Most of the group were ecstatic at the sight of a buffet table laden with fish and chicken, not to mention ice cream and chocolate sauce. The ashram food was good and wholesome vegetarian fare, but we were ready to cut loose. The immaculate bathrooms were also cause for celebration.

After lunch we were scheduled to go to Brindavan, Baba's summer ashram which is close by. We were to stay in the homes of devotees overnight, experience a 4:00 A.M. fire *puja*—a special worship service—with a Brahmin priest, leave our mattresses as the service project, and head into Mysore by bus to see Baba's orphanage, the site of famous miraculous manifestations. Kurt and a few others were down with the flu and high fevers. Others just wanted a rest. The thought of international CNN and room service was more alluring to me than a night on the floor and early morning activity. More important, my husband was sick and I wanted to stay with him. About half of us decided to forgo Brindavan and check into a business-class hotel in Bangalore. We dubbed ourselves the rebels.

Those rebels well enough to travel boarded our very own bus for Mysore in the morning. Our driver didn't know the whereabouts of the orphanage, and most of us were content to skip it and get on with the business of seeing the maharaja's palace. As we tooled down the road, the bus carrying the other half of the group from Brindavan appeared suddenly on the right. We pulled over and stopped, having arrived at the orphanage despite our collective indifference. This is a famous site of Baba's miracles, generally pooh-

poohed by the skeptical inquirers who feature him on their "debunking" Web site. It bothers materially minded people that Baba seems to manifest rings, huge necklaces, ten-pound gold statues, steaming meals for the multitudes and the like, apparently out of thin air. The rings might be explained by sleight of hand, even though they are always a perfect fit for the recipient. But like the loaves and the fishes, the manifestation of large quantities of hot food, enough to feed everyone present, with no kitchen handy, is a little tougher to write off.

The orphanage is home to a huge picture of Baba, perhaps twenty inches wide by thirty inches tall. Sacred ash accumulates between the frame and the picture, obscuring all but Baba's face. As soon as the priest shakes the ash out to give it away, more forms. There is also a bowl—maybe two quarts in size—in which *amrit* spontaneously manifests. *Amrit*, which means "immortal" in Sanskrit, is a term for the nectar of the gods. A sweet, very fragrant substance the consistency of thinned honey, the *amrit* is indeed delicious.

We watched as the priest fished out two tiny oval pictures from the bottom of the bowl with a spoon. They looked like little campaign buttons. On one was the face of Sai Baba. The other bore the likeness of Shirdi Sai Baba, of whom the current Sai Baba is said to be the reincarnation. The holy man of Shirdi died in 1918, promising that he would be reborn eight years later in southern India. Sai Baba was born in 1926 in the obscure rural village of Puttaparthi, where Shirdi Sai Baba was unknown.

At thirteen young Sathya, as he was known then, declared that he was leaving home. He was Shirdi Sai Baba and his devotees were waiting. His schoolmates must have missed him, since the young boy made a habit of pulling sweets and pencils out of an empty bag for his friends. He recited Sanskrit scripture that he had never been taught, and sang beautiful devotional songs known as *bhajan*s. He soon became known throughout India for his miracles. He says they are his calling card. They get people's attention and turn their thoughts to God. They inspire faith.

The priest drained the little campaign buttons on the side of the bowl and placed them on the heel of a hand of one of the women in the group. Streams of nectar flowed from them, through her fingers. It pooled in her other hand, which was cupped underneath. The priest motioned for her to drink the nectar, transferring the buttons to another hand and another, several times. The nectar kept flowing. The priest then gave it away, pouring it into little bottles that people had brought. Some in our group had plastic film containers. I had nothing. I ran out to the lobby where there was a souvenir stand selling Baba pens and keychains, pictures and plastic *vibhuti* containers with holographic images. Turn it one way you get Shirdi Sai Baba, the other way his more recent, Afro-topped incarnation. I bought one and returned to the priest for *amrit*. But alas, since the container was not watertight he refused to give me any. Instead, he filled it with what it was made for—the sacred ash.

Many hours later, having sung every song we knew in the bus, we arrived back in Bangalore. Kurt was sick in bed and I thought of feeding him *vibhuti*, which is known for its healing powers. I tried to open the plastic box, but the thing was stuck shut. I couldn't figure it out. It was, in fact, meticulously sealed all around the edge with a white film. It took several minutes of holding it under hot running water and banging it on the sink to pry the thing open. I stood triumphantly over my sick husband, ready to feed him some spiritual penicillin, freshly manifested from Baba's picture. But when I opened the box, it contained *amrit* instead. My busy mind went completely blank with the pure shock of the discovery.

The usual thoughts occurred to us. Is *vibhuti* temperature sensitive? Could the ash have melted? Had I made some mistake? Had a sly pickpocket gotten into my carefully latched purse? We could reach only one conclusion. A miracle had occurred in my lowly pocketbook.

I admitted to the miracle sheepishly at breakfast the next morning. The conversation turned to the obvious. Why me? What does this mean? The transmutation of ashes to nectar was clearly not a gift to the faithful. Not only did I border on Baba irreverence for a week, I crossed the border many times. Seeing all the *vibhuti* at the ashram store, for example, I conjured up the image of poor Baba staying awake every night waving his beautiful little hands over giant vats. It turns out that the store-bought ashes are remnants from a sacred fire that Baba blesses, however, rather than miraculous apports from the Spirit World. At the orphanage, a black granite statue of Shirdi Sai Baba's feet is enshrined in a little temple enclosure, down by a river. They are known to leak *amrit* on occasion and have a perfumed smell. I sniffed them all right, wisecracking that the priest probably anointed them with Chanel every morning.

The miracle was certainly not a reward for good behavior or a boon to the faithful. That would have made it far less interesting. Furthermore, it didn't feel all warm and fuzzy, the way we might think miracles should. My heart didn't melt with divine love when I discovered the *amrit* in my purse. I didn't lose my boundaries and enter blissful nondual awareness. Not even a single tear escaped eyeballs that normally drip at the drop of a hat. My only reaction was unadulterated surprise. I would say disbelief, but I had to believe my own eyes.

What do I think it means, this transmutation? people kept asking. My meaning-making apparatus was working overtime, but to no avail. I prayed for a dream the very night that the ashes turned to nectar. I was looking for clarity. Baba didn't show up in the dreamtime. Instead Gurumayi Chidvilasananda, whose ashram I visited on a trip to India ten years before, came gallivanting through the dreamscape. I woke up remembering her visit, but not her message. Confusion was still the order of the day. I was not comfortable in the "don't know" state of beginner's mind. I would rather have wrapped the whole thing up like a snapshot taken of a holy site. I realized with painful clarity that I really was jaded. I would rather have the picture than the experience, and this made me sad.

THE MYSTERY OF NOT KNOWING

The next morning several of us went for treatments at an Ayurvedic clinic, run by an Indian physician colleague of mine. Andrea, the other Jewish woman on the trip, and I went together for a reflexology appointment. Andrea is a physician interested in complementary medicine, and thought she might enjoy observing a session as well as receiving one. Our reflexologist noticed my necklace, which was from the Israel Museum in Jerusalem. Three silver charms are covered with Hebrew letters. She read them to me. How odd, I observed, that she knows Hebrew. Not really, she replied, because she is a Jew who lived in Israel for twenty-two years with her former husband, an Orthodox rabbi.

Andrea and I perked up. We asked how many Jews lived in the city of Bangalore, population roughly 7 million. There are four, we were told. Andrea and I had just increased the Jewish census by 50 percent. Seemingly out of the blue, our therapist launched into stories about Sai Baba, and how his guidance had helped her. I asked her the avatar question, the idol worship thing, the $64,000 Jewish question. She didn't know or care what he is. It didn't matter. Words, she said, are just that. Whatever Baba is, she counseled, you know it is good by his effect on your life.

She was comfortable with not knowing. Like my friend Angela, the reflexologist had arrived at a faith rooted in mystery. I felt the arteries in my left brain relaxing as they were given permission to stop trying to figure things out. As my stranglehold on religious pigeonholing began to lose its grip, I became content to wait and see about Baba. I didn't need to make the miracle into a snapshot that could be put in a drawer. I didn't need either to become a devotee or to renounce him. I could live in faith, trusting that since my journey and Baba's had intersected, I could travel on a while and see what the experience was like. The feminine path, after all, is ultimately experiential and mystical. I could feel the gentle wings of faith beginning to flutter within my heart.

This reflexologist was an angel of the feminine path, a *dakini* of not-knowing, and a total surprise. Who would have expected to meet another Jew in Bangalore, let alone one who knew Baba? What were the odds? We bonded in sharing our stories, and the ineffable experience of deep belonging and faith in the goodness of the human heart spread its spiritual perfume over us. In that moment I felt closer to God than during our time in the ashram, when witnessing the miracle, or in all the mental peregrinations over its meaning. I was content, resting in the arms of a relationship with a stranger, recognizing that God is never closer than when the space between two hearts narrows. In the instant of joining, spiritual mathematics hums the music of the spheres. One and one makes a wiser one.

This familiar unity, wrought suddenly from the threads of difference, doesn't have to make sense to the mind. As the Buddhists chant each morning in the Heart Sutra, *Gaté gaté paragaté, parsamgaté bodhi svaha.* "Gone, gone, gone beyond the beyond."

Relationship is an invitation into a parallel universe where fear, doubt, and separation are unknown. There are no miracles in the house of belonging, other than the homely reality of love. The path to God doesn't require scaling mountains, slaying dragons, or living in caves while dining on meager rations of locusts and wild honey. It only requires the eyes of the mind to recognize what the heart has always known. The Ground of our Being is love. I began to feel the frozen spring in my heart thaw a little bit.

We flew next to the ancient city of Cochin on the west coast of India to visit a four-hundred-year-old synagogue. It is at the end of a narrow cobblestone street crowded with antique shops, called Synagogue Lane or Jew Town. This district feels far more European than Indian, even though the antiques are Indian tea leaf sheaves used for divination, temple friezes of Hindu gods and goddesses, and giant statues of Ganesh and Shiva, Lakshmi and Hanuman. Even in Jew Town idols abounded.

Built in 1568, the synagogue is still open for worship, although the Jewish community has dwindled to only seventeen members. This handful of survivors can trace their history through several periods of extermination. As many as eighty thousand Jews originally landed in Craganore, India's only port city in ancient times, after the destruction of the Second Temple in Jerusalem by the Romans in 70 C.E. Jewish astronomers and mapmakers created navigational systems that were the heart of a prosperous trade route in their new home. After a thousand years in peace, the Jewish community of Craganore was decimated by the Moors, who burned their homes and synagogues, subsequently taking over their commercial interests. Miraculously, the maharaja of nearby Cochin granted the Jews protection and land for a small town and synagogue.

Even under the protection of the maharaja, the Jews of Cochin were hunted and tortured mercilessly by the influx of Europeans who tried to kill them off one by one, particularly those from Portugal and Spain. Things improved when the Dutch appeared on the scene in the 1660s. By then only 128 families remained. The rest had been killed. Those families worked and worshipped in Cochin through the time of the British Raj, until the state of Israel was established in 1947. The bulk of the community then returned to their homeland, which their ancestors had fled two thousand years before.

The seventeen remaining Jews of Cochin are old. Ten are women, which means that there are only seven men, three short of the ten required to form a *minyan*, the minimum number of men needed to pray. Andrea and I joked about "pulling a Yentl," pretending to be guys. Then we could help them toward a minion which, these days, is entirely dependent on male Jewish tourists.

This minion business is part of what had made me an all-but-dropout Jew, hanging around the fringes of my religion at best. I attended temple only every few years, even though I am fascinated by the more mystical elements of Judaism. Why only men for a minion? How come the Shacharit, the Jewish morning prayers, has a section where the men actually thank God for not having been born a woman or a slave? This is where I got off the bus. But I stopped wasting any anger on it a long time ago, or so I thought. For the third time since our arrival in India, a religious wound that had been surreptitiously draining my faith surfaced for healing. The issues of betrayal by a Hindu guru, anger at the Catholic Church for its history of torture, killing, and persecution in the name of God, and anger at the patriarchal nature of Judaism had arisen like a three-headed Hydra from the waters of my unconscious.

No wonder my spiritual life felt dry. While I counsel other women to heal their religious wounds so that spirituality can find fertile soil to grow in a loving heart, my own wounds had been swept under the rug. The miracle of seeing them was more subtle, but no less powerful than the transubstantiation of ashes to nectar.

There in the temple I forgave the guru for leading me astray. I forgave myself for going down a dead-end path and for giving my power away to another person. The part of me that feared repeating that same error with Baba had taken refuge in avoidance and irreverence. His mission was clearly not about power or money, but about service and healing. But could I trust myself to walk down the path hand in hand with him, wounded as I was? The old religious roles of women had us look up to male mediators, authority figures, and images of the Divine. Even an avatar who announced himself as Divine Mother and Father, packing people off to worship the God of their own understanding, looked suspiciously like the patriarchy at first glance.

In the sweet grace of forgiveness I realized that thanking God for not being born a woman was, unfortunately, a reasonable prayer in biblical times. Religions only mirrored the devaluation of women in the culture. Male minyans and male rabbis are culture-bound traditions from another time and place. They are a small container for an unlimited Mystery beyond time or space, culture or custom. I decided that I could drink the Jewish Mystery without having to eat the box it was packaged in.

The hardest part of my impromptu forgiveness ritual concerned the persecution and holocaust of people worldwide by the Catholic Church. The experience in Chennai, where I could not bring myself to take communion, was still raw. I continued to be haunted by the images of parents without eyelids forced to watch the torture of their children. I am still working on forgiving the Church, which like any substantial act of forgiveness, is ultimately a gift of grace. While my intellect knows better than to throw out the Baby Jesus with the dirty bathwater, my heart still grieves for those who have suffered in the name of faith.

The synagogue had worked its healing spell in just a few moments. It felt so good to be there, to be home in a familiar place of worship. The Torah was in a simple red ark. The holy days had left their footsteps on the old tile floor. The songs that were sung and the prayers that were chanted in this faraway place were inscribed indelibly on the pages of my heart. I felt the arms of an invisible community wrap around me. I felt the visible community of witnesses as well. Apparently you can take the woman out of the temple, but you can't take the temple out of the woman.

Andrea thought that the sweet little synagogue felt lonely. She wanted to sing it to life. Other than our group, there were only four or five other tourists. Two were Jews from Tel Aviv. Andrea drafted them, and we begin to sing a medley of Hebrew songs beginning with "Yerushalayem, Yerushalayem." Jerusalem, Jerusalem. We were so overcome with emotion that we were practically drowning in tears. I was grateful that my eye makeup was in the luggage still lost two weeks into the journey. The eyes of several of our women friends were on us. They began to leak in empathetic understanding. Their presence brushed our souls like gentle feathers.

I walked into the foyer of the synagogue with Andrea. We put rupees into the donation box and bought souvenir postcards of the synagogue decorated for Purim. The women filed out in twos and threes, silently. They left us alone. There was no need to process what we had shared, no words that would be sufficient. Finally Andrea and I wandered back out into the street and went our separate ways. We met up a few minutes later in a store and began to shop for spices and shawls, wall hangings and earrings. We didn't have the vocabulary to discuss the experience, so we shared a lighter form of camaraderie.

A peace that the Bible tries to describe as that which "passeth understanding" enveloped me as we boarded the bus for the trip back to the hotel. It was a kind of contentment born paradoxically both from fullness and emptiness. There was no need to figure out what happened in the synagogue. For a while the thought waves that busily construct reality slowed down. The ocean into which they merge moved subtly from the background to the foreground. In emptying of the self that thinks, I became the ocean that is.

God was meditating me. No empty place cried out to know, to be filled with meaning that must eventually be cast off like shoes at the door of a holy place. To Baba or not to Baba was no longer the question of the hour. Content in the Mystery, I felt sad that Kurt wasn't there to share this epiphany. My quirky, silly, beautiful beloved was back at the hotel, still resting up from the flu. I knew that no words could really convey the depth of my experience to him. To the restless mind that must be assured that it is taking the right path Home, spiritual experience is maddeningly mute. The heart cannot speak. It can only sing, which we did for the duration of the bus ride. The tour guide was a devotee of Baba. She led us in chanting the Gayatri mantra, which most of us had memorized pretty well after a half hour of singing. Arriving back at the hotel, the best I could do was to smile at Kurt like the Cheshire cat. It was a rare and sweet moment, this renewal of faith. It was contagious. I could feel it in the sunlight of his smile.

Like my friend Angela, I grew and healed through a crisis of faith. Rather than developing more certainty about God, my renewed faith has made me more comfortable with less certainty and more mystery. God is ineffable, knowable only through the love we share on the journey. Since the trip to India, and the forgiveness of Judaism, Christianity, and Hinduism that I experienced in the synagogue, I have added more Jewish ritual to my practice. It speaks to me. The old prayers and melodies are in my bones. Every night before sleep I call down the Shekhina, the feminine face of God, and wrap myself in her gentle wings. I pray to the Ein Sof, the Infinite Mystery, in Hebrew and to Wakan Tanka, the Great Mystery in Lakota when Kurt and I make prayer ties together in the evening. Sai Baba visits occasionally in my dreams. I am always delighted, inspired, and blessed to have his darshan.

TRAINS TO GLORY

Religion and Spirituality

While some women find spirituality within religion, others need to make a distinction between the two. If they are religious dropouts like I was, they may even need to heal old religious wounds before they can find an authentic spiritual path of their own. For those who ultimately make the journey of return to their childhood religion, there is an additional process of winnowing out the spiritual wheat from the religious chaff. What was most nourishing and authentic for us as children holds a clue to those things that can still sustain our souls as adults.

The following is a memory of a childhood spiritual experience that occurred in a religious context, reconstructed during a relaxed reverie. You may enjoy searching your memory for a spiritual experience from your own childhood.

I am twelve or thirteen years old, my face lifted to the dappled sunshine that traces the outline of ancient pines. Sitting on a rough-hewn bench, sneakered feet sinking into a mat of pine needles, I am dressed in Sabbath whites. My eyes are closed and I am listening to Susan Abramowitz, a girl from our bunk, who is giving the Saturday morning sermon. The words that flow from her mouth are like honey on the tongue. They seem to come from some mysterious well of wisdom, much older than Susan.

There is an almost imperceptible shift in the quality of attention, a kind of focusing in which the group becomes one rapt and eager organism. Little girls and teens, we move into the same satisfying dimension of pleasure and belonging as when we trade neck rubs or trace our initials on each other's backs. Nothing could be more delicious than this moment. The pine grove is completely still but for Susan's voice, the cooing of doves, and the soughing of the wind through the pines. Even the bubot, *Hebrew for "dolls," only seven or eight years old, sit transfixed. Although we have no words for this moment of wonder and completeness, our bodies and souls will remember it. We are on holy ground.*

In the forty years since Susan's childhood sermon, I have never been so moved by another speaker. Although the words she spoke that morning are long forgotten, their effect is still vivid. She opened our spiritual eyes to the presence of the Shekhinah, the feminine face of God, Who graces us with Her presence on the Sabbath. We felt held in gentle arms, inspired to serve others with the love we ourselves were receiving. The boundaries of ego erased, we felt our unity as part of a larger identity. That identity was not only religious—Jews bound by the intention to engage in *tikkun olam,* the healing of the world—but spiritual. The latter is hard to put into words. It is numinous. It is an invisible force that is realer than real, more present than hands and feet. The spiritual is a sense of union with the Ground of our Being, a precious sense of connectedness. Spirituality is the glorious destination that the train of religion is bound for.

Religions have words to describe themselves, but spirituality has none that do it justice. It is an experience of deep belonging in which all traces of fear, judgment, guilt, separation, and doubt disappear just as darkness is dispelled by the sunrise. Religion has forms, precepts, rituals, rules, and stories that can sometimes deliver us to this place of unspeakably sweet wholeness and belonging. But it is only the vehicle that gets us there. We have to jump off at the destination, while the train continues to make its rounds.

If we mistake the train for the destination, we are liable to keep riding around in circles. And if we are angry that the train has run over people in the past, burned them at the stake, cut off their eyelids, demeaned women, or even failed to inspire, we will waste energy that could itself be a vehicle for spiritual experience. For while we don't necessarily need religion to be spiritual, religion can block spiritual experience if we find ourselves hanging on to the train, hijacking the train, or trying to blow up the tracks.

RELIGIOUS DROPOUTS

Spiritual experience at my beloved Camp Pembroke was as natural as breathing. We all loved the ritual of dressing in white, purifying ourselves of worldly concerns, before assembling in the pine grove on Friday evenings to welcome the Sabbath Queen. We showered and changed into whites on Friday afternoons and wore them until *havdalah*—which means "separation"—was sung and celebrated on Saturday night. The separation of sacred and secular time was a poignant ritual. We mourned the passage of the sacred time apart that marked the Sabbath, just as we celebrated the return to the world, which meant that we could once again "work." As children, work meant making arts and crafts, writing letters, and going to the roller rink or the Dairy Queen on special outings. There was a comfortable rhythm to the week. We rolled along in high gear until Wednesday or Thursday, when thoughts began to turn to the rest and healing of Sabbath.

I even loved the precamp shopping for whites. As my mother and I bought and name-taped the ritual clothing, the special sweetness of the Sabbath reached across time and space to enfold me. There was special food at camp on Friday night—chopped liver, challah, and roast chicken. There was the lighting of candles both on Friday night and at *havdalah* when a special twisted candle with three wicks was kindled as soon as the first three stars appeared in the deepening navy blue of the sky.

Sabbath is a woman's ritual. In homes across the world, the candles are kindled by women. The great-grandmothers, grandmothers, mothers, and little girls form an unbroken lineage. Celebrating the Sabbath made me feel as though I belonged to a tradition that valued women.

But back home my mother didn't light the candles. We were secular rather than religious Jews. Since the entirety of my Jewishness resided in a camp run by a woman, Hadassah Blocker, who was my first spiritual teacher, I associated not only the Sabbath but the whole of my religion with the gentleness and wisdom of women. But on the few occasions when my family went to temple—bar mitzvahs, funerals, and the High Holy Days of Rosh Hashanah and Yom Kippur—women's participation was visibly lacking.

As a child it seemed that the temple smelled stale, like sweaty gym socks and old cigars. It was close and dark, not like the sweet fragrance of a pine grove at all. The rabbi mumbled rapidfire prayers like a slick and facile auctioneer speaking in Hebrew, and the congregation kept up the fevered pace. I struggled fruitlessly to find the right place on the page. In the Conservative Jewish synagogue of my youth there was a lot of skipping around in the prayer book. Only the regulars knew which pages were read and which were omitted. But I loved it when the cantor sang. And I nearly passed out with pleasure when the congregation joined our voices.

Hebrew melodies are haunting. An invisible choir of ghosts seem to join the chanting. There are the women at the well, drawing the living waters from the dust of the desert. Generations of bearded men stand behind us, studying the Holy Torah and her gift of compassion. Then there are the children, too many dewy faces turned to dust and ashes in the pogroms, the Inquisition, the ovens. This is no ordinary music. Equal parts love and longing, praise and gratitude, fear and trembling, it summons up the joy of life. It also pierces the heart with the sadness of thousands of years of persecution and destruction. "By the waters of Babylon," we sing in the ancient tongue, "we sat and we wept." Even the most alienated Jew is moved to tears by these ghost songs.

The music was my only connection to the numinous in the temple. Tired of the dry and empty services and the women whose major interest seemed to be in one another's clothes, I gave up going to temple except for bar mitzvahs. In the late 1950s girls didn't receive a bas mitzvah in our temple, or any temple I knew of in our Boston suburb. Coming of age was exclusively a guy thing. I used to sit there during the bar mitzvahs and chant the blessings in my head. I knew them all by heart and longed to get up in front of the congregation and let those ancient melodies stream out of me, blessing friends and relatives. I got impatient when many of the boys could hardly pronounce the words of their part in Hebrew, stumbling along while I could have sung like a bird. I was jealous, plain and simple. My mother was proud that I knew all the prayers. She'd pat me on the head and tell me that I'd make a good *rebbitzin*—a rabbi's wife. I'd stomp off fuming, "I don't want to be the *rebbitzin*, dammit, I want to be the rabbi."

"Jesus, Mary, and Joseph," she'd reply, having been tutored by generations of Irish Catholic housekeepers. Hands on hips and lips pursed, obviously hurt by my impassioned outburst, she would put me in my place. "You don't have to get on your high horse, Miss High and Mighty. I was just giving you a compliment. And don't swear."

I wish I could have explained why that compliment inflicted such exquisite pain. The spiritual community that had sustained me, from the time I was a *bubot* to the year I left camp at age fifteen, was missing. I had come to depend on it in the way we depend on air. We don't know how important oxygen is to life until there isn't any. Attending temple services was like being suffocated. Becoming a rabbi's wife seemed like a death sentence. But if I could become the rabbi—and at camp all of us were empowered as little rabbis—perhaps I could recover the spiritual once again. It would be many years before women could become rabbis even in the more liberal Jewish denominations. The Orthodox still will not ordain us.

After my last year of camp, before our group of girl Hebrew-schoolers got confirmed, we each had an obligatory meeting with the rabbi of our temple. Emerging from my usual reticence and eagerness to please, I managed to find a voice for the burning questions that plagued me. Why was there so little room for women in Judaism? Why was a prayer minion composed of ten men, rather than men and women? Why couldn't women become rabbis?

The rabbi smiled as he explained that women were naturally spiritual. We shared our stories, we healed the sick, we cared for children and the elderly. Our daily lives were sacred. We were priestesses of the hearth and home. Religious ritual and study was the domain of men because they were not naturally spiritual. They needed religious structure to deliver them to the place where women started from. Their prayer and study was like a remedial course.

I was intrigued but suspicious that I was being had by the prover-
bial silver-tongued devil. Even if the rabbi were right, most people
didn't share his point of view. Women were clearly second-class religious citizens. Furthermore, we needed a structure in which our
innate spirituality could be celebrated. And at fifteen, there was no
longer the succor of Camp Pembroke. It was time to spend summers
in more worldly pursuits, like learning to program computers in
FORTRAN and haunting the coffeehouses of Harvard Square.

I received a sterling silver *kiddush* cup at our confirmation ceremony, to be used in blessing the wine for celebrating the Sabbath.
It seemed a bitter cup, and I threw it into the junk drawer underneath the bathroom sink. The year was 1960. I tossed away my gir-
dle and my religion in one neat package. I let my perfectly coifed
hair grow long, donned dangling earrings and brown leather sandals that laced up the leg, and learned to play the guitar. My cheat
sheet consisted mostly of mining disaster songs and other laments
that mirrored my own inner sadness. I was bereft. My spiritual connection was gone. I could relate to those miners trapped deep beneath the earth with no air to breathe.

For a few years I made a little spending money by playing my
lugubrious repertoire at bar mitzvah parties. Guitars and folksongs
were in. On one of these occasions a prototypical Jewish *bubbe*—
an old-style grandmother who hailed from the shtetls of Poland—
came up to me at the end of a set. "Vot's duh matter, *bubbeleh*? You
depreshed? Can't you zink zomtink heppy? Life is hard enough
vitout you remind us of gloom on a day of joy."

That was the end of my career as a folksinger. I kept my angst to
myself, seeking spiritual solace and meaning in the local Unitarian
church. This first, tentative foray into apostasy was soon discovered
by my horrified mother, who issued one of her fierce maternal
edicts. "Thou shalt study no religion other than Judaism." The
corollary of this was, "Thou shalt date only Jewish boys."

I tried to argue that she, of all people, was no role model for religion. Other than the holiday feasts to which she committed weeks of planning and cooking, she had no interest at all in Judaism. She had her reasons, and the Holocaust was high on the list. Were there a God of love, she reasoned, holocausts around the world would not be common currency. If we are made in God's image, heaven help us all, because He must be a sorry piece of work. She articulated what many studies have demonstrated. The more religious people get, the more intolerance is spawned. Supposed to teach us love, religions are more often schools for persecution. Anti-Semitism had knocked the wind out of her sails, stolen the lives of her relatives. Nonetheless, a member of the immediate post-Holocaust generation, I was taught pride in my Jewish heritage. Ethical conduct, charity, and good works were the secular expression of a religion of compassion, misunderstood by most of the world, including my parents and myself.

Like one-third of the population of this country, I became a religious dropout. While my mother was alive, she served as a focus for our quasi-religious family holiday feasts. When she passed on, my brother, Alan, and I continued the tradition until we both moved out of Boston. By that time my sons were grown. Feeling free from the responsibility of passing on our Jewish heritage, I let it all go. The train to glory, the train to Auschwitz, could go steaming right on down the tracks without me.

My story is a familiar one to many women and men as well. The spiritual retreats and lectures that form the backbone of my work usually begin with a poll, inspired by the research of Wade Clark Roof. "How many of you are religious loyalists," I ask, "finding nurture in the tradition in which you were raised?" About 20 to 25 percent of the hands go up.

"How many are religious dropouts?" Sixty to 70 percent of the hands shoot up for this question, usually with a lot of energy. There is some charge associated with being a dropout, an emotional valence. The remaining 10 or 15 percent of participants identify themselves as returnees. They have returned either to their religion of origin or to some other religion, for a multitude of reasons. These range from giving structure to their children, to remarkable and numinous conversion experiences, to missing a spiritual community in which to worship.

At a health-care conference, I was giving a workshop called "A Peaceful Heart in a Busy World." It was to be a day of prayer, contemplation, and rededication to Spirit. As typical of such workshops, 90 percent of the participants were women. We were hungry to form a temporary community of worship, to find the spiritual roots from which the world religions have flowered at different times and in widely diverse cultures.

"Who is in mourning for the absence of spiritual community in your life?" I asked. Almost all the hands went up, even those of many loyalists and returnees.

"Who is angry that your religion of origin could not, or cannot, connect you to the spiritual?" Most of the same hands went up.

"How many of you are angry at God?" You could hear a pin drop in the room. I asked people to share their stories in groups of three. When we finished, some were eager to offer the insights of their small group to the rest of us.

Violet spoke first. She was schooled by nuns that she referred to as the Sisters of Perpetual Guilt. Many in the room tittered in understanding. These lapsed Catholics, of all ages, are the angriest group. Some remember kneeling on hard grains of rice. Others recount having to make up sins to feel competent in the confessional. Some never recovered from the sense of betrayal they experienced while reading about the horrors of the Inquisition both in the Old World and the New.

One woman in the group, Rosemarie, a woman in her fifties,

nodded knowingly, finally volunteering that she was a nun. Still a sister, she had been plagued by the common doubts and fears about the Church, with sadness over its treatment of women as sinful and unworthy of the priesthood. Nonetheless, she continued to find spirituality and beauty in her tradition. The Catholic sisters in her community were a steady source of light and joy to her as was their work with battered women.

"There are problems in Catholicism like in all religions," she finished. "But the rituals, the saints, and our beloved Mary and Jesus sustain me. They ministered to the poor, and that is my joy, too. When I don't know how to help, I pray to the Blessed Mother and she always inspires me to do the right thing."

When Rosemarie finished speaking, a Jewish woman talked about being raised in a Reform temple, and then becoming a religious, Orthodox Jew. Although she learned a lot about the religion, and loved the close community, she felt stifled by rules and regulations, by having to cover her hair with a wig to go out in public. She is now part of a Jewish renewal community, which she characterized as a kind of mystical, egalitarian, New Age Judaism.

The loyalists who come to my classes and retreats tend to be liberal. Three Sephardic Jewish modern Orthodox women from Brooklyn, New York, took turns speaking next. They found happiness through close community, the yearly cycle of holy days, the weekly rhythm of work and rest that revolved around the Sabbath, and God-centered ideals. These women fall into the loyalist category, but they are liberal in their understanding of and respect for other religious traditions and for people like me who are spiritual but not particularly religious. This type of inclusiveness is one of the hallmarks of feminine spirituality. Each of us has the inalienable right to worship in our own way, within or outside the walls of religious institutions.

The room bristled with stories, with inspiration, and with angst.

I talked about dying patients I have had the privilege to work with, and how religious beliefs often come into bold relief when we face our mortality. I told the story of a young gay man with AIDS who, having forsaken his fundamentalist Christian, fire-and-brimstone childhood, reverted to it suddenly in the face of death. He concluded that the Bible was right. Homosexuality was a sin, and AIDS was the first installment of punishment. He had nothing to look forward to but an eternity of damnation and suffering. "But isn't God also merciful?" I asked. "Isn't forgiveness always the promise of grace?"

"Only if you repent," he replied. "And I cannot repent of finding love. My partner and I have a relationship so beautiful and caring."

What is wrong with this picture? How can love in any form be less than the road to salvation? The young man eventually shelved his belief in a punitive God, in favor of a love that could heal. But he made a common error. He equated healing with curing. Even though he forgave himself, forgave his parents, and learned to live in the present, nonetheless his disease progressed. He was healed, but not cured of AIDS. In his hunger for life he decided, once more, that God must be punishing him by withholding a cure. He had not yet healed the most primary relationship we have outside of our parents—our relationship to God.

He called me from the hospital, dying and hopeless. "I was right in the first place," he wept. "God is punishing me for being gay. I am on the way to hell."

As I related this anecdote, a hush fell over the room. It became clear that reconciling ourselves to God is not only critical as health-care providers but also for us to be fully alive and whole as human beings. The gravity on many of the faces mirrored the inner understanding that forgiving God and religion was going to be hard work. Having spent years counseling people who have survived every sort of abuse that twisted minds can devise, I am convinced that some of the deepest pain we suffer as human beings is alienation from God. Until that is put right, peace of mind is an elusive dream at best.

Women's anger at God is generally directed at two targets: the general failure of the religious institutions to provide nurturing spiritual growth and "the patriarchy," literally the religious orientation of the fathers underlying the Judeo-Christian worldview. Far and away the angriest group are dropout Catholics, many of whom feel deeply wounded and betrayed by institutional religion, and some of whom long to be priests.

Holding spiritual retreats in Catholic retreat houses, which I have done on many occasions, has a way of bringing up anger and religious wounds that need healing. In many convents crucifixes hang over each bed. This ancient symbol has provoked unexpectedly rich discussions, and several times the crucifix has been an agent of healing.

Jewish women are often put off by Catholic retreat houses, by the statues of Mary and the crucifixes. I remember one woman in particular. In light of the terrible persecution of Jews by Christians ranging from pogroms to the Holocaust, from accusations of being Christ killers to being charged with controlling the world economy for personal gain, she felt unsafe sleeping under a crucifix. Yet she respected Jesus as a teacher and didn't want to do anything offensive.

After careful thought, she laid the crucifix on a towel in her dresser drawer and covered it gently with a tissue. Many women in the group resonated with her story. A dropout Catholic woman was infuriated that the patriarchal religious structure, in the form of a crucifix, was invading her spiritual retreat. She steamed and raged inwardly until late Saturday night when she ventured into the church that shared the convent grounds. The smell of incense and the sight of a statue of Mary and the Infant Jesus moved her to tears, called her beyond rage to a tender inward place that yearned to be filled.

Alone with her longing, she underwent a kind of spiritual conversion experience in which she felt the nearness and presence of God. The comfort and inspiration that others had received there seemed to stream over her like a balm, anointing her with peace and love. In a highly emotional epiphany, she forgave the Catholic Church for its shortcomings. She didn't plan on becoming a returnee but was relieved to be healed from years of anger.

ANGER AS A FIRST STEP TO HEALING

Whether we can tolerate the crucifix on the wall or not, the deep-seated anger so many women have about religious patriarchy has scant outlet. Without an egress, anger builds up like steam in a pressure cooker, and we eventually explode. The little bird of faith is likely to get its tailfeathers singed in the process. So how do we learn to recognize and heal the anger? Women burned their bras in the 1960s. Are we to burn our Bibles in the next millennium?

Fortunately, there are role models to guide us. Even in colonial times women responded strongly to the religious institutions that infantilized them and cast them as morally inept. In this section, we can relate to the story of a small group of women who sat down to tea one day and planted the seeds that gave us the vote some seventy years later. Members of this same group produced the provocative book, *The Woman's Bible*, published a century ago. It was an angry book, focused on the moral ineptitude of men characterized as religious paragons of virtue. Perhaps it is time to write a new *Woman's Bible*, one that focuses on compassion, one that includes the untold stories of biblical women. But, in order to do that, we still need to heal the anger first.

Only in relatively recent times have women been able to voice their frustration with teachings about a patriarchal and vengeful God. In colonial times any dissension from dogma was the cause of shunning, hanging, or even burning as a witch. Nathaniel Hawthorne's heroine Hester Prynne got off lightly by having to wear a scarlet *A* publicly as shaming for adultery. In 1637 Anne Hutchinson was banished from the Massachusetts Bay Colony for heresy. She dared to criticize Puritan theology with her belief that once a person had accepted God's grace in their heart, there was no need for priestly intermediaries. An outspoken nurse with a respected presence in the community, she soon attracted a large following of women to her independent spiritual thinking. Unfortunately, her eloquence during her trial only served to convince the Puritan elders more firmly of her danger to the party line.

By the 1830s women like the Grimké sisters, Sarah and Angelina, were demanding their God-given right to participate in the abolition movement alongside men. The Grimkés were Quakers who believed that an "Inner Light," a Divine Spirit of conscience and guidance, was present in both men and women. And they contended that both genders were morally bound to use that light for justice. Unfortunately, religious ideas about the moral inferiority of woman, as well as laws and customs of the times, constrained women's choices in a dangerous way.

"Such obstacles to women's freedom, they asserted, not only limited woman's moral life to a slavelike existence dictated by the desires of men, but threatened women's immortal life as well. If women could not act and speak according to individual conscience, they could not fulfill the moral duties necessary for salvation."

The theological basis for women's political oppression led Elizabeth Cady Stanton who, along with Susan B. Anthony, was a pioneer for women's suffrage in the mid-to-late 1800s, to gather a small group of women Theosophists, Freethinkers, and New Thought leaders, the so-called Revising Committee, to write *The*

Woman's Bible at the turn of the century. Stanton, the daughter of a judge, was raised in a wealthy Boston home by a father who constantly lamented the fact that she wasn't a boy. Her cousin Garrett Smith was an abolitionist who introduced her to runaway slaves, Oneida Indians, and her future husband, abolitionist Henry Stanton, whom she married in 1840 and accompanied to London to attend the First World Anti-Slavery Convention. There she was profoundly influenced by the speech of the famous Quaker abolitionist, Lucretia Mott.

Mott had been an abolitionist since the 1820s and was a radical Quaker in the sense that she gave authority only to the guidance of the Inner Light rather than to the elders. She was outspoken about the need to oppose male hierarchy in religion. In the days when there were few women public speakers, Mott was well known and frequently addressed "mixed" audiences of both genders.

By 1848 Stanton and her young family of three children had moved to Seneca Falls, New York, where Mott and her husband were summering among the Seneca Indians. It seems that these two women were affected, although researchers are only now trying to figure out the extent, by the egalitarian position of Indian women compared to white women of the times. Whereas white women were considered the property of their husbands and had no legal right even to the wages they earned, Indian women were respected members of their communities whose wisdom was integral in every way to their clans and tribes.

In July of 1848, Mott and Stanford, along with Mott's sister, Martha Wright, and another Quaker, Mary Ann McClintock, were having tea when they hatched the idea of a women's rights convention and sent off a notice to the newspaper that it would take place later that very month. McClintock, while a Quaker, was also a spiritualist, which was greatly in vogue, especially among the intelligent women of the times. People commonly confuse spirituality with spiritualism. The latter is a literal belief in the spirits, the souls of the dead, who can be communicated with and asked for guidance. That the women's movement arose from a milieu of both spirituality and spiritualism, and was most certainly influenced by Native American culture, is a fascinating historical fact.

Stanton and her colleagues immediately set out to rewrite the male Declaration of Independence to address the liberties of women, in time to be presented and ratified at the convention. Their document was called the Declaration of Sentiments. Just as the Declaration of Independence had listed eighteen grievances with regard to the domination of the male colonists by England, Stanton listed eighteen grievances whereby women's freedom was curtailed through domination by men. This included the fact that married women had no legal rights—they were "dead" in the eyes of the law. Women had no vote. Divorce and child custody laws were entirely in favor of men. Women weren't allowed into colleges and universities and were thus barred from professions like law and medicine, and so it continued. These, of course, were just the grievances of white women. The situation was much worse for black women, many of whom were still slaves.

At the convention, the Declaration of Sentiments and twelve resolutions were unanimously endorsed. The only part that caused heated debate was women's suffrage. Less than a hundred years ago women lived in such a repressive climate that they were actually shocked at the very prospect of voting. Stanton's pleas for suffrage weren't enough to move the assembly. Ironically, it was Frederick Douglass, a black male abolitionist, who swayed the women by making the point that suffrage was the foundation of the power to make laws and choose those who would govern.

The press had a field day with the Declaration of Sentiments, making fun of it throughout the thirty states of the Union and referring to the writers as unattractive "old maids" or "mannish women, like hens that crow." These epithets strike a familiar note. Modern criticism of feminists as bitches, ball biters, and dykes isn't much different. But the strategy of the press backfired as women in every state became aware of the document and turned out in great numbers at women's rights conventions from Massachusetts to Ohio. These continued until the Civil War.

Central to the Declaration of Sentiments was the opposition to the commonly held doctrine that women were inferior in moral judgment compared to men, and therefore had to be kept out of all decision-making positions. Stanton held the opposite position. She had learned from her Quaker friends that it was the God-given right and obligation of women to use their Inner Light to intuit God's will and change the world for the better.

As she put it in one of the eighteen grievances against men, "He has made her, morally, an irresponsible being, as she can commit many crimes with impunity, provided they be done in the presence of her husband. In the covenant of marriage, she is compelled to promise obedience to her husband, he becoming, to all intents and purposes, her master—the law giving him power to deprive her of her liberty, and to administer chastisement." She went on to write that half the population of the country was, in fact, disenfranchised and degraded socially and religiously, oppressed and "fraudulently deprived of their most sacred rights."

The misogynist position of the organized Christian Churches became the prime target for Stanton. Her position eventually distanced her slightly from Susan B. Anthony and other feminists of the time who felt that the women's rights agenda might be compromised by a frontal attack on religion.

Stanton kept on. She spent the last twenty years of her life researching, writing, and lecturing on the oppressive nature "of orthodox Christianity and its interconnectedness with women's subjugation in the home, economy, state and church." Her inspiration came from Transcendentalism, Quaker ideals, Unitarian thought, Freethinkers, Spiritualists, Native American values, and the burgeoning New Thought movement, the spiritual groups of her day. But in adopting their approaches, she often alienated mainstream women in the Christian fold. In fact, her lectures about the need for birth control raised less opposition among women than her condemnation of orthodox Christianity and its presumption of women's moral inferiority. Nonetheless, *The Woman's Bible* with its pithy combination of theological criticism, women's sensibilities, and political commentary relevant to the times was a hot seller that still makes a provocative read.

The introduction to *The Woman's Bible* states: "The Bible teaches that woman brought sin and death into the world, that she precipitated the fall of the race, that she was arraigned before the judgment seat of Heaven, tried, condemned and sentenced."

The Revising Committee was an intelligent and outspoken group of early, and angry, Bible exegetes. They recognized that many of the horrific tales of man's inhumanity both to men and women were simply glossed over in the so-called Good Book. And that's true. No Sunday school teacher points out the shameful episode in which God's angels, disguised as a couple of good-looking male strangers, show up at Lot's front door. Their mission is to tell Lot's family to get out of town before God sends the fire and brimstone to destroy the wicked. Now, Sodomites were a lusty lot, and a large crowd of men gathered outside Lot's house intent on sodomizing—what else?—the two angels. Lot immediately had a great idea. He'd toss his two young daughters out the door to the ravenous crowd, thus protecting the two strangers. That's quite a plan for the only man in Sodom who was thought of as righteous.

The story makes it clear that women had very little value, and that their abuse was no big deal.

The women on the Revising Committee for *The Woman's Bible* had plenty of common sense. They wrote plainly of the brutishness of King David. You may recall that David fell in lust with the beautiful Bathsheba, even though she was married and he already had a large harem. So he sent her husband, a poor and honorable soldier named Uriah, who "had but 'one little ewe lamb,' one wife he loved as his own soul" to the front lines of battle in the successful hope of getting him killed. This accomplished, he added Bathsheba to his harem.

The Revising Committee writes of King David: "He was ruled entirely by his passions. Reason had no sway of him. Fortunately, the development of self-respect and independence in woman, and a higher idea of individual conscience in religion and in government, have supplied the needed restraint for man. Men will be wise and virtuous just in proportion as women are self-reliant and able to meet them on the highest planes of thought and action. . . . No magnet is so powerful as that which draws men and women to each other. Hence they rise or fall together. This is one lesson which the Bible illustrates over and over—the degradation of woman degrades man also."

PARTNERS IN RELIGION
AND SPIRITUALITY

The circumstances of women in the United States have changed dramatically in the century since *The Woman's Bible* was published. We got the vote in 1920. And since that time women have become full partners with men in a variety of spheres, although there is still a great deal of progress to be made. We are doctors and lawyers, ministers, rabbis, and Episcopal priests. While it is unlikely that women will be Catholic priests any time soon, Mary may become coredemptrix with Jesus. But in spite of the progress that has been made, too many women are still angry at men. And we all lose energy because of that. As the writers of *The Woman's Bible* said, "We rise and fall together." There may be reason for anger, but, without forgiveness, old patterns stay locked in place.

Writer Brenda Peterson, in her fine book *Sister Stories*, speaks of what we need in order to establish a workable feminine spiritual tradition. "A rediscovered language of sacred sisterhood can change the world. One way to begin this work is to reestablish and claim the lost, feminine traditions of spiritual practice: to know ourselves, and mirror each other, without blaming our brothers. In fact, the brotherhood should no longer be our standard or focus. In the way that the women's movement began with rightful outrage, it is now moving into a more visionary period in which women re-imagine the feminine as distinct and powerful in itself."

The emerging women's spiritual movement is also distinct and powerful in itself. It is not meant to abolish religion or to create divisiveness between women and men. As we come into the power of the she-bear, and become comfortable walking a path of our own, so will the brothers that we meet along the way.

FROM RELIGIOUS ANGER
TO SPIRITUAL EXPERIENCE

Once we have expressed our anger and grief over the failings of religion, the question remains of how to find a spiritual community of like-minded others who have gone beyond blame to love. By sharing our hopes and dreams, wounds and stories, we continue to grow and heal. My own spiritual community is mobile, composed of temporary women's gatherings around the country. It is also home based. Kurt and I often make prayer ties at night or have pipe ceremonies in which we pray out loud. Community sweat lodges are another precious opportunity to pray out loud, and at length, both with loved ones and with strangers who often become friends. Jewish holidays with friends and services with the Boulder Jewish Renewal community round out my dropout/returnee brand of spirituality.

An important part of my religious healing has been the inclusion of Jewish rituals in the potpourri of spiritual practices that sustains me. As much as I have been angry at Judaism and find solace and meaning in mystical Christianity and Eastern religions, something in my DNA is set to the Jewish wavelength. I cry when I hear Hebrew songs. My heart smiles when a Jewish grandmother pinches my cheek. Yiddish phrases send little shivers up my spine. I love it when I find Jewish meditation practices and evidence that the very things that attract me to Christian mystics and Eastern thought are also present in Judaism. Like it or not, I was born a member of that particular tribe.

I believe that everyone has tribal roots that are imprinted on their bodies, minds, and souls. In honoring our tribe we make conscious or unconscious contact with a lineage of elders who, in some subtle way, seem to be there to help us. I am convinced through years of experience that even religious dropouts can have profound spiritual experiences by choosing a prayer or ritual from their birth religion and making it part of their current spiritual practice. If nothing else, one's degree of resistance to this suggestion is a good barometer of the amount of religious healing left to accomplish.

Every night before bed, I repeat a short version of the practice called the bedtime Shema. *Shema* means "listen." It is the first word in Judaism's holiest prayer, Shema, Yisrael, Adonai Eloheinu, Adonai Ehud. "Listen, Israel, the Lord our God, the Lord is One."

The word Yisrael, or Israel, does not refer to a geographical region or a modern Jewish state. It is a state of consciousness. When Jacob wrestles with the angel all night long, on the way home from his long exile, God renames him Israel. Israel means "one who wrestles with God." This is exactly what we do in our religious healing and in our pilgrimages to find faith. We whine, complain, reason, bargain, rail, scream, make amends, forgive, and look for a way to be present to God.

This process of anger and reconciliation makes room for the spiritual. The Shema prayer reflects that fact. Listen, you who wrestle with God, the Lord our God, the Lord is One. This is a reminder that God is everywhere, part of everything. There is no place where God is not. There is no journey to God, despite the title of this book. Just an opening of heart and mind to what is always and already present.

My bedtime ritual has three prescribed parts. The first is reconciliation. You review your day and look for places where you were hobbled by guilt, judgment, or anger. These are emotions that are limiting and toxic because they pull us out of present time. They are inherently isolating. Since spirituality is about connectedness, coming back into present time is a necessary requirement for making the short journey to God, who dwells within our own hearts. So we forgive other people and ourselves.

In the second part of the ritual we repeat the Shema, having opened ourselves emotionally to the experience of Oneness. The final part of the ritual consists of calling upon the four archangels. Uriel, Hebrew for the "light of God," stands before us. Raphael, the healer of God, stands behind. Michael, the likeness of God, stands to our right. Gabriel, the strength of God, stands to our left. Above our head, falling over us like a blanket of light, is the Shekhina, God's feminine aspect. Wrapping ourselves in this love and divine protection, we then commend our soul to God to keep for the night.

Upon arising, there is a special morning prayer, sung in Hebrew, which thanks God for returning our soul to our body once again in divine compassion. Even though these two rituals require only about five minutes a day, they are deeply nourishing. They are in my bones and the bones of my ancestors. They are ancient thought forms of worship and belonging.

Margaret, a woman who attended a retreat with me several years ago, wrote of her experience in adopting a prayer from her Christian background. A dropout from a fundamentalist Christian sect, she was infuriated with God the Father and the patriarchal, woman-degrading nature of her religion. Yet, in her heart of hearts, she loved and respected Jesus. She missed him. He'd been knocking on the door for quite some time, she reported, but she simply could not let him in, fearing that the whole church would barge in on his heels.

Although the Lord's Prayer, the Twenty-third Psalm, was written well before the birth of Jesus, Margaret always thought of him when she said it. This may not be the exact version of the Lord's Prayer that you remember. Different churches adhere to either modern or archaic language. But it is the childhood version imprinted on Margaret's soul.

The Lord is my shepherd,
I shall not want;
He makes me to lie down in green pastures.
He leads me beside still waters;
He restores my soul.

He leads me in the paths of righteousness
  for His name's sake.

Yea, though I walk through the valley
  of the shadow of death,
I shall fear no evil; for You are with me.
Your rod and Your staff, they comfort me.
You prepare a table before me in the presence
  of my enemies.
You have anointed my head with oil;
My cup runs over.
Surely goodness and mercy will follow me
  all the days of my life,
And I will dwell in the house of the Lord forever.

She began the practice of repeating the Lord's Prayer morning and night. For the first few weeks she experienced waves of deep grief. In leaving the church where she was born and raised, she had effectively been shunned by all but her closest relatives. Repeating the prayer brought that grief back to life.

Then, imperceptibly at first, the prayer began to comfort her. The community was gone, for better and for worse. But Jesus was always there. Three months into the practice, the presence of Jesus had become palpably real. The prayer began to repeat itself spontaneously in her mind during the day when things got rough. It became a life raft whereas before it had felt like a cement coffin. Margaret began searching for an ecumenical, liberal, Christian spiritual community. She went from trying to blow up the tracks to appreciating the train of religion as a vehicle that could—when her heart was open—deliver her to a spiritual destination.

Sabbath whites, religious songs, the crucifix, the rosary, the Lord's Prayer. These and other useful remnants of religious ritual may be lying in a Goodwill bag in the dusty closet of your memory. Rather than give them away, why not shake them out first and try them on again? Even though you may have jumped from the train they came on, the religious rituals of your ancestors remain in your bones. They may have an almost uncanny power to deliver you to God, once you give yourself permission to use them in your own authentic way, letting go of whatever anger you may have about your childhood religion.

INTUITION AND REASON

Jacob's Ladder and Sarah's Circle

The journey to God is one of spiritual connection to a greater whole. That whole is not somewhere above us, a place to which we ultimately ascend. It is found within us here and now. Whatever our image of God and way of worship, the journey is one of connection to our own deepest self. That connection enables us to access and utilize our gifts and strengths. It guides us in recognizing and overcoming our weaknesses. It helps us to develop compassion and free the energy of the she-bear who protects life whenever it is threatened. Spirituality is the result of thoughts, words, and deeds that culminate in the ability to take our place in a universe where every thread is important to the integrity of the final design.

Spiritual growth is inextricable from psychological growth. And psychological growth is, in part, a gender issue. Men and women are different, our bodies as well as our brains. In this chapter we will consider gender-specific patterns in information gathering and the development of a sense of self. In the arena of psychospiritual growth one size does not fit all, a fact that religious systems based on male sensibilities fail to take into account.

As a medical scientist and psychologist I have been amazed how often data about men's bodies and minds are extrapolated to women as though we were cut from the same piece of cloth. And as Carol Gilligan once quipped about the story of Adam and Eve, when you try to make a woman out of a man you are bound to get into trouble. This troublesome gender blending has been just as true in our path to God as in the rest of life.

JACOB'S LADDER

Our blueprint for male spirituality is laid out in the story of Jacob's ladder in the Book of Genesis. It is a powerful story of intrigue, betrayal, individuation, and redemption. Jacob is sent away from home to avoid the murderous rage of his brother, Esau, whom he and his mother have tricked out of his birthright. Midway through Jacob's journey to find a wife in a distant land he makes camp, places a stone beneath his head, and falls asleep:

> And he dreamed that there was a ladder set up on the earth, and the top of it reached to heaven; and behold, the angels of God were ascending and descending on it! And behold, the Lord stood above it. . . .

In this luminous, revelatory dream God makes a bond with Jacob, promising the land where the dream took place to Jacob's descendants.

The archetype of male psychospiritual development is encapsulated in this biblical hero's journey. Jacob must leave home, die to his old self, face tremendous challenges, find new meaning, and then return to give wisdom and direction to his people. In all modern-day conceptualizations of the male life cycle, the central theme of development is the separation and autonomy that Jacob's story represents. As the late Yale psychologist Daniel Levinson writes in *The Seasons of a Man's Life*, "Leaving his home the man must set out on a path of individuation during which he dreams his own dreams, finds appropriate mentors and finally leaves his mark upon the world."

Step by step, according to psychological theorists as diverse as Jean Piaget, Erik Erikson, and Daniel Levinson, men ascend the ladder of psychological development. The goal is an autonomous, separate, self-reliant identity. Several male Jungians, among them James Hillman and Thomas Moore, likewise conceive of spirituality as an autonomous journey traveled in a vertical dimension. Spirit is up there at the top of the ladder, and soul is down here. Spirit is transcendent, transformative, brave, and heroic, like Icarus flying to the sun. Soul, in contrast, is portrayed as more nitty-gritty stuff, that which lies below the surface and which men in particular are not acculturated to diving into.

While plumbing the depths is surely an exercise in soul making, I can't think that Spirit is lurking up above, disconnected from the process, while we dig in the fertile darkness of the Underworld. Were it not for the indwelling Spirit that guides and inspires, we would probably perish from the despair and depression of the darkness. The framework we will develop in this chapter encompasses both the realms of darkness and the constant presence of the light.

From my feminine perspective, the spiritual journey is less a matter of climbing up than of looking in and discovering the Inner Light that has been there all along. And once we have discovered the Light, its dissemination is more natural than heroic, more circular and relational than an autonomous, ladderlike process. Rather than spreading a messianic message of salvation, women's lives and relationships become a subtly transformative presence that has no need to return victorious and wise from a grand adventure.

Let me state from the outset that frameworks can be valuable. But they can also lead to stereotypes and half-truths. Jung pointed out that the animus and anima, the male and female principles, reside in both women and men. Depending on which aspect of our wholeness is individuating, or emerging into focus at any given time, we may find ourselves on either a hero's or heroine's journey. But since most theological systems are based on the expression of the animus, and those practices and experiences that strengthen its emergence, more is known about the male journey to God than its female counterpart. Yet both are inextricably interwoven in the lives of all human beings, regardless of gender.

Almost all spiritual exercises and systems were developed by men, for men. It is implicitly assumed that they apply equally well to women. The assumption that what's good for the gander is good for the goose is untrue not only for spirituality but also for psychology and medicine. A little-known fact is that the original research on breast cancer was done in men although the incidence of the disease is one in a million for them and one in eight for us. In terms of spirituality, it is similarly easy to say that we have no path of our own, and that, misleadingly as in the case of breast cancer, gender is irrelevant.

THE DARK NIGHTS OF SOUL MAKING

In speaking of the male spiritual journey, Hillman refers to soul stuff as what goes on internally, in the depths of the psyche, when the upper dimensions of achievement and triumph aren't realized.

The trip up the ladder is thwarted, and a dark night of self-examination begins. But for women the dark night is more likely to occur when feelings of separation and relationship problems arise, not only our relationships to other people but our relationship to the God we know most personally and effortlessly—the Inner Light of intuition. Since I was a former hyperachiever in the male world of academic medicine, the ladder was normative for me. And while I've certainly had dark times when success seemed out of reach, these were not the stuff of soul making.

I was at a workshop at a health-care conference, part of a panel discussing dark nights of the soul as turning points in professional life. One of the panelists was a successful young male cardiologist. He was vibrant, optimistic, a shark at the top of the academic food chain. He had not yet tasted the bitter medicine of despair, or at least did not speak of it. The other panelist was a psychologist and psychophysiologist. A gentle, thoughtful man, he shared that academic success was a turning point after a nightmare of childhood abuse at the hands of an alcoholic father. Through success he discovered that he was a worthwhile human being after all. That's where healing began for him.

It was my turn to speak. I found myself back in the early years of hospital practice. A young patient of mine, a delightful lawyer named "Arthur" discovered that the cancer he had been told was surgically cured had recurred with a vengeance. He was riddled with tumors that would, in all likelihood, end his career, his marriage, and his fathering of two small girls. Arthur tried to commit suicide and failed. Since he was remarkably successful at other things, I concluded that he really didn't want to die. If he had, he wouldn't have botched the attempt.

I told him this, and we had one of those holy moments when two souls meet through the eyes in an instant of truth and recognition. You can feel a peculiar shift during these experiences, a sense in the body. There is often a prickling sensation at the back of the neck and a sharpening of perception. Clock time is left behind and eternal time takes over. Colors become more vibrant and the moment seems realer than real. This is a spiritual experience in which both parties have accessed an authentic sense of Self, an Inner Light. There is no posturing or artifice. In this state, information can be accessed from the larger whole, and a revelatory quality takes over.

I spoke to Arthur from my heart, guided by that Inner Light. I told him how my father was driven mad by high doses of cortisone given as treatment for leukemia. The manic stranger that the treatment created was entirely foreign to the family. It was like living with a stranger for a year—a golem, a double. He looked like my father but was possessed by some other spirit. The grief our family experienced was nearly unbearable. Weaned off the steroids in preparation for surgery, my father came back into his right mind. But our relief and exuberance were short-lived. Apparently determined to save the family from further suffering, he managed to crawl out of bed in the middle of the night a few days after his release from the hospital. He successfully jumped to his death more than thirty stories below.

My mother was never the same. She had survivor's guilt. Her response to my father's suicide was self-blame. She had failed to watch over him and protect him. He had died on her watch. She responded by locking herself away, shutting out the world other than the immediate family. For the last thirteen years of her life my formerly gregarious, funny mother was a hermit. Although I never doubted that my father's suicide was motivated by compassion, in the end it was not a skillful choice. I left cancer research after the tragedy, more interested in the real world of people than the fascinating microcosm of tumor cells growing in petri dishes. Cancer cells in isolation from human beings had lost their meaning.

Now I was sitting opposite a young man who also had tried to end his life to spare his family. I told him honestly how my father's suicide had affected me. We wept together. We hugged. He went home and got his wife. We all talked with sincerity and candor. The young man agreed that life, at that moment, seemed a more compassionate choice than death. The couple spoke of how precious every moment is. They vowed to be present to one another and their children in whatever time was left to them as a family. Then they held one another for a long time, in silence.

My supervisor was appalled when I related these happenings. I had shared a personal story with a patient. This was a major no-no. In his eyes I was transferring the grief over my father's death onto the patient. My frontal lobes, the superego part of the brain that governs morality and self-comportment, went instantly into a major spasm of guilt and self-loathing. My mind was intent on beating me up. How could I have been so stupid as to violate basic protocol? But my heart remembered the young man and his wife in my office. It resonated with the deep level of intimacy and empathy that had blossomed between them due, in part, to my theoretically inept intervention. I had followed my intuition, guided by the Inner Light, the spiritual connection. Now I was being told that I was wrong.

This was truly a dark night. My frontal lobes, which my friend psychiatrist and neuroscientist Mona Lisa Schulz assures me are of double-D cup heft, took a long time to stop blaming and berating my therapeutic skills. For a while I resisted every impulse to listen to my intuition. I might, after all, be wrong. And there were rules for successful therapy developed by people much more knowledgeable. I folded my wings and dragged them sulkily behind. I relied solely on logic, instruction, supervision, and theory to guide the therapy. There were precious few times of spiritual connection with my own Inner Light or that of patients. But the Light resists being hidden under a bushel. Despite one's best efforts at ignoring it, it peeks out from time to time. These were the juicy moments when patients were likely to make breakthroughs. These were my finest moments as a therapist. I learned to trust and value my intuition and keep my methods to myself.

When women share their dark-night experiences, they are often of a relational nature like mine was—the relationships involved are of three kinds: the relationship we have with ourselves, the relationship we have to another person, and the relationship we have to the indwelling God who speaks to us through intuition and whose Presence is felt when the walls between two hearts crumble. Healing our relationship to God is not only a matter of coming to grips with theologies that may have wounded us. It is learning to trust that God is in the center of the circle of our lives, in the center of our hearts. We can count on that Presence which makes itself known through feelings, dreams, and synchronicities. Intuition is a natural state of consciousness in which our small isolated mind opens up to the Big Mind of the Divine.

TRUSTING THE INTUITION

I was at yet another health-care conference. Just after I arrived I got the bad news that I had lost the opportunity to host a radio program on women's spirituality. I had been psyched up by the prospect and had a good shot at being chosen. Right after the phone call I went to an early dinner with friends, so that I could deliver the opening keynote speech at 7:00 P.M. One of my trustiest psychological coping strategies is compartmentalization. Although disappointed and grieving, I was able to tuck that away for later and put on my perky, professional face. I was not even thinking about the lost opportunity when I showed up at dinner, yet the women at the table immediately picked up on the fact that something was wrong. They asked, and I gave them the thirty-second version. It was not yet time to talk it through.

The next day one of the friends reported that she had begun grieving for me the afternoon before I arrived, before I even knew of the lost opportunity. When Naomi saw all my books and tapes on display in the conference bookstore, she burst into tears. The difficulty of my demanding travel schedule washed over her. She realized that I needed to find a way to bring my work to more people without carting my body around the face of the earth. This revelation was body centered and deeply emotional. In fact, it gave her a headache. The "knowing" that I was in trouble was as close to her as her own cells.

When we met at dinner she understood that her intuition had been right on target. And it continued to flood her with information. That night she had a dream on my behalf. In the dream she was trying to get to a meeting about a radio show. It was one of those frustrating dreams in which obstacles keep arising. You just can't get where you want to go. She finally arrived at the meeting late. Everyone was gone and she lost the show. When she got home it turned out that the reason for the obstacles was that there was no paper in her fax machine. The symbolism of the missing paper became clear the minute I told her that the woman chosen to be the host of the radio show had a divinity degree whereas I do not. "Ah, you were missing the right piece of paper," said Naomi. Goose bumps rose on both of us, and our bodies agreed that her dream had gone right to the heart of the matter.

I cried in her arms as she told me more about what she had been dreaming, feeling, and thinking about my life. We are the kind of friends who don't see one another often, but when we do there is a particularly deep connection and affection. The Inner Light in both of us connects, and we feel the Presence of God through one another. That Divine Presence, the Big Mind, contains all information. By connecting to her deepest self, through her own journey, my friend was able to access information about me. Her connection to the Inner Light effortlessly drew me into the same place within myself, and we shared the kind of connection I had with Arthur.

The Inner Light, the Divine Presence, the Big Mind, the intuition, or whatever metaphor we use to describe it, is filled with intelligence that gets decoded and comes to conscious awareness through our nervous system. Strong emotion often facilitates the decoding, perhaps because emotions are body centered and help us to focus our attention. Women are generally more body aware and attuned to their emotions than are men. Although the same information is potentially available to both genders, I believe that intuition is frequently preceded by the word *women's* because our superior attention to emotional cues acts like magnifying glasses that bring a larger world into focus.

The downside of intuition as body awareness is that women easily take on the problems of other people as if they were psychic sponges. My friend Naomi had both a headache and a stomachache during the two-day period when she was receiving intuitive information about my problems. Not only is our individual body connected to our mind, it is potentially connected to other minds as well. By accessing intuition we become part of a circle in which knowledge flows from the center to the surround and back again, touching many people who are part of both a visible as well as an invisible network.

SARAH'S CIRCLE

Jan Maier is a choir director, vocalist, workshop leader, recording artist, and social activist who often facilitates the music for the

Gathering of Women retreats. As part of discussing the phases of growth that constitute the female life cycle at a midwest gathering, the group was walking around four altars that we had constructed to the Maiden, Mother, Guardian, and Wisewoman stages of life. Jan spontaneously began to sing, "We are walking Sarah's circle." She had once heard Pete Seeger sing these words, substituting them for the traditional "We are climbing Jacob's ladder," at a women's gathering years before. The metaphor seemed immediately right. The ladder is a linear, logical step-by-step process. The circle is relational and intuitive.

Abraham, Isaac, and Jacob were the three patriarchs of Judaism. As is typical in biblical tales, we hear a lot about the men but very little about the women. The story of Jacob's ladder is explicit, but the story of Sarah's circle has to be ferreted out, intuited. Explicitly, Sarah was Abraham's wife and the matriarch of Judaism. In her postmenopausal old age, due to the miraculous intervention of God, she bore a son named Isaac. Isaac, in turn, married Rebekah, who bore twin boys, Esau and Jacob, Sarah's grandsons. The entire Jewish lineage is part of Sarah's circle in that they are her descendants. She is the elder, the grandmother, the kin keeper, the invisible matrix out of which a new tribal religion grew.

An interesting query about Sarah's story concerns its most salient point. What does it mean that she was postmenopausal when she gave birth to Isaac? Certainly it would give the Israelites a leg up to trace their origins to a miracle. But in a more basic sense, Sarah's restoration to fertility is as much about the possibility of instantaneous, surprising change as it is about the birth of a special child. The ladder process, the hero's journey of psychospiritual individuation, is a measured course of logical steps. The goal and destination are obvious. The circular process is more unplanned, unexpected, intuitive and irrational. It leaves room for God to change our path at any time and suggests that we are not always the "doer." Unseen forces and circumstances can provoke sudden transformation that comes through us, rather than from our own will.

Men, in general, are more goal directed than women about getting things done. For a brief time in my career, I planned to become a management consultant. The creative process was intriguing. I attended a business seminar given by the company that was going to hire me. Goal setting was one of the main agendas, and it made perfect sense to the group of men who were being trained. But when I reflected on my own life, I realized that goal setting only worked as a short-term strategy. When it was time to write a research grant, and one's career was entirely dependent on grant funding, I rarely knew what the topic would be. Instead, I would go to the library a few weeks before the deadline and would invariably come upon a journal article that related perfectly to my current work and suggested some totally new slant. Then things would fall into place. Phone calls, articles in the mail, and corridor conversations would all fit together like pieces of a puzzle. I found this chaotic but reliable process no less miraculous than Sarah's sudden fertility.

When I was in college, my boyfriend asked what I thought I would be doing at forty. Out of the blue I replied that I would be writing a best-selling book. He joked about my narcissistic grandiosity. But I don't even know where the idea came from. I never planned to be a writer, or had that as a goal. I was thirty-nine when I attended the management seminar. One of the exercises was to decide upon a one-year goal. It dawned on me that I would soon be forty, and although I hadn't thought of it in years, the conversation with my college boyfriend came to mind. I told my partner in the exercise that my goal was to write a book, although I had no idea about what. Part of the exercise involved agreeing to contact your partner at the end of a year to see if they had taken the steps necessary to meet their goal.

I lost interest in becoming a management consultant and soon forgot all about the exercise. When my partner called a year later to ask about my progress on the book, I had taken no steps at all. Nonetheless, the first phone call the following Monday morning was from an agent who wanted me to write a book about stress. In my fortieth year I wrote *The New York Times* best-seller, *Minding the Body, Mending the Mind.* I was such a neophyte to the book world, and so lacking in goals even after the book was written, that when the publisher called to tell me that it was going to be on the *Times* list, I asked, "Is that good?"

Like Sarah, some Higher Power seemed to have had a plan for me in which I was a willing participant, but certainly not the doer. I was not at the center of the circle alone, directing the shots. God was with me. The Inner Light guided me. Writing that first book was no hero's journey to fetch the Golden Fleece. The idea itself was a pure intuitive hit that occurred twenty years prior to its publication. The events and people who were important to the book were not consciously courted and contacted. They arrived, as if on cue, as part of the natural flow of life. An interconnected web of small, seemingly unrelated circumstances all circled round to birth a book.

The majority of men set goals and measure success by achievement. The majority of women tell me that the major accomplishments of their lives came through a confluence of unexpected events. They see themselves having intuited the right path as it opened in front of them, rather than consulting a map that led to a specific destination. Some men complain about women's "circular, fuzzy thinking." The fact is that we tend to see relationships between things that may not be obvious to men. Our intuition may even bring up ideas that seem unrelated to the conversation at hand.

While a circle is defined by its center, a ladder has no central point. Each rung is either closer to or further from the top. In a circle there is no above and below, ahead or behind. Everything is equidistant from the center. The center of the circle for a woman is her heart, the Inner Light, the intuition, the voice of God. Her journey is one of orienting to the center of the circle so that she can hear the guidance that always comes from within and use it wisely for the greater good.

There is an old adage that God is a circle whose circumference is everywhere and whose center is in every person. While there are different intensities of experiencing the center of the circle—ranging from the kind of touched-by-the-Light stories people recount in near-death and other numinous experiences, to the everyday shift into expanded consciousness that we call dreams and intuition, to the kind of relational experiences I had with Arthur and Naomi—all forays into the center of the circle are marked by wisdom and healing power. And when anyone in the circle touches the center, information flows to everyone else. Sarah's circle is a relational journey in the company of other travelers.

Whereas in a ladder model spiritual experience proceeds step-by-step, according to precepts and practices that are well worked out, in a circular model spiritual experience can strike anyone at any time. No previous experience is needed. If the former model is one of works, the latter is one of grace. One doesn't have to be holy and healed to experience Divine guidance. In fact, such guidance often comes as a result of pain and problems. And why not? When things are coasting along smoothly, we don't need guidance. The sudden flashes of intuition and dreams we have in our darkest hours, however, are capable of renewing our lives, changing our course, and mending a broken spirit.

Researchers Sherry Ruth Anderson and Patricia Hopkins spent five years studying patterns of spiritual growth in women. They summarized their findings in the book *The Feminine Face of God.*

In their magnificent study, based on over a hundred in-depth interviews lasting two or more days, each with women all over America, they discovered that spirituality is natural for women, rather than a sequential series of steps to be mastered as it is for men. They write, "We had heard and read so much about spiritual development based on systems formulated by and for men, systems built on successive stages of realization, that we had begun to think of development as some achievement like the development of pectoral muscles or shopping centers."

Walking Sarah's circle is another way of saying that our spiritual journey—and thus our lifetime development—is a circumambulation of the center, of that Spirit that the Quakers call the Inner Light. The Buddhists call this *rigpa*, one's own true nature. Jews call it the Shekhina, "She who dwells within." The Christian mystic Meister Eckehart called it the Godseed. The Hindus call it the Atman. The Seneca tribe calls it the Orenda. The theological debate over whether God is immanent or transcendent doesn't make sense in a circular model. Everything is related and interdependent. In a nonlinear universe, either/or gets replaced by both/and. By grace, at any time during the journey, we can touch the center and know God.

Like particles and waves, the energy of the universe is forever taking different forms. Sometimes we climb a ladder. Other times we walk a circle. Sometimes grace sweeps us into the center. The ladder and the circle are both valuable models of the journey to God. But they are only models. Yin and yang, male and female, unite to form a circle in which one half is black and the other is white. There is a small black dot in the white side, a small white dot in the black side. A little of the ladder pertains to women, and sometimes the circular path is walked by men. One way is no better than the other, just more suited to us by biology and development. When the two symbols intersect, and men and women respect and support one another in their own authentic spiritual paths, we will help to carry one another home.

A BRAIN OF OUR OWN
FOR A PATH OF OUR OWN

While Tufts University psychologist Zella Luria has reminded us that we are two different genders, not two different species, the biological differences between men and women are nonetheless real. It is the most basic fact of life that I am a woman, not a man, and that femininity comes with its own gifts as I have discussed at length in *A Woman's Book of Life*.

Women are wired neurologically as receivers, attentive to the nuances of voice, expression, sight, and sound around them which register in our bodies as feelings and sensation, health and illness. Even without the aid of the five physical senses, women come wired for intuition, the sixth sense that speaks to us regularly in dreams, "knowings," flashes of insight or feelings. Men can and do develop these sensitivities, but for women they are a natural gift of our gender.

Intuition is not a startling gift that is the province of a few psychics. Too often portrayed as the stuff of seers, fortune-tellers, and people with their heads wrapped in bedsheets, it is less about divining the future than it is about entering more authentically into the present. Intuition is always operative, so common that it often evades conscious recognition.

It was bright and sunny, the warm Colorado sun streaming over the earth like liquid gold. I was hot as I fired up the trusty four-wheel-drive car for a trip down the mountain to Boulder. Suddenly I flashed on my winter parka hanging in the hall closet, and before my feet knew what hit them, they were walking back up the steps.

The jacket got tossed in the backseat, and by the time I got to Boulder it was snowing. Jane was working on a business plan and the ringer on her phone was turned off. Before her fingers knew what motivated them, they had turned it on again just in time for a call from one of her children. Bethany picked up a picture of a friend that had been lying on her table for months, and prickles went up her spine. There was an uneasy feeling in her stomach. Bethany called her friend, who had just walked in the door from the hospital. Her husband had been in a car crash. Sue is struck by a sudden lust for soy burgers, normally as appetizing as marinated sawdust. She then buys a bottle of vitamin E without knowing why. After two days her hot flashes disappear. The body knows.

Mona Lisa Schulz, M.D., Ph.D., a psychiatrist, neuroscientist, and medical intuitive, writes about how women are wired for "knowing" in her groundbreaking book, *Awakening Intuition:*

> The left half or left hemisphere of the brain, is the seat of logic. It's sequential, rational, linear, fact-based and focuses on the external world. It constantly searches for value in the information it receives. Its strengths are speech and language, and it's usually thought of as the masculine half of the brain. The right hemisphere, on the other hand, is more irrational, receptive, visual, and gestalt oriented. It's interested in beauty and aesthetics. Its focus is on emotions and the state of the body, and it's generally designated as the feminine half. . . . Some people are left-hemisphere dominant, and some are right-hemisphere dominant. Women, on the whole, have greater access to the right brain and a greater ability to move back and forth between the two hemispheres simultaneously. Men, as a general rule, are apt to use one hemisphere or the other but not both at once: they tend to stay more in the left hemisphere.

The right hemisphere is also more compliant and submissive than the left, as well as receptive. Mona Lisa tells a wonderful story about a scientist who noticed something striking about hemispheric dominance while driving with his wife in England, where the steering wheel is on the right side of the car instead of the left. When his wife was in the passenger seat talking to him, his left ear received most of the information. Since hearing is wired contralaterally, in other words what goes into the left ear registers in the right brain, he was much more receptive to her point of view than usual and found himself remarkably compliant. When they got back to driving in the United States, however, his wife was once again speaking to his left brain through his right ear, and he was less receptive to her suggestions. Maybe that's why intuitively I have always chosen to sleep on the left side of the bed so that my suggestions are received by my husband's more emotionally attuned, receptive, and compliant right brain.

The right hemisphere is also the source of what we think of as paranormal events like out-of-body experiences, near-death experiences, mystic experiences, and meetings with the Light. When people enter these altered states, they can often correctly report their observation of events happening at distant locations and are privy to worlds of wisdom and meaning that are ordinarily unavailable. The research on these phenomena is extensive and robust. Stimulate the mesial (middle-facing) right temporal lobe during surgery and they are readily reproducible. The fact that we can know about events occurring at distant locations is what physicists call a nonlocal phenomenon. Physician and author Larry Dossey writes about the mind as a nonlocal consciousness that can tune in to a larger reality. It is rather astonishing to think that the hardware for omniscience is installed in our brains. Like television sets, they are capable of picking up invisible signals from a multitude of sources.

The mesial aspect of the right temporal lobe is the circuit board for mysticism. It is closely connected to the emotional brain, or limbic system. Almost every mystical experience I have had, ranging from dreams of Divine Light to entering the Light with my mother when she died, have been accompanied by strong, highly charged emotions. Anger, frustration, grief, and fear have been my tickets to heaven. It amuses my oppositional nature that mystical experiences rarely result from meditations in which I am peaceful and centered, although meditation increases right-brain activity and may prime the pump. It is the push and pull of daily life, the normal anguishes and difficulties, and the fervent wish that things might be better that seem to trigger God's grace. My renewal of faith in India, for example, followed a dry and difficult time. Anguish rather than spirituality is what led to the breakthrough.

Like all women, my intuition and receptivity increase during the second half of the menstrual cycle, after ovulation, when research has shown that women become more right-hemisphere dominant. Interestingly, the left hemisphere is more upbeat than the right. It likes joyful words and a happy world. The right brain is less optimistic and more in tune with emotions that are uncomfortable and which the left brain filters out during the first part of the menstrual cycle. Psychophysiologist Margaret Altemus and her colleagues, using something called the dichotic listening test in which words are presented to different ears, discovered that premenstrually we hear many more negative words than in the first part of the cycle. Most women routinely experience this monthly increase in negativity, but now we know why. Right-brain activity is increased before our periods. But we can think of this hemispheric shift as a gift rather than a curse because it calls our attention to what we know intively but tend to repress, especially when that information might goad us into making a major life change.

WOMEN'S WISDOM:
THE INTUITION NETWORK

My husband can tell exactly where I am in my menstrual cycle by my moods, dreams, and preoccupations. Things that I haven't mentioned all month, because I haven't thought of them much or at all, escalate in the last two weeks of the cycle from minor concerns to crises of Armageddon-like proportions. This is the intuition's built-in attention-getting method, and like much of women's wisdom it has been discounted: "Don't listen to that, it's just PMS. Take a few pills and get over it." But an important part of spirituality is action. If your intuition is pointing out problem areas where action is necessary, you can think of it as the voice of the Spirit that dwells within, calling you to create a better future.

As women mature past the childbearing years into menopause, intuition increases. Dr. Christiane Northrup calls this going from an AC, or alternating current of wisdom—two weeks on and two weeks off—to a DC, or direct current of wisdom after menopause. She relates this to the neurohormones FSH, follicular stimulating hormone, and LH, luteinizing hormone, which fluctuate premenopausally, controlling estrogen and progesterone levels during different parts of the cycle. But the secretion of FSH and LH doesn't decline postmenopausally like that of estrogen and progesterone. They get stuck in overdrive. Traditional medical thinking attributes the striking increase in these neurohormones to a vain but valiant attempt of the brain to goose the aged ovaries into coughing up a few last eggs. But nature isn't so wasteful. A better hypothesis is that these neurohormones, like others secreted from the anterior pituitary gland, are neurotransmitters. It is a reasonable bet that they are part of the information-processing network and that their increase underlies the flowering of intuition that ancient cultures ascribed to the postmenopausal wisewoman.

My mother was forty when I was born and postmenopausal by the time I was a teenager. She was a fine medical intuitive although there was no word for that skill in her day so she simply called herself "the brain surgeon" or "the witch." Before she rendered a diagnosis she would preface her comments with "mark my words." When finished she would say, "I have spoken," like a true oracle. She probably would have been burned as a witch in medieval times. The same intuitive powers that can allow diagnosis may also operate in the domain of treatment. Before the days of modern medicine, midwives were herbalists who had a much better track record at healing than male physicians, whose bleeding, purging, and cupping killed enormous numbers of people. Although today's modern medicine is truly miraculous, it has overshadowed important intuitive knowledge that was common currency for the effective healers of earlier times and more "primitive" right-brain-dominant cultures.

Which herbs might be helpful for a particular condition? In some Native American tribes, for example, healers dream of the correct plants to use for the conditions of specific patients. Rather than following a rational, linear outline that dictates this herb for that cure, the plants themselves "speak" to the healer in the context of which plant medicines can best restore balance and wholeness. The left brain finds this kind of "knowing" irrational and potentially dangerous. It is offended by the ability to know things without benefit of logical process. Nonetheless, scientific breakthroughs are often based on right-brain intuitive hits that are later dissected and described by the left brain, which then takes credit for them. The German scientist Kekulé, after much puzzling, finally figured out the circular structure of the benzene ring by dreaming of a snake with its tail in its mouth.

By menopause a woman not only has a growing number of potentially disruptive "knowings," she also tends to vocalize them. Due, in part, to the relative increase in testosterone as estrogen declines, women get more ballsy and brazen at midlife, speaking out about what is important. The urge to protect life in all its forms, to be a she-bear, surfaces. This may be unpopular, since it can buck the tide of societal behavior or the corporate vision where she works, and may lead to criticism or even ostracism. In past times, speaking our truth may even have led to burning at the stake.

Over the years I have been struck by the number and consistency of reports I have heard from women concerning emotionally chilling memories of being burned at the stake. These may occur in dreams, in reveries, or in sudden flashes during situations when the woman is trying to assert herself for some greater good. Most younger women have considerable difficulty speaking out, even when they know they are right. And almost every woman I have asked is almost phobic about anger. Many will do just about anything to prevent people from directing anger toward them.

The common psychological explanation for fear of anger and resistance to speaking one's truth is that we would rather be people pleasers than risk disapproval and possible abandonment. But I think something more pervasive and nonlocal is at work. I am certainly open to the possibility of past lives, that some women really were once persecuted as witches. But even without invoking past lives, perhaps women tap into a morphic field of ancient memories, of the persecution of women from former times. The intuitive powers of women have long frightened men, particularly when they threaten the established social, economic, scientific, or religious order of the day. This may be one of the reasons why women's intuitive, circular spirituality—and the ancillary powers of healing that arise from it—have been forced underground, ignored, or ridiculed.

I experienced some of that ancient fear of women's healing wisdom when running a mind/body clinic at one of the Harvard Medical School teaching hospitals. I was standing in the oncology outpatient department when "Martha," a graduate student in physics from mainland China who was in one of my programs, walked out of her doctor's office. She flashed a conspiratorial grin at me. The cancerous tumors that had been completely nonresponsive to treatment were suddenly melting like icicles in the sun. The doctor was mystified. We were not. But neither of us told him what we believed was causing the remission.

Martha had come to me to learn meditation to calm herself down and help strengthen her body's defenses. Chemotherapy was not working for her, and at twenty-five she was ready to prepare for death. She arrived at one of our sessions deeply depressed. An old woman herbalist in Boston's Chinatown had taken her by the hand, looked into her eyes, and given her the message that her ancestors were angry. When Martha's family had left their rural village for the city, no rituals had been performed for the ancestors. Until they were, the old woman explained, Martha's treatment would not work. I asked whether her family could still arrange such a ritual. Martha nodded her assent. But it would take several months to accomplish, and by then she might be dead.

"Do you believe in the living presence of your ancestors, in their ability to change the present?" I asked this brilliant young scientist.

She heaved a sigh, and met my eyes. "Of course I do. This is my culture."

"Even though you are a scientist?" I continued. Martha gave me a short lecture on quantum physics. She explained a little about Bell's theorem and how particles once in association continue to respond to one another across time and space. When you salt your food and the sodium chloride breaks down to a molecule of sodium and a molecule of chlorine, the two halves of the molecule still respond to each other. If the sodium ends up in New York, it will adjust its spin to the chloride, even if that molecule resides in Czechoslovakia. Theoretically, every atom in the universe is part of a great network, in constant communication. It was a short leap for Martha from Bell's theorem to the continuing presence of her ancestors and the ability of the past to change the future.

"Well, then. If the consciousness of the ancestors is nonlocal, not bound by time and space, why can't we contact them right now and explain your predicament?" This made perfect sense to Martha. The energy in the room seemed to move up a notch as our intentions joined.

I took a candle and a stick of incense out of my desk drawer, where they waited for just such occasions. We arranged them near a plant, creating an impromptu altar. Pushing the chairs out of the way, Martha and I placed my small Oriental rug in front of the altar. Kneeling down, we closed our eyes and went into meditation. I then asked politely, and with great respect, if the ancestors would join us. I explained Martha's problem and asked if they would accept her prayers right now, before the formal village ritual, so that her body could heal. Martha spoke to them next, praying in the village dialect she had learned from her parents. The singsong rhythm of her words created a bridge to an ancient world, an explosion of feeling. We began to sway and shiver. Tears welled up. We invited the ancestors to visit at any time, and Martha promised to stay in daily connection with them.

Within a week she was responding to the chemotherapy. The left brain is tempted to invoke the placebo effect. Martha had a powerful belief in the ancestors and in the prayer ritual we had devised together. Her belief may have changed her body. I'm sure that it did. But I'm also open to the possibility that the old woman from Chinatown tuned in to real ancestors, as did Martha and I. Perhaps the old woman actually saw or heard the spirits. We did not, yet we prayed and acted with belief and respect. In joining together spiritually, we walked through that doorway between linear and eternal time, what the Greeks call chronos and kairos. Healing occurs in kairos, a place of limitless possibility where energy has not yet collapsed into either a particle or a wave. What is created there manifests here.

Some of my left-brain colleagues would probably call me foolish for the "intervention" I designed with Martha. They might also ascribe her remission after the ritual to coincidence. As we scientists hasten to say, one anecdote does not data make. Nonetheless, for over thirty years I have observed cases like Martha's, where intuition was a guide to both diagnosis and healing. At times the healing was physical—a cure. At other times it was emotional and spiritual. At all times it occurred through the agency of relationship where the Divine Presence entered through the door of an open heart.

A few weeks after our ancestor ritual I was standing in the outpatient oncology department once again. Martha's physician, who had been openly hostile to my behavioral medicine approach, walked up with a big smile. He slapped me on the shoulder. I had been miraculously accepted as one of the guys. Before I could recover from the shock, he introduced a patient to me and told her that she should sign up for our cancer group. "I have no idea what they do in there," he explained, "but people love it. They come back peaceful. Treatment seems to go better. It's probably witchcraft," he winked at me, "but it seems to help a lot."

An important part of our spiritual development is learning to trust our ability to see and feel deeply and directly beyond our usual experience. During the years when I was most miserable, undergoing the period of healing that women move through in preparation for menopause, my intuition was in high gear. Mystical experiences and "big" dreams fell like rain. I became addicted to them. When my wild and instructive dream life grew quiet, and Light experiences stopped coming, I thought that I had done something wrong. Perhaps I was not trying hard enough, not committed enough to spiritual practice. It was those insistent goody-goody frontal lobes again, trying to get me to climb the ladder and do things "right."

The process of spiritual development is more subtle now. There are fewer fireworks and more steady warmth. The Light no longer appears to me but shines out of my heart to others. Its wisdom is liable to come through in conversation, in lectures, in writing, in quiet times. Perhaps this developmental process is why I have come to love the company of women so much in midlife. Those of us who have done the healing work of overcoming regrets and resentments, forgiving the gods of our childhood and making peace with life, are an unexpectedly wise, spacious, tolerant, and funny group. It is good to be on the journey together.

WOMEN'S RELATIONALITY: WIRED FOR EMPATHY

Women are relational stars. We love company and conversation. We empathize easily with others and internalize their experience as our own. Like Naomi, who immediately deduced that something was wrong even though I gave no overt signal, we have an uncanny ability to read subtle cues about people's internal state. An emotionally healthy woman can then match her responses to the other person's inner experience. As a result, deep and meaningful interaction follows.

A study reported in the prestigious journal *Nature*, and promptly picked up by the international wire services, investigated whether the superior sensitivity that women display to social cues like facial expression and voice modulation is a result of nature or nurture. British psychiatrist David Skuse and his colleagues at the Institute of Child Health in London studied eighty girls and young women with Turner's syndrome, a genetic disorder in which women have only one X chromosome rather than two. Young women who inherited their single X chromosome from their father had normal social skills, while those who inherited it from their mother apparently irritated people, hurt their feelings, and had trouble sustaining friendships according to reports filled out by their parents.

The reason, according to Skuse and his group, was a putative gene on the X chromosome that carries the coding for relationality. They believe that this gene is switched on, or operative, in the paternal X chromosome but is switched off in the maternal X chromosome. Genetically normal women with an X chromosome derived from both parents are innately relational. Men, with a single X chromosome from the mother containing the inactive gene, and a Y chromosome from their father, are not innately relational. And as research demonstrates, neither are women with Turner's syndrome who lack a paternal X chromosome with the switched-on gene. Skuse comments of men, "We've got to learn social skills, whereas women just pick them up."

I believe that some of the differences between men's and women's journeys to God can be explained by Skuse's comment. Walking Jacob's ladder in different religious traditions provides men with a rational, step-by-step approach to learning the relationality that is inherent to women. For example, almost every religion stresses ethical relationship practices as a first step, as a foundation for reaching God and holiness. These ethical considerations are based on an empathetic understanding already hardwired into women by virtue of the chromosome that Skuse's group studied.

After the Ten Commandments are outlined in Exodus, there are detailed explanations for a variety of interactions, including a section on how to treat slaves fairly, both the ones that are bought and those who are sold. "When a man sells his daughter as a slave, she shall not go out as the male slaves do. If she does not please her master, who has designated her for himself, then he shall let her be redeemed; he shall have no right to sell her to a foreign people. . . . If he designates her for his son, he shall deal with her as a daughter. If he takes another wife to himself he shall not diminish her food, her clothing, or her marital rights. And if he does not do these three things for her, she shall go out for nothing, without payment of money."

Exodus goes on with a long list of punishments for unethical behavior, many intended to keep the aggressive behavior of men in line. Whoever steals a slave is put to death as is anyone who strikes a parent. If men get into a fight, the winner has to pay the loser for the time lost from work while he was healing. If men gang up on a pregnant woman and beat her, causing a miscarriage, her husband can set an appropriate fine. If a man seduces a virgin, he has to offer her father a bride-present and marry her. If the father refuses him as a son-in-law, the seducer has to pay a different amount of money. The laws in regard to worship are likewise outlined. Any person caught making sacrifices to some other God gets the death penalty as does any "sorceress." So much for women's intuition in a patriarchal society.

Yet many of the laws are compassionate. "You shall not wrong a stranger or oppress him, for you were strangers in the land of Egypt. You shall not afflict any widow or orphan. If you do afflict them, and they cry out to me, I will surely hear their cry. . . . If you lend money to any of my people with you who is poor, you shall not be to him as a creditor, and you shall not exact interest from him. . . . If ever you take your neighbor's garment in pledge, you shall restore it to him before the sun goes down; for that is his only covering."

While I don't want to imply that women are always kinder, gentler, and more relational than men, societies that honored women, such as many of the pre-Columbian cultures, had no need of laws to legislate fair and empathetic behavior. Although the men may have been fierce warriors, their relationships were the model of the Golden Rule, as they exempted their enemies' women, children, and elders in war. Every conqueror, from Christopher Columbus to the English, French, and Dutch colonists, left records about the gentle godliness of the Indians, and how they would willingly give away everything they owned to strangers. Their indigenous spirituality was not a ladder but a circle in which relationship to other people, to the earth and the animals, the cycles and the seasons was a guiding light. These Indian men and women were biologically distinct from each other in terms of the number of X chromosomes they had, yet nurture provided the men with some of the same relational skills that are inborn in women.

Psychologist Janet Surrey, of the Stone Center for Women's Research at Wellesley College, has written about the fact that women mature differently from men. Men develop a sense of self through autonomy and separation from their mothers. They make a psychological Declaration of Independence. Freud thought that all human beings ought to develop that way, and, according to him, women were inferior because they didn't. Lacking male sexual parts, he reasoned, women don't develop the Oedipus complex, as a result of which young boys withdraw from their mothers fearful of being castrated by dad, a rival too big to scrap with. Instead, we cleave to our mothers and learn to be relational. Perhaps this is why Elizabeth Cady Stanton and her colleagues wrote what they called a Declaration of Sentiments as a counterbalance to the male Declaration of Independence.

Rather than seeing relationality and empathy as a one-down position, Surrey has discovered that women mature through a continual process of "self-in-relation." Our very sense of self comes from an openhearted desire to know another, to put ourselves in their place and to empathically experience the world through their perceptions. Surrey describes how girls and women individuate in relationship by being received and mirrored by another person, and then receiving and mirroring them back. We've all experienced that. You are having an intimate conversation, and an insight springs up that you would not otherwise have had. Some new part of yourself is brought forward by the interaction. Surrey describes this as a case of the whole being greater than the sum of its parts.

There is security in intimate conversation, in experiences of self-in-relation, a sense of being accepted, valued, and appreciated. When we are involved in self-in-relation, the sacred Other is a soul friend, a connection to the spiritual. John O'Donohue writes of deep friendship, an experience of self-in-relation, in his poetic book on Celtic spirituality, *Anam Cara*. "In this love, you are understood as you are without mask or pretension. The superficial and functional lies and half-truths of social acquaintance fall away, you can be as you really are. Love allows understanding to dawn, and understanding is precious. Where you are understood, you are at home. Understanding nourishes belonging. When you really feel understood, you feel free to release yourself into the trust and shelter of the other person's soul."

Both women and men are capable of deep friendship. But if Skuse's research is correct, men may have to develop the sensitivity to self-in-relation over time, whereas it is the woman's innate way. The relational skills that allow us to grow by releasing ourselves "into the trust and shelter of the other person's soul" are as natural as breathing to women who have had healthy childhoods. But if we have not, and our hearts are closed, then we will have to go back into the depths to heal the soul. Experiencing one's depths, through pain and healing, helps develop relational skills. This, I think, is what Hillman and Moore are really talking about when they describe male soul growth as a dive into the depths.

Sarah's circle is a relational, intuitive mode of being. The Golden Rule is a biologically inborn gift of empathy. So, unlike men, emotionally healthy women do not have to study ethical practices as a series of rungs in the ladder of spirituality. Unlike men, women do not generally need to suffer dark nights of the soul to bring us into our own depths. We do that for one another in the course of everyday interaction.

What those of us walking Sarah's circle do need to learn is trust. Trust in our intuition, the Inner Light, trust in the illogical, irrational flashes that guide us on the journey. These skills have been devalued in a left-brain society where the logic of Jacob's ladder, and its step-by-step approach, has been assumed to apply to women as well as to men. Women are born with prodigious relational gifts. The ladder is superfluous for our gender. But as men walk the ladder, they can and do learn about relationality. It is a perfect map for their journey. Women, on the other hand, need only to celebrate and trust what we have already been given by virtue of our nature. When we willingly enter the world of another, we ourselves are entered. Even our breath synchronizes. We conspire—literally breathe together—to be something more in relationship than either of us is alone. We find ourselves blessed by each other's presence, at home in the garden of the soul.

NAMING THE MYSTERY

Father, Mother, or Other?

Once women have recognized that our journey to God is a circle rather than a ladder, freeing ourselves from culture-bound concepts, the next step is to reevaluate our image of God. Is that, too, culture bound, or have we arrived at a way of naming the Mystery that resonates deeply with our own soul and sensibilities? Does our image of God feel personal and real? Every woman needs to find an authentic link to the Divine, to name the center of her circle in a way that makes God most accessible to her.

For years my inability to connect with a meaningful image of God made prayer and the cultivation of a day-by-day relationship difficult. While I was most comfortable with the idea of God as consciousness and Mystery, these abstracts were too slippery to be an anchor for the center of my circle. I tried out many different images of God. Unlike friends who worshipped God the Father or Mother, Kuan Yin or Jesus, Buddha or Mary, Saraswati or Krishna, my Jewish roots kept trying to put up shoots. The idea of a God that is both male and female is part of the Jewish mystical tradition. Baruch Ha Shem, meaning the "Blessed Holy Name," is male. His consort is the Shekhina. It is the spiritual duty of every person through prayer and good deeds to reunite these two aspects of God, which somehow fell out of union with one another.

The Lord's Prayer that the rabbi Jesus taught in the original Aramaic actually addresses the Cosmic Birther, Mother-Father God. I can relate to that. I like the Aramaic words, *Abwoon d'bwashmaya*. They feel like music in my body. It took me many years to arrive at this focus, and it is my hope that this chapter will help you get to yours, especially if you are a dropout who is out to sea without an anchor or if the image of God you were raised with causes pain or grief.

Almost every child who goes to Sunday school learns that God is a male person rather than a mysterious force of creation, guidance, conscience, love, intuition, healing, and transformation. Even the deity's shape-shifting powers are played down. We forget about God as a burning bush, a whirlwind, or a pillar of smoke. Such images are evocative of Mystery. The light of creation. The stuff of stars. A moon that waxes and wanes, its full face reflected on the waters. The neutrons and positrons that swirl in the center of an atom. The elegance of mathematics. The fragrance of the earth after a rain. John Donne's "force that through the green stem fuses." The cosmic mother who gives birth and nurtures. The insistent maw of death, the fearsome power of renewal that turns the wheel of life.

I was introduced to the original, old-time lemonade-stand version of God the Father of the white people on the first day of Sunday school. We were given coloring books of Genesis. God was drawn as an old man in the sky, a kindly grandfather who looked like an emaciated Santa Claus with a long white beard. His cheeks puffed out as he blew a stream of breath that condensed into the land and the seas. Then He breathed life into trees and flowers, a vast array of animals, and finally a handsome young man. Then he put Adam to sleep and pulled a smiling, beautiful Eve from his side. The coloring book had been G-rated for kids, since Adam and Eve both emerged from the mists of creation fully dressed in vines and fig leaves.

I arrived home with the coloring book, exuberantly acting out the creation story. My father sat me down on his lap and began to make one of his most impressive noises, a buzzing like an airplane that came from moving his index and middle fingers up and down so rapidly that they seemed a blur. He zoomed his magic fingers through the air, finally landing on my belly button. As I laughed, he chortled, "If God is a man up in the sky, do you think that airplanes are flying through his belly button all the time?" We rolled around on the old green velvet sofa, hysterical with giggling. The image of the sky man began to develop holes.

I lay awake that night, the light of the full moon streaming through the window and across my red woolen blanket, illuminating dolls and teddy bears. I knew that the man in the moon was not real, even though I liked to pretend that he was. The sky man with the long white beard wasn't real either. I knew that God was, whatever God was. But I couldn't get my mind around it. Night after night I pondered the paradox. Where did God come from? Was there nothing before creation? How could something arise from nothing? So began the search for a way to describe the indescribable. Even though I knew that descriptions of God were impossible, even at seven, the left brain with its penchant for arranging the world with linguistic certainty would not cease from trying.

My father taught me that God could not be imagined. If anything, God was the act of imagination itself. But, for many people, a concrete image of God was installed during childhood, and no amount of effort can purge it from the hard drive of our neural circuitry. It lives on as an icon that pops up every time we open the folder named religion. Whether a source of nurture or a perpetual thorn in the side, the icon has a life of its own. A Buddhist friend of mine, who as an adult has no belief at all in a personified God, still can't shake off the icon of "God the Peeping Tom." This peevish deity who rewards good little girls and boys and punishes bad ones lives on in her imagination. She is still angry at this image, although she knows that she is boxing with a shadow. In order to heal our relationship to God, so that we can get on with our spiritual development, old images that are toxic need to be retrieved and recast.

THE LIKENESS OF THE DIVINE

In Genesis God said, "Let Us make man in Our image, after Our likeness. . . . So God created man in His own image, in the image of God He created him; male and female He created them." Had my father and I discussed this verse, I can imagine what he might have said to appeal to my childhood logic and imagination. "If God is a white man, and we are all supposed to look like him, how did all the other colors of people get created? What about the Chinese and the Eskimos? They are yellow and they hardly grow any beards at all. Certainly not the long, bushy kind that God has. And women don't even grow mustaches."

Had my father lived to see his daughter mature out of young adulthood, our discussions would surely have been less concrete. As we mature, so does our capacity for metaphor and paradox. If we are nurtured sufficiently, we leave the childish need for black-and-white certainty behind. Then we can ask whether the biblical words "image and likeness" refer to physical form at all. Perhaps they are metaphors for God's creative powers or loving consciousness. As an adult, the only concrete "image" I have of God is as a force of creative power, love and mercy, a cosmic birther. The center of my circle is an unspeakably generous fountain of infinite compassion and encouragement blending male and female principles, *Abwoon d'bwashmaya.*

As children our parents are our first concrete images of God. They have the power to create and destroy, to love us or to leave us. If you were lucky enough to have a father like mine, a masculine image of God might evoke giggly, warm, safe feelings. The image of God the Father might serve you well as an adult, and be a powerful connection to the spiritual. Lynne's father, on the other hand, was a brutish drunk who routinely beat up her mother and older brother. He started sexually molesting Lynn when she was eight. The idea of God the Father scares her to death. He is a cosmic bogeyman who can always find you, so that you can never be safe. For her, God the Father is a poor image for the ineffable Light of love. Genesis could be rewritten from a human perspective. "Let us make God in the image of our parents, after their likeness. . . . So girls and boys created God to mimic their caretakers, in the image of these powerful beings God was created."

A study of one hundred Roman Catholics revealed that, regardless of similar religious training, people develop idiosyncratic ideas about God. Those with high self-esteem, the products of good parenting, tend to believe in a merciful God. Those with low self-esteem, the children of less capable parents, are more likely to imagine God as punitive. Until the wounds of childhood are healed, images of God may be distorted and painful. Spiritual growth, and the capacity to love, is a reflection of psychological maturity. It is no surprise that many fire-and-brimstone preachers began their journey as abused children. As adults they are still locked into black-and-white thinking, the eye-for-an-eye and tooth-for-a-tooth mentality of early childhood. The bearded white man in the sky is a nightmare to be kept at bay by a rigid set of rules and compulsive rituals. He is the personification of fear rather than of love.

Once the left brain settles on an icon for God, the right brain gets busy creating the stories that bring it alive and provide a context that gives meaning to life. Every culture has evolved its own set of creation stories and icons suitable to its environment and social structure. For example, it is unlikely that an African culture, nurtured by the verdant jungle or expansive savanna and keenly aware of the spirits of plants, animals, ancestors, and nature, would evolve a representation of God as a bearded white man. One image of God is no Truer, with a capital *T*, than the other. The pre–European-contact Native Americans, comprising over five hundred tribes, knew this. Many tribes had different creation stories. Rather than make one another's beliefs wrong, there was delight in the Great Spirit's ability to appeal to different peoples in ways that were most meaningful to their culture.

Icons can be dangerous and powerful as projections of the human need for conquest and domination. But they can also have salvific power when they embody the love and compassion of the Nameless One. Our ability to love God in any form or image, as long as we allow others to worship in their own way, opens our heart and ultimately enhances our relationship to our own self and to other people.

Specific wisdom teachings are also associated with different gods and goddesses. The Buddhist goddess Tara is a teacher of compassion. The goddess Saraswati is a sharpener of intellect, the Hindu equivalent of a patron saint of books and writing. Mary is a warrior of the heart, of love and worship, hope and healing. Jesus is like a gentle thunderbolt, brass knuckles in a velvet glove. He calls us to throw the charlatans out of our inner temple and stand up for what we know is right. White Buffalo Calf Woman is the renewer of faith. She brought seven sacred rituals to the Lakota at a time of great need. At times I pray to all these icons and more, because they are focused rays of power that help me bring forth the qualities I need at the moment.

As we begin our generic consideration of God as Father, God as Mother, and God as both Mother and Father, pay close attention to what your body tells you. Are you comforted or anxious, inspired or disinterested, angry or curious? This process of attention to your intuition and feelings is an important part of the woman's way to God. It is your truest guide to the image of God that has the power to draw you into the sweet and mysterious depths of your soul. It is also your guide to healing old images of God that may have hardened your heart.

GOD THE FATHER

My dear friend and retreat partner in the *Gatherings of Women*, Elizabeth Lawrence, is a pastoral counselor and a cradle Catholic, meaning that she was born into and baptized in that faith. Beth lost her father in World War II. She was only five, and remembers the funeral. She remembers the soldiers in their fancy uniforms and colorful ribbons folding up the American flag that had draped his coffin, and presenting it to her. She remembers her family's tears. Beth misses her father. And for many years she found him in a heavenly Father to whom she went in a personal way, seeking the same kind of comfort and guidance that her own father might have given her.

On several occasions dropout Catholic women, still angry at the Church, asked how Beth—such an erudite and liberated woman— could love what they consider a patriarchal God. But, to Beth, God the Father had nothing to do with the patriarchy that has exploited and devalued women. He was the One who saw her soul most clearly. He watched over her and protected her. He wanted her to inherit the Kingdom. His love was dependable and sweet. And He would never die and leave her fatherless.

"Do I have to give up God the Father to be spiritual?" Beth wondered as we walked the beach one day in the early spring many years ago. "Is He too small a God, too childlike? I know that God is a Mystery, but I would miss Him as a Father. I even like to call the priests in the parish 'Father.' It doesn't bother me at all. It comforts me." I understood her need for a personal God who can hold you in the palm of His hand. It is hard to cuddle up with the void, the nameless, formless Mystery. Sometimes it's nice to have a shoulder to lean on, even when—in your heart of hearts—you know that God is bigger than your image.

Coming to terms with what Sara Maitland calls "a big enough God" is a struggle for some women, a gradual evolution for others. For Beth, the image of God the Father evolved and enlarged in a very interesting way. She is a healer of prodigious talent, often helping clients who have been in therapy for years make stunning breakthroughs in only a few sessions. I can vouch for her, having been one of her earliest clients and having referred hundreds of people to her over the years.

Beth is the founder of a system of healing called the LuMarian method. *Lu* means light. *Mary* refers to the Divine Mother. And *ian* represents the balance of male and female. Beth works specifically with the energy and presence of Mary. That Mary actually appears in the sessions I have no doubt. The scent of roses associated with her often wafts in, seemingly out of nowhere. With Mary's guidance, Beth uses her intuition and the sensitivity of her palms as she passes her hands above the body with deep attention. She simply asks what the client sees or feels at certain energy centers and quietly waits to see what emerges.

Almost invariably, deep grief wells up for people. They suddenly remember scenes from childhood or traumatic experiences later in life. There is often a powerful release of sobs and shuddering. Beth then does insightful psychological work, coupled with spiritual work, to help the client forgive, release grief, and find a new meaning that transforms the problem, usually within the parameters of a one-hour session. I find it absolutely remarkable that such a technique can almost instantly access a person's worst shames and deepest fears that might take years to come up in traditional therapy.

Each session begins with prayer, an invocation of God, Mary, the archangels, and the particular guiding spirits and angels assigned to each person. Being a cradle Catholic who related to God as Father, early in her practice Beth naturally invoked a male deity. She was astounded by the intense negative reaction that some of her clients had. The overwhelming grief that came from many women in response to a simple prayer had such a powerful effect on Beth that, out of consideration for her clients, she began to address God simply as the Divine or as both Mother and Father. With time, her own image of God gradually mutated to that of Mother-Father. It is interesting that the name LuMarian came to her in a meditation before she had consciously changed her image of God. Her unconscious was already speaking to her of the balance of male and female.

For some women their tradition of origin, and the God of their ancestors, remains a strong anchor that is stable through life. A male deity is not a problem for them. A Lakota woman, Wawokiya Win, writes of her relationship with God in *The Divine Mosaic: Women's Images of the Sacred Other.* In her tradition God is not only a Mystery, Wakan Tanka, but a Grandfather, Tunkashila. She walks proudly in her religious tradition, with none of the baggage so many *wasicu* (white) women carry about a male God. Her culture is one in which women have always been revered. The anger about male dominance endemic to some sectors of white society is missing in her own traditional Lakota upbringing.

She writes of the old ways of her people, of their respect for women and love for the children. She talks of the lavish praise they heap on one another. Her descriptions of Lakota spirituality illuminate their reverence for the earth as Unci Maka, Grandmother Earth, a female creation of the Great Spirit, Wakan Tanka, who in turn nurtures creation and gives life.

She writes, "To my people, God is the Creator, Our Grandfather, the Great Spirit, and we see him everywhere in all his creation. For us, walking a spiritual path is not something to be taken lightly. Unlike a one-day-out-of-the-week ritual, every day is a day of worship for us. . . . From the time we wake up with the morning sun (Ata—father), and pray to a new day until the sun goes down, we give thanks to the Creator for life. . . . To balance our life we need to depend on faith in our Grandfather, the Great Spirit."

There are obvious cultural differences in the way that women image God. And there are also differences within cultures. Some Lakota women grew up in the traditional ways. Others grew up with the combination of Christianity and traditional religion common to indigenous cultures in which missionaries preached a Western notion of a pale, blond Jesus and a bearded Father God. These white icons are incorporated into indigenous cultures through reimagining them within a completely different cultural context. They have developed ways of embracing God the Father without buying into a patriarchal, male-centered theology.

EMBRACING THE PATRIARCHY ON OUR OWN TERMS

Many women are distanced, sad, or furious with the biblical image of a Father God who devalues women and the earth. At every retreat I have ever facilitated, someone wants to discuss the patriarchy. A few want to bash it and trash any idea of God as Father. But as Sister Rosemarie commented in Chapter Two, we don't have to throw the baby out with the bathwater. We can love God as Father or adore Jesus without subscribing to the dogma that women are the weaker sex or that Eve was the source of all humanity's troubles. I learned this lesson in a most unexpected way in the early 1990s, when I participated in a three-week journey to Chiapas, Mexico, to learn about the spirituality of Indians of Mayan descent.

These Indians practice an astonishing blend of Native ritual and Catholicism that would most likely make the pope's hair stand on end. Early one Sunday morning in the cool, crisp air of mid-December, we arrived at a Catholic church several hundred years old, situated in a remote mountain village. Most people were barefoot and very poor, the women wearing long cotton dresses and colorful shawls, the men threadbare pants and shirts open at the neck. Small groups were gathered outside in the dusty courtyard that doubles as an outdoor market, sitting on the bare earth, drinking a strong alcoholic home-brew as part of the preparatory ritual for worship.

The harsh winter sun glinted off the stained-glass windows and the white stone of the church, which is where any resemblance to Western churches ended. Inside there were no pews, only a hard-packed dirt floor on which the waxy residue of thousands of candles formed glistening pools and little stalagmites. There was no service, no priest or sermon, and no collection. A priest, in fact, served the church only one Sunday a month to offer the sacrament of baptism. Even then, we were told, he did not conduct a service. No one would listen. Those receiving baptism gather at one end of the church, and the others continue with their own private rituals of worship.

People clustered in family groups with their elders or, in some cases, with shamans from the village. Each group conducted its own ceremony at its own pace, the only common denominator being their presence in the church at the same time with the intent to honor Jesus, God the Father, the saints, and the most beloved of all religious figures in Mexico, Our Lady of Guadalupe. With meticulous care they held flame to the bottom of dozens of candles, creating hot pools of wax on the floor to attach the tapers. When several rows of candles had been lighted, they began to intone ancient Mayan chants in honor of the ancestors as well as adopted Christian deities, finding parallels between the old ways and the new.

African American women's spirituality also has its roots in a religion that grew out of traditions that were blends of missionary Christianity and African spirituality. Gloria Wade-Gayles, in her acclaimed anthology, *My Soul Is a Witness: African-American Women's Spirituality*, writes of the missionaries, "Nor did they understand that in worship they called 'primitive,' we were respecting and connecting to/with the unseen power that governs the universe. Nor did they understand that we imaged ourselves as a people imbued with spiritual power, a belief we retained from our African culture. They did not know we appropriated the religion they gave us, invested it with Spirit, and transformed it into a force that kept our humanity intact."

In the United States, the slave years were a call to a spirituality that could lift the dispossessed African people above oppression, giving wings to their souls even while their bodies were shackled.

My stepdaughter Natalia went to college at the State University of New York at Purchase. One of her assignments was to find a place of worship other than her own, attend the services, and write about her experience. She chose a black Baptist church in Harlem, and was surprised and delighted when her worship experience began a few blocks from the church, while she was trying to find her way there. A black couple stopped her, an out-of-place white girl looking tentative and confused, and asked if they could help. Was she lost? Did she need directions?

With open hearts and good humor, they escorted her to the church. She loved the service. The music was compelling and soulful. It spoke not so much of a God out there but a God among the people. "There was such Spirit there," she told me. Much more so than in the Catholic church of her childhood. Her faith was renewed among these strangers who treated her as a friend and invited her back.

Contemporary African American women, like white women, worship God in many ways, both within religions and outside of them. They are Christians and Muslims, Buddhists and Hindus, and adherents of traditional African religions. A few are Jews. Catherine Goboldte studied the role of African American women in a particular community, the Imani Faith Temple in Philadelphia. In her study, she sought to understand women's spirituality both in terms of how it affects their lives within religious institutions and outside of them. Her study is an excellent model of how women can embrace the patriarchy on their own terms.

Goboldte chose to study a contemporary African American Catholic congregation founded in 1989 by Reverend George Stallings, a Roman Catholic priest who formed an independent congregation as a protest against racism within the Church. The pastor of the church at the time of the study was Reverend Rose Vernell, and there were other female clergy as well. As a researcher, Goboldte participated in mass and special functions and was even invited to preach.

The mass incorporates elements of African ritual and Roman Catholic ritual. It includes "prostration of the priest, pouring of libations, invocations of saints and ancestors, African instruments, African American spiritual and gospel songs, and the Eucharist. . . . The liturgy began with the procession of worship service participants including the choir. They were accompanied by the music of drums, bells, and rattles. An explanation in the bulletin stated: 'These are traditionally used in African ceremonies to call upon the Divine. Also, this heralded the arrival of an important personage; here, Jesus who comes to feed us with his Body and Blood.' "

Each week the Liturgy of the Word is read by different members of the congregation. The first reading is taken from the Bible; the second from the work of a great African American spiritual leader. In the spirit of participation so evident in the Imani Temple, all people, regardless of church affiliation, are invited to partake of the Eucharist. Goboldte reports that the majority of the congregation are women and that women are involved in leading all the rituals.

The women she interviewed all spoke of the liberating and empowering experiences of their faith, and their delight in realizing that many of the saints were black. Moses was a black Egyptian. One of the interviewees, a cradle Catholic, spoke of the deep connection with Jesus and the Trinity that the Imani Temple had facilitated, how she can really pray now through the Holy Spirit. Another spoke of how the makeup of the church was what she imagined as "fairly typical," in that there were more women, fewer men.

While the Imani Temple is certainly not your typical church, it is a much-needed experiment in women's spiritual expression within a religious context. We can only hope that more such "experimental" churches will be founded for diverse religious and cultural groups. My beloved Camp Pembroke was, in its own way, an experimental temple. Although all the members were white girls, we were practicing a male-oriented religion that had developed in a desert culture over six thousand years ago, in a way that was relevant to the needs and concerns of a contemporary feminine congregation.

Within modern Jewish culture, there is a renewed movement for women to celebrate and worship outside of temples. God the Father is not thrown away. He just becomes one part of a larger picture. Some women participate in Rosh Hodesh (new moon) groups, a ritual that God gave to women at the time when Moses was receiving the Ten Commandments up on Mt. Sinai. According to Jewish lore, the men freaked out when Moses was gone so long. They reverted to pagan beliefs and collected jewelry to melt down into the famous idol of the golden calf. But the women kept their faith and their jewelry along with it. In appreciation of their steadfastness, God gave the women a ritual of their own, a celebration of the new moon, which marks the beginning of each month in the Jewish calendar.

Rosh Hodesh is connected to nature and the pull of the moon on women's bodies and emotions. It is a celebration of the most obvious form of renewal that human beings witness, the waxing and waning of a heavenly body. In the only Rosh Hodesh ceremony I have attended, the ritual was participatory and earth centered, involving tambourines and hand drums, singing and dancing as it must have been celebrated in the ancient Middle East. The prophetess Miriam was a drummer and dancer. As a community, we were reclaiming our heritage as women without forsaking an essentially patriarchal religion.

Women outside the United States are also on a journey of finding an image of God that fits their culture and temperament. One of the most interesting accounts concerning a Father God was written by Akiko Kobayashi, a Shinto priest in the region of Kamakura, about an hour's drive out of Tokyo. *Shinto* means "the way of God." She presides over the Goryo Shrine, which was established nine hundred years ago and is dedicated to a rather fierce samurai, Lord Gongoro.

She explains that Japan has over 82,000 shrines to different gods and goddesses, ancestors, or the spirit of particular human beings like Gongoro. When her young daughter asked whether shrines existed for idol worship, since there were so many gods in the Shinto tradition, Kobayashi realized that she prayed to one God, rather than a polytheistic pantheon, to the "extreme principle of God manifest in the image of Gongoro." In just this way, many women pray to a greater principle manifest in a Father God image.

Kobayashi serves a male deity as part of an inclusive theology, without any angst or apology. Like my colleague Beth, her relationship to men is warm and loving so that a masculine image is nourishing, rather than a spiritual stumbling block. Even though women can be priests, and no particular image of a Father God exists in her tradition, many wise old men are part of Japanese folklore, and ancestor worship is very important. Far from being a sign of patriarchy, to Kobayashi the thought of God as an old man is profoundly beautiful. She writes, "Even I, who live in modern times, feel like worshipping an old man whenever I see one praying silently in a temple or a graveyard because it reminds me of the great spirit of the space into which he will soon dissolve."

GOD THE MOTHER

Tikva Frymer-Kensky is an Assyriologist and Sumeriologist, a professor at the University of Chicago. Mother of two children, she is the author of a book called *Motherprayer*, a compilation of scholarly translations of ancient prayers about birth, pregnancy, and motherhood from Latin, Hebrew, Sumerian, Akkadian, and Aramaic.

When she had to be rushed to the hospital in 1977 for an emergency cesarean section, she scooped up a bunch of magazines to take with her. Mixed in with them, most fortunately for her situation, was a Babylonian birth incantation she had translated for her dissertation. It gave her courage and solace to appeal to a nurturing Mother God for help with childbirth, an experience that no man has ever had. It was this experience, in part, that led to the writing and publication of *Motherprayer.* And it is these deep experiences of the feminine that women want—religions, God, rituals, incantations, and prayers that relate to the body, to birth and death, to the earth, to the seasons. For women, spirituality is less a hero's journey to a distant land than a finding of our center in a God who is present in the homely practicalities of day-to-day life.

There is a wealth of myth and story, as well as archeological evidence, about ancient Goddess worship. At the time of Jesus, Judaism was still waging a battle against worship of the Babylonian goddess Asherah. Mary, who was not originally venerated in early Christianity, gradually drew a following because she was a natural extension of the Goddess. Since the "pagan" fascination with goddesses could not be wiped out, the church fathers allowed it to be transferred to Mary and wisely coopted the earlier forms of worship and veneration. Although Mary is not technically a goddess but the Mother of God come to earth in human form, she is nonetheless worshipped as divine by many people around the world.

When we hurt, the mother understands. Unless we had a conflicted relationship with our mother or other female caretaker, it is mother who comforts us. When a small child is lost or hurt in the company of strangers, the little one will almost always run to the nearest woman. And kids under five nearly always want mom rather than dad. Somewhere in the neural circuits a program runs in which women are viewed as more accessible and nurturing than men. Whereas the sky god can be angry and vindictive, the mother is a symbol of love, at least in Western culture. In the Hindu pantheon there are many goddesses representing different aspects of the ultimate Godhead, Brahman. Kali is a fierce goddess, portrayed as giving birth and then eating her children. That, of course, is exactly what Mother Nature does.

The Mexican story of Our Lady of Guadalupe is a cultural counterpart to that of the Virgin Mary. It emphasizes that the mother Mary was not simply a historical character who came and went but a living Presence who cares for her children. Appearing just as the indigenous Indian cultures were being brutally wiped out by the Spaniards in the name of Jesus and the Apostles, the gentle Lady of Guadalupe became the salvation of an oppressed people. She allowed them to adopt a new religion in its gentleness, rather than with the violence that the conquistador's actions exemplified.

Dr. Jeanette Rodriguez, a Hispanic woman of Ecuadorian descent, focused her doctoral thesis on Our Lady of Guadalupe. She was working with Mexican and Mexican-American women in California, hopeful of understanding the spirituality that empowered them to overcome difficult circumstances. There are over 12 million people of Mexican descent in the United States, and God the Mother, in the form of Our Lady of Guadalupe, is their most important icon and guide. She first appeared to the people of Mexico in 1531, shortly after Hernán Cortés began the decimation of the Aztec empire and the Nahuatl Indians in 1519. The indigenous people were hunted like animals, raped, massacred, and dismembered all in the name of God. Some of their children were baptized and their skulls smashed in with rocks to assure their "salvation," ostensibly a fate preferable to living a "pagan" life. Other children were simply ripped from the arms of their mothers and fed to the hungry dogs of the conquistadors who then raped and murdered the shrieking mothers.

In a few short years the conquered people were disheartened and guilty, wondering if they had displeased their gods. Soon enough the missionaries appeared to convert the Nahuatl to a new god. While the Spanish Christians believed in individual salvation, the Nahuatl believed in the salvation of the community group—its wholeness and preservation. The Spaniards believed that intellect was paramount in abstracting the Truth; the Nahuatl believed that truth came only through the understanding of the heart. Rodriguez writes, "The Christian Spaniards felt that space-earth had been given to humanity by God and that humans had a right to claim it, to use it for their own good. The Nahuatl people held space-earth sacred, believing it belonged to the gods. Humans could only use it and had to live in harmony with it. The concept of private property was sacrilegious and incomprehensible to them."

It was in this cross tide of conflicting cultures that the miracle of Guadalupe occurred. In northern Mexico City, early on Saturday morning December 9, a peasant by the name of Juan Diego was on his way to church. He was on a hill called Tepeyac when heavenly music permeated the air, and an apparition of a heavenly Lady, cloaked with the radiance of the sun, came to him. According to Rodriguez, she identified herself as "the Mother of God, who is the God of Truth; the Mother of the Giver of Life; the Mother of the Creator; the Mother of the One who makes the sun and the earth; and the Mother of the One who is near. She told Juan Diego that she wanted a temple built for her where she could bestow love, compassion, strength, and defense to all those who came to her. She wished her house to be at Tepeyac, a site of great significance, for the spot previously housed the shrine of Tonantzin, one of the major Earth Mother divinities of the Aztec people."

Juan Diego went to the bishop with his story but, as you might expect, got nowhere. He was heartsore at the thought of disappointing the Lady. But she simply sent him back to try again. This time the bishop told him that in order to build a house for the Lady, she would have to provide Juan Diego with a sign. The sign was twofold. She cured the peasant's uncle, who was mortally ill. And she sent Juan Diego to the top of Tepeyac to pick roses for her, which were out of season, and which he nevertheless found in profusion. She arranged the flowers in Juan Diego's *tilma*, or cloak, and sent him back to the bishop.

When the *tilma* was opened, the flowers fell to the ground, and the image of Our Lady of Guadalupe was imprinted on the cloak in radiant colors that gave the image a three-dimensional quality. The original image is enshrined today in a cathedral in Mexico City where millions go for pilgrimage each year. Anyone who has ever traveled to Mexico will be familiar with the compassionate, joyful face of the Lady, composed, it is said, of scientifically unknown pigments that refract the light and give her visage its olive-toned hue.

Her eyes have been the subject of careful study with infrared photography and computer digital imaging. The pictures reveal several reflected images, as if people had been looking at her. One is a bare-chested Indian, sitting cross-legged in prayer. Another is the face of the Spanish bishop Juan de Zumarraga. Another is an unidentified black woman. And although blacks were rare in Mexico at that time, the historical record indicates that two black women were indeed slaves in the bishop's household.

One of the most interesting aspects of the image of Our Lady of Guadalupe is that she is wearing the *cinta*, a tassel or maternity band, around her waist. She is a pregnant goddess. Other aspects of the image are distinctly Aztec in symbology: the stars on her turquoise mantle, golden sun rays that emanate from her form, a moon beneath her feet, and an angel who holds her aloft on the crescent moon. Contemporary Mexican and Mexican American women relate to her very personally. She is their mother. They can talk to her about their problems, just as they would speak to an earthly mother. They are women. She is a woman. She hears and understands. She is a protector and an intercessor with the more remote, male aspect of God.

Our Lady of Guadalupe is only one apparition of the Divine Mother that has come when people were oppressed or troubled. Numerous other apparitions of Mary are occurring worldwide with ever-increasing frequency. Fifteen-year-old Melanie Calvat and eleven-year-old Maximin Giraud saw a globe of radiant light that opened up to reveal an apparition of Mary in the French town of La Salette in 1846. Bernadette Soubirous was fourteen years old, in the year 1858, when she saw apparitions of Mary in a grotto in the French town of Lourdes. When Mary told her to dig in the dirt to find a healing stream of water, the townspeople laughed. But Bernadette dug and a stream bubbled up. Thousands of healings have been reported by those taking the waters at Lourdes, and nearly seventy bona fide miracles—impossible according to science—have been validated by a meticulous medical board.

In 1917 Mary appeared again to three small children in Fatima, Portugal, where she promised to return on the thirteenth of each month. While there are twelve months in the current solar-based calendar, the original calendars counted thirteen months in the year because they were lunar. These have been called menstrual calendars, moon based. And thirteen has traditionally been regarded as the number of the feminine. So Mary's choice to appear on the thirteenth of each month is a redemption of the disowned feminine.

At Fatima, Mary requested that people pray for world peace and, promised a miracle that would convince the world that her apparition was real. The "miracle of the dancing sun" was subsequently witnessed by over seventy thousand people, skeptics and believers alike. The sun began to whirl in the sky, illuminating everything with rainbow light, then shone gently, without hurting the eyes. It repeated this cycle three times over twelve minutes and then appeared to fall to earth, as though it would crash into the terrified crowd that exulted as the sun ascended majestically back to the heavens.

Apparitions of Mary continue unabated, in greater and greater numbers, worldwide. Appearances on a hillside in Medjugorje, in what was once Yugoslavia but is now Bosnia, have continued since 1981. The message to the six "visionary" children at Medjugorje is ecumenical: "Respect your own religion and everybody else's." Like Lourdes, there have been many healings at Medjugorje, and, as at Fatima, the sun has danced. A team of scientists has repeatedly studied the six children, whose gaze rivets on an apparition that no one else can see, always in synchrony. The visions have been declared authentic scientifically, if not by the Catholic Church, which may perhaps resent the apparition's ecumenical message of the truth of all religions.

Mary has given the children at Medjugorje (now young adults) ten predictions concerning the future. She says of an event that is supposed to occur near the millennium, "What will come to pass is something so great that it will exceed anything that has taken place since the beginning of the world. It will be like a Judgment in miniature, and each one will see his own life and all he has done, in the very light of God."

When I read this prophecy I was reminded of the accounts of people who have had life reviews in the course of near-death experiences. They report that "the Judgment" is actually a kind of self-reflection that occurs in the Divine Light. Surrounded by the loving light of wisdom, people claim that they review the events of their lives from the perspective of how their thoughts, words, and deeds affected others. They actually experience themselves through other people's emotions, the most profound type of rationality. From this vantage point they can appreciate how their behavior got passed on from person to person, like ripples in a pond. This understanding functions as a healing, because it awakens compassion.

Physician, philosopher, and near-death researcher Raymond Moody has reported cases in which hardened criminals who experience life reviews as part of near-death experiences immediately repent of their actions. I can't think of a faster way to a change of heart than the whole world having such a firsthand experience of interdependence, interconnectedness, and relationality. Since one in twenty Americans, between 8 and 12 million people, have indeed had a near-death experience, and about a third of those have had a life review, perhaps the prophecy of Mary is not as far-fetched as one might think.

HEALING OURSELVES AND OUR IMAGE OF GOD

Mary's prophecy about a healing in which we review our lives and turn our wounds into wisdom doesn't have to wait for a worldwide miracle. The ordinary, painful, and inspiring process of psychological growth is no less miraculous. A period of healing from childhood wounds frequently occurs for women in their midthirties and early forties as the profound changes leading to menopause begin. In *A Woman's Book of Life*, I call this seven-year period in the feminine life cycle "spinning straw into gold."

Therapists often notice that old memories of emotional and

physical abuse surface during this period preceding midlife. At menopause we enter a time when we find our own voice and have the courage to speak it aloud. It is a miracle of feminine biology that we undergo a major mental housecleaning in preparation. For if we enter midlife without healing, the voice we raise may be bitter and angry. But if we do our work, our voice will be the compassionate, strong voice of the she-bear.

The prompt for healing is often a sense of disconnection. We may feel disconnected from our bodies, from our work, or from relationships. Our relationship to God is no exception. A woman named Chris ran out of the sanctuary in which we were holding a *Gathering of Women* retreat. She was in tears. The venue was an old stone Jesuit monastery in Virginia, and I was leading a meditation on the invocation of the four archangels. When the session broke for lunch, I went outside to find her and ask what was so upsetting.

Chris was sitting on a wooden bench, under a bower of purple lilacs in full bloom. Their sweet, spicy fragrance floated around us like healing balm, creating an atmosphere of safety and beauty. "The archangels are all men," Chris finally spat out with great vehemence. "I'm sick and tired of hearing about men. Aren't there any woman angels?"

As a therapist I realized that some deep wound concerning men had to be the source of that much anger. As tenderly as I could, I explained that the angels are, in fact, genderless. Their Hebrew names denote aspects of God like light (Uriel), compassion (Michael), healing (Raphael), and strength (Gabriel). The fact that they are often portrayed as male is just another example of projection. When God is imagined as Father, his minions tend to be cast in the same gender.

Chris blew her nose and calmed down a little. She apologized for running out of the sanctuary and hoped that it hadn't been disruptive. She just couldn't stay. She had left to seek solace in nature, the only place where she felt close to God, although she didn't like to use the G word. It had too many bad associations. The beauty of the trees, the faces of the flowers, the feel of the wind in her hair, and the seasonal cycles of renewal were the face of her Higher Power. But at thirty-eight she was experimenting with a more personal face for God. She said that she had come to our retreat because she was hungry to introduce more organized ritual and worship into her life and liked to participate in spiritual community.

She had been a member of a Goddess-centered women's group for about two years. Along with a small group of friends, Chris celebrated the solstices, equinoxes, and other seasonal holidays that she felt organically drawn to as an expression of the life force. One of a growing number of women intent on escaping the clutches of the sky god, Chris thought that she might relate more authentically to Goddess rituals and the nature-oriented celebrations of Goddess cultures. Of Irish descent, Chris could relate to the spirit of holidays like Beltane, celebrating the union of the Goddess with her consort to bring the blessing of new life and fertility in the spring.

Yet she confided that she was not quite at home with Goddess rituals either. She felt they had a "make-believe" quality, as if the participants had dressed up to put on a play. In other words, the rituals didn't feel authentic to her. There was no heart connection. They were more like putting on a mask and pretending to be someone she wasn't. The quality of nurture, associated with God the Mother, seemed curiously lacking as she told her story. Instead, the rituals felt to Chris more like the practice of some kind of arcane white magic.

Had I asked other women in her Goddess group about their experiences, there would surely have been many who found the rituals nourishing, inspiring, and real. As we continued to talk, the reason why Chris felt disconnected finally surfaced. With some pain and hesitancy, Chris revealed that she had been molested repeatedly by her father as a child. Her reaction to men, whether in the flesh, as archangel, or as God, was consequently fraught with pain.

We got up to walk as Chris got to the most painful part of the story, making our way down a trail in the woods, through dappled sunlight. Chris told me that she had never really forgiven her mother either. Like many women in her circumstance, she felt that her mother should have realized what was happening and protected her from harm. Nonetheless she needed her mother and had remained close to her, even though their relationship was conflicted and strained. Her father had died several years ago, but her mother lived close by. I asked whether they had ever discussed the abuse.

Chris looked down and stopped, pushing a pine cone around with the toe of her sneaker. "Once, a long time ago. I was in college then and she came to visit. She wanted to know whether I had a boyfriend. I told her that I didn't and that I never would. That I hated men because of what Dad had done to me. She was shocked. She defended him and told me that I had imagined the whole thing. That nothing ever happened. So I let it go. There was nothing else to do."

We were silent for a moment, and in the pregnant pause, I asked, "Do you still think that there's nothing you can do, Chris?"

"Oh, Joan, I know what you're going to say. My friends have said it, too. It's time to get some help and resolve this whole thing. I'm not a kid anymore and I'm tired of hurting. I don't know if I can ever forgive my father, truly, but I guess I've got to at least forgive my mother. Maybe then I can trust the Goddess, do you think?"

That's exactly what I thought. And I told Chris that the process might take a long time, but that whenever we have a willing heart, grace comes in to give us a boost. In the meantime, Chris could find

God in nature, and that was an authentic connection to the center of her circle. It was a source of strength that she could draw upon as the painful process of healing got under way.

GOD AS MOTHER/FATHER

I don't know whether Chris ever worked through the anger at her mother and was able to feel connected during the Goddess rituals. It is unlikely, given her history, even if she does eventually forgive her deceased father, that she will be able to connect with a uniquely male image of God. But she may eventually relate to an image that many women find organically whole, a God who is both Mother and Father. This icon may even provide a kind of corrective emotional experience, providing the ideal parents she never had.

My friend Lynnclaire Dennis, author of the fascinating book *The Pattern*, refers to God as the Goddessence. God, Goddess, and the Divine Essence within are encompassed in her neologism. A similar view of God as both male and female was beautifully expressed by Julian of Norwich. A fourteenth-century English nun, she had a thrilling series of divine visions and revelations that spanned a twenty-four-hour period in 1373 when she was thirty years old. They were published in a text called *Showings*, the first book in English ever written by a woman.

Although Julian sometimes referred to God as Father, she also referred to the divine as Mother. This was not a new idea in Christianity. Even St. Augustine referred to God as Mother at times, or more typically used maternal metaphors for being comforted and nurtured by God. Julian's contribution was the unification of the male and female aspects of God. She didn't want to replace the Father with the Mother, she wanted to convey the unity of both.

She wrote, "This fair lovely word 'mother' is so sweet and so kind in itself that it cannot truly be said of anyone or to anyone except of him and to him who is the true Mother of life and of all things. To the property of motherhood belong nature, love, wisdom and knowledge, and this is God."

Julian was, in her way, a healer. In the terminology of mystical Judaism, she was trying to bring back the exiled feminine aspect of God and reunite it with its masculine counterpart. This is what many contemporary women, lay people and religious alike, are also trying to accomplish. Dr. Zhang I Hsien, known in the West as Lily Siou, is a Taoist woman philosopher and doctor of Chinese medicine. She writes that all the elements are in harmony in the Tao. Above is heaven, called the Father. Below is earth, called the Mother. And from their union spring all the elements.

In this ancient philosophy Siou writes, "Female and male, called yin and yang in Tao, give joy to each other. They support each other and give life to the next generations. . . . A universal law of Tao is that when the yin is complete, it gives birth to the yang. When yang is complete, it reaches satisfaction and gives energy to the yin; yin is the mother of yang. Both reach the fullness of their potential and give birth to the opposite. This is the law of nature. . . . All things in the universe, when reaching their potential, give birth."

Even the Lord's Prayer, which begins in English with the words "Our Father Which art in heaven," is in fact a psalm of praise to the birther, Mother/Father God. Neil Douglas-Klotz, an Aramaic scholar, has retranslated the Lord's Prayer out of the original Aramaic, which was the vernacular language in Judaea in the time of Jesus. The Aramaic words *Abwoon d'bwashmaya*, usually translated as Our Father, are more properly translated "O Birther! Father-Mother of the Cosmos."

The process of birthing, which requires a balance and harmony of universal forces too large to reduce to a name or image, inspires a feeling of the sacred for me. It is the authentic center of my circle. Night births day; day births night. The seasons die and are born again. Ashes turn to flesh. Flesh goes back to ashes. Spirit births matter and as matter we reflect Spirit back to itself. God knows itself and grows itself less through the act of creation than the act of relation. After each creative act in Genesis God pauses to note that it is good. How much more magnificent when creation itself sings the praises of the continuous process of birthing through which the universe expands.

One of the hallmarks of feminine spirituality is the permission to celebrate God in any form. Our image of God may be abstract and impersonal—a life force, consciousness, nature, Mystery. It may also be personal and gender based. Whether that image is of God the Father, God the Mother, a Goddessence that combines the two, Wakan Tanka, Gongoro, Mary, Jesus, or any other form, the most important thing is that the God of our understanding feels real and authentic. Otherwise worship—which is a profound relational experience, perhaps the quintessential relational experience—falls flat. There's no juice in it. It is not possible to relate to an evanescent shadow or to an image of God that makes us angry, anxious, or uncomfortable.

It is my hope that in reading this chapter you remembered to pay attention to your body, the most direct connection to intuition. Perhaps you already had an image of God that you're comfortable with. If not, you may have found some clues that will be helpful on your journey. What really caught your attention? Were the feelings positive or negative? Is there something you need to heal before you can trust in God? Is there something you need to heal before you can trust yourself?

Summing up our discussion so far, we have spoken about faith and how it provides the passion that keeps us focused on the journey. We have distinguished spirituality from religion and defined the latter as a deep sense of connectedness and belonging, the destination that the train of religion is bound for. We have distinguished the ways in which men and women make the connection to God. They climb Jacob's ladder while we walk Sarah's circle where our natural relationality and intuition are the built-in connectors to the Inner Light, the God within who is at the center of our circle. Who, or what, dear reader, is at the center of your circle?

DEVELOPING A
RELATIONSHIP TO GOD

Friendship and Intimacy, Sensuality and Sex

I f God is the center point that defines the circle of our lives, we can think of the spiritual journey as the process by which that center becomes accessible and familiar to us. When we have a strong connection to the God within, when we are on intimate terms with our intuition, when we have a strong and inspiring image of the Divine, we can trust that our life is guided by the highest principles. We feel that our life has meaning and purpose and that we are taking our part in the cocreation of a better and more beautiful world.

So what would it actually feel like to have an intimate relationship with God? I asked this question of a group of women at a retreat. Nineteen-year-old Ashley, an outgoing young woman who had been delighting us with her participation all weekend, was pragmatic. "I wouldn't feel so anxious all the time, so jumpy. I'd be able to take a breath and focus on God. I'd feel quieter. I'd feel loved. Then I could tell God what was really on my mind and ask for help and guidance. I guess the most important thing is that I would hear the answers."

Florence, a woman in her seventies, stood up and started to clap. Then the rest of the group joined in. We were proud of the young woman with the nerve to speak first about a topic that she told us wasn't generally discussed in her circle of friends.

Florence spoke directly to Ashley. An elder sharing her precious experience is always a touching moment. "I can't add much to what you said, dear, but I can say that the last part, about hearing the answers, isn't so easy to learn. And it's the most important thing. For me, that's where faith comes in. The stronger my faith, the more I believe that God is really there for me. The more I believe, the more I take spirituality and my relationship to God seriously. We're not just talking out of our hats here, ladies," she turned to address the rest of the group with a wistful, inward smile and a soft, dreamy voice.

"There really is a God who listens and guides, who loves and holds. My relationship to God is the most intimate, personal thing in my life. I love this teaching from the New Testament. I'm not sure which gospel. Jesus is talking about how the Father wants you to inherit the Kingdom. He asks what earthly father, if you ask for bread, would give you a stone? And if we can count on an earthly father, how much more can we count on a heavenly Father? Faith. That's the crux of any intimate relationship. You have to have absolute trust in the one you're relating to."

Cindy spoke next. A redhead with big dimples and a quick smile, she replied, "Asking for help. That's such an important thing to remember. If God is just an idea you don't ask for what you need. Why bother? But if you have a real relationship you do ask. I forget about God a lot of the time, and I'm really good about getting worked up over things. It's this red hair, they say. Makes me passionate about life. But when I remember that God is really here— as they say, closer than hands and feet—I calm down and ask for what I need. And help comes pretty fast a lot of the time. Not always, but I think that's because I'm such a whirlwind that I don't take the time to listen for a response and to check in on what my body's telling me. I get a lot of information through the body."

Wendy was nearly jumping out of her chair. "Everybody talks about intuition and guidance as a body thing. Is something wrong with me? My guidance comes in totally different ways like synchronicities. Sometimes I turn on the TV and it's like whatever's being said is the answer to my prayers. Or I pick up a magazine and whatever I need to know pops out at me. God is pretty cagey. I think that divine intelligence uses every possible channel of communication."

"I guess that's why mindfulness is so important," a fifty-something woman with a beautiful gray shag haircut added. "If you're tuned out you don't hear what's coming in whether it's through dreams, conversations with friends, the TV, billboards, or even the shape of the clouds. Did anyone ever try talking to God and then watching the clouds for an answer? It works great for me. I was once worried that my husband was having an affair. He seemed so distracted and snippy. So I decided to talk to God before I confronted Jack. I sat in front of the living-room window, and since our house is high on a hill we have a terrific view of the passing clouds right from the sofa. What happened was that two clouds passed by. One looked like a dove and the other was heart shaped. Then I felt so much peace, such deep peace. I just knew Jack couldn't be having an affair. Later that day, with a lot of love in my heart, I told my husband what had happened. He actually broke down and started to cry. He told me how much he loved me, and that he'd been hiding a problem all right. But it wasn't a woman. He'd been given notice at the bank where he works and he wanted to find a new job before he told me so that I wouldn't worry. God's answer helped both of us, but I would have missed it unless I was tuned in. Like with any relationship, you have to give God time and attention."

"God speaks to me mostly through other people," said a midlife woman in a T-shirt that announced I'm Out of Estrogen and I Have a Gun.

"I pray to God a lot. When I wake up, when I go to bed, when I say grace or thanks for anything, and especially when something's bothering me. And when I have a question, I do expect an answer, just like I'd expect one from a friend. If the conversation was a one-way deal I'd have given up on a relationship with God a long time ago. But mostly I get my answers through talking to my friends. It's uncanny how I'll have a problem and someone will start talking about the very same thing and what helped her or someone she knows. So for me God's a cosmic ventriloquist."

Having a relationship to God, as these women expressed, is very similar to relating to a friend. We need faith and trust in that friend. For a relationship to grow we have to take it seriously and give it time and attention. And we have to be mindful of the way in which God talks to us. Wendy made an excellent point. While many women tune in to their intuition, the Inner Light of God, through their bodies, other people receive information in ways as different as synchronicities and messages on billboards.

As we focus on a relationship with God, relationships with friends and lovers also deepen. That's the beauty of walking Sarah's circle. When our heart is open to God all life pours in more abundantly. And, conversely, when our heart is open to friends and lovers, we feel the nearness and Presence of the Divine. Wisdom and delight pour through us to one another and we feel that closeness to God that is the true essence of love.

Even sex gets better. Twenty-five years ago my former husband and I were part of a mystical Christian community where we tried to live the teachings of Jesus. When the priest told me that I should make love to my husband as if he were Jesus I thought he was a nut. I was not yet mature enough to understand what he meant.

God is the Divine Beloved in every person. Making love to that Holy Being within a spouse or a lover, relating to the Divine in flesh, is a sacred act. We do this unconsciously in that first phase of a love relationship when we are infatuated with one another. The lover has no faults yet. They are perfect, and our physical loving is guided by that perfection. So sex is at its best. But later, when we realize that our lover is human after all, we lose some of the passion and sweetness of the initial physical intimacy. To reclaim the ardor we once felt, we have to relate to the God within our lover.

Rabbi Zalman Schachter-Shalomi talks about God as a verb rather than a noun. Just as love is better understood as a relational, active exchange than as a passive noun, so is God. Whenever we are relating intimately with open hearts, we are God-ing. We feel that process as love. Love is the greatest longing of every human being. To love and be loved, said Mother Teresa, is the reason why we take birth at all. Showing up fully in all relationships is God-ing, lov-ing. It is the way that we walk Sarah's circle. Every time we bask in the joy of an intimate relationship, and love suffuses our body with that precious sense of belonging, we are feeling the Presence of God, whether we recognize that consciously or not.

THE *ANAM CARA*: SOUL FRIENDS

One of the most deep and beautiful writings on the more intimate and lasting nature of friendship is found in the book *Anam Cara* by John O'Donohue. He writes, "Human presence is a creative and turbulent sacrament, a visible sign of invisible grace. Nowhere else is there such intimate and frightening access to the mysterium. . . . *Anam* is the Gaelic word for soul; *cara* is the word for friend. So *anam cara* means soul friend. The *anam cara* was a person to whom you could reveal the hidden intimacies of your life."

This process of revealing hidden intimacies is actually the pathway for self-in-relation through which women develop psychologically and spiritually. As we come to trust a friend, we reveal more of ourselves. Our idealized mask falls off as we realize that she loves us, warts and all. We can be ourselves. And in being listened to with an open heart, a deeper sense of self actually emerges. What may have been unconscious comes into the light of awareness. We know ourselves better. We become more authentic and wise. Since relationship is circular, and we feed on one another's insights, the friend becomes more herself in the process. Once again, we find ourselves anointed with the nectar of divine belonging.

In the progressively more rushed and hurried lives we live, we are losing some of the intimacy that is the heart and soul of women. The time required for intimacy is just not there for many of us. In the mid-1980s I made the acquaintance of a psychiatrist from India who was taking a sabbatical at Harvard. In 1989 we met again in Bangalore, at the First World Conference for Holistic Health and Medicine. I asked him what his primary impression had been of the United States. He looked sorrowful. "The terrible quality of life for the women," he observed. "You're so busy that there's no time for yourselves, not enough time to be with other women. You're isolated from each other and that's heartbreaking. Women can't survive like that, it's contrary to your nature. And I don't think your society can survive the decimation of its women."

I was taken aback. For an instant I wanted to defend our society. "The sad state of our women," I thought, "well, at least we haven't burned any brides over here lately." But I thought quietly about what he had said. I had felt that sadness, that loss of time to spend with other women, particularly during those years when I was a working mother rushing back and forth between what amounted to two full-time jobs.

The fact that women have lost something vital in our busyness is now big business. In the 1990s a whole genre of books and movies about the importance of women's friendships appeared. *Steel Magnolias*, starring Shirley Maclaine and Julia Roberts, was not only about the relationship between a mother and a daughter but especially how their circle of friends—gathered in the local beauty salon—gave them strength and courage in times of crisis. Books like Rebecca Wells's *Divine Secrets of the Ya Ya Sisterhood* likewise celebrate the importance of women's friendship as the soil in which we grow and the glue that holds us and our families together. Judy Blume's book, *Summer Sisters*, explores how the unhealed hurts of childhood prevent true intimate friendship from maturing.

During those years when I was a busy working mother without time for friendship I tried to put aside a little time each day to pray and meditate, to cultivate a relationship to God. But the meditations felt dry. Friendship had not yet allowed me to enter the deeper realms of myself where I would be most available to God. I came to meditation not as a person secure in her own depths but as a child who thought that I could hide my pain and insecurities from God. Rather than showing up as who I really was, I hid behind the mask of what I thought God wanted me to be. The experience of self-in-relation, whether with God or with another person, can occur only to the extent that we trust the friend to love us as we are. Only then can we mature into something more.

When I facilitate women's retreats, or give talks to groups of women, I always stress the importance of friendship. So many younger women, in particular, are caught between conflicting demands on their time. Work, children, and aging parents often take precedence over friendship, and the women find themselves anxious and stressed. Even research in health psychology glorifies friendship. The most important factor for a healthy heart and a strong immune system turns out to be what the researchers call social support. It is also the best buffer against stress. We are not meant to be alone.

Friends can act like angels, messengers of God, not only by provoking feelings in us and then acting as a mirror but also by patiently listening to our stories, which reveal the true feelings that we may have been avoiding. Carmen Renee Berry and Tamara Traeder, in their wonderful book *girlfriends*, write, "Our mothers told us that we should wait for the right man to come along. But few told us that we may have to wait for the right women friends as well. How do we recognize these women? What is the common characteristic that distinguishes our closest and best friends from our acquaintances? The answer seems to be, in part, that they mirror who we are."

I am fortunate in having several friends who act like mirrors and afford the experience of growth through self-in-relation. I was walking down Boulder's Pearl Street Mall on an April day, enjoying the tulips and daffodils poking out of the brick-rimmed flower beds, gathering the energy to burst into bloom. Ducking past crowds of people drunk on the warm weather and early spring light, I was trying to finish errands quickly so that my friend Janet and I could meet at Pasta Jay's for dinner. To have lunch or dinner with someone in our society is often a euphemism for another agenda. Business may be the real focus, especially at lunch. But with women, friendship is the agenda just as often. This dinner was about grieving, about crying over a glass of wine with a friend who could hear even the unspoken words of the heart, giving them voice.

There was a kiosk that sold flowers at wholesale prices, just a few blocks down the mall. It was in the opposite direction to Pasta Jay's, but if I hurried I could buy us each some roses and still get to dinner on time. What a deal. Twenty-five big, heavy, dusky red Peruvian roses for $13.99. Clutching the bouquets, intent on being timely—people with double-D-cup frontal lobes hate being late—I ran right past Janet, who was waiting for me on a bench on the sidewalk outside the restaurant. She looked at me quizzically, placing a gentle hand on one shoulder to stop me. We tried to hug, but the flowers got in the way. She had already divined my state of mind, ten seconds into the interaction, and hugged me with her eyes.

We asked the waitress—in this kind of establishment our "server for the evening"—for a quiet spot where we could talk. It was early and we had our pick of seats. We chose a table by the window, overlooking the pedestrians strolling down the mall, but we didn't see them. Our eyes were 100 percent on each other. Janet Quinn is a medical scientist and nurse, like me a frequent presenter on complementary medicine and healing at hospitals and conferences around the country. She is the author of an honest and compassionate book that is a worthy mirror of who she is, *I Am a Woman Finding My Voice.* We are also partners in women's silent prayer retreats and courses on spirituality and healing. Her commitment to honesty and intimacy in relationship, including her relationship to God, makes her a real *anam cara*, a spiritual mirror.

Janet's meditation practice is centering prayer, a form of waiting patiently for deep relationship with the Divine. Quieting down in sacred space, you hold the intention of sharing intimate time with the Creator. When the mind wanders, you repeat a prayer word, a sacred word, that brings you back to your intention to be present to God. There is a lot of waiting in this practice. God is always there, but it takes time for the veils that cover the mind and heart to fall away, so that we can meet the Divine Beloved in the innermost room of our being.

Father Thomas Keating, Janet's spiritual director—a Catholic term for a spiritual guide—teaches that centering prayer is like a declaration of readiness, a preparation for divine union. But the sacred marriage is ultimately a gift of grace. We can't storm the gates of heaven. Keating also points out that the meditation practice itself may seem quite ordinary, most of the time spent bringing your mind gently back to its intention to wait for God. The actual experience of divine union may take us by surprise some other time—walking through the supermarket, watching the clouds, sitting with a friend. Janet's long practice in sacred waiting makes her a receptive, patient listener.

We talked long and slowly about what was in our hearts. Our server knew that we were more interested in one another's stories than in dinner. She brought the wine right away and then waited a commendable period of time before sidling up to the table, asking in a hushed tone whether we would like to hear about the specials. Janet had just ended a relationship. It took time to tell the story, to let the feelings wash between us like the tide coming in, the story touching progressively higher ground. Every wave sank a little deeper into the sand on the shores of our understanding.

After a time the tide turned to me. I was still grieving about the lost opportunity to host the radio show that might have slowed my life to a more manageable pace, given structure to where I was on any day of the week. In the course of conversation I realized that this peripatetic lifestyle, more than half of the year away from home, had not been good for my still-new marriage. How could this simple truth not have been evident before? This was what I was really grieving about.

We talked about the kind of intimacy that gives us permission to be honest with ourselves, that provides the mirror for word and gesture that calls the deepest truths into awareness. We spoke of the need to meet the men in our life at the same place we meet our women friends and God. Somewhere in that silent time after a wave of words had gone out, and before the next had broken on the shore, there was another insight. I was not entirely available for intimacy with my husband, Kurt. Not just because my body may have been two thousand miles away in a Holiday Inn, but because I am ever self-contained and self-sufficient.

I am an independent woman who often keeps troubles close to my chest. I don't mind talking about things once they are resolved, but I have a hard time admitting to problems while they are active. They embarrass me. A part of me still wants to pretend that life is perfect and so am I. Vulnerability is not my strong suit. That's the value of friendship with people like Janet. She is such a good mirror that I cannot hide from myself. The veneer of strength melts away in the sunlight of her understanding, and I am willing to stand naked in the truth.

That night at Pasta Jay's, Janet's deep listening created the space into which honesty could flow. I was no longer crying over the radio show at all. It didn't really matter in the scheme of things. The tears were an admission that the strength of independence, like all strengths, turns into a weakness when carried too far. We traced the childhood and adult threads that had woven this independence into a sturdy fabric of identity. The price of intimacy is vulnerability, and I realized that I didn't even know where to begin making holes in the fabric of my safety net.

The conversation about intimacy eventually came around to sex. I recalled what an intimate experience sex is in the first months of relationship when our brains are churning out quarts of the neurohormone phenethylamine, which magically dissolves boundaries. Everything the beloved says seems like a revelation. We dote on one another's words. Even if you have the libido of a paperweight, lust consumes you. But as we all know, this chemical intimacy is short-lived. Boundaries firm up again, and, if the relationship is to grow, it must be tended with care. At the end of a long day, or a long trip, it takes effort to make love with words or bodies. It is easier to curl up with a book and a cup of tea, content in the comforting, if remote, presence of the other.

We spoke of how intimacy is particularly difficult in the tender realm of sexuality, where we are most vulnerable. We are not only physically naked but emotionally naked as well. Why is it so hard to say, "Yes, yes, more of that. It feels good over here," and "No, no, that's annoying. Let me show you what I want."

In the beginning, when the phenethylamine is flowing, everything feels good. We are, after all, drugged. We are intoxicated by one another. But after the initial grace period we are on our own, cold sober, forsaken by the chemical Cupid. If we admit that the bells are no longer ringing, perhaps our partner will take this as a rejection rather than as an invitation to know our body and mind more intimately. Intimate relationships of all kinds take time and commitment. They take trust. And there is no more intimate a relationship than sex.

HOLY, PASSIONATE SEX

One of the most interesting aspects of facilitating women's retreats is the witnessing of midlife women to that desire for holy, passionate sex that Janet and I spent the rest of our dinner discussing. Sex is the life force. It is the creative power. What better place to find an intimate relationship with God? Perhaps sex can be a kind of centering prayer, a commitment to waiting for God by making ourselves totally present to the body, mind, and soul of another person.

"Candles, music, flowers, and wine—these we all know are the stuff of romance, of sex and of love. But candles, flowers, music and wine are also the stuff of religious ritual, of our most sacred rites. Why is there this striking, though seldom noted, commonality? Is it just accidental that *passion* is the word we use for both sexual and mystical experiences? Or is there here some long-forgotten but still powerful connection?" So begins Riane Eisler's erudite treatise on sex, myth, and the politics of the body, *Sacred Pleasure.*

Riane maintains that women's sexual parts, our vulva and vagina, were once revered as magical, the portal of life. Our furry, sacred triangle was an object of adulation and worship. In Sanskrit the vagina is called the *yoni*, the cosmic door to creation. In Chinese it is referred to as the jade gates. In modern parlance the cosmic door has suffered a serious demotion. Cunt, snatch, beaver. These are hardly the words of mystery and magic, of respect and worship.

Although I won't romanticize ancient Goddess cultures, in which, according to Tikva Frymer-Kensky, the Goddess had to hold her ground in patriarchal turf, there was at least some place for sacred sexuality. In Sumeria and Baylonia, temples to the Goddess were attended by priestesses who ritually made love to men as a form of communion with God. The woman, in such instances, represented the mystery of creation made flesh. To enter her mysterious portal was to unite with the life force itself, to assist the feminine in its act of creation. The cosmic joining of male and female recapitulated creation, ensuring that the world would continue to spin on its axis, that the stars would progress through the heavens, that the seasons would appear in cosmic order, that the crops would prosper, and that children would be born in the human and animal realms. The act of sex was a sacred union, the human partners representing their divine counterparts.

Before we can think of sex as an act of deep communion with God, it has to be reclaimed from the sterile desert of puritanical religion. This may require healing if our religion has taught us that sex is dirty and ungodly, a nasty necessity for procreation in those without the commitment to lead a celibate, religious life. In one joke that speaks to this issue, the pope died and went to heaven. He was met by St. Peter at the pearly gates. "You were such a good pope," St. Peter said, smiling. "Tell me what would make you happiest and I'll see to it that you get it."

The pope was thrilled. "I'd like to read the original words of Jesus, his instructions to people for living a godly life. Who knows how they might have been changed through the years."

"You're in luck," St. Peter said. "We have a library here containing the original words of all the holy people from every religion." The pope settled in to read. A few hours later St. Peter heard terrible moans and wails coming from the library. The pope staggered out, bereft.

Holding his head in his hands, he blurted out to St. Peter. "I can't believe it! The word wasn't celibate at all. It was celebrate."

As a Catholic woman at a Gathering of Women retreat put it, "I can't believe I've wasted fifty-five years thinking that the body was evil. I must have been out of my mind. It's beautiful and pure. So sensual and intimate, this giving and receiving. Sex is holy. And," she added with a sly, conspiratorial smile, "there's not a minute to waste." But a full-bodied celebration of the sacrament of sex requires not only healing of religious ideas that the body is evil but also a healing of the wounds in our own sexual pasts.

As we reaffirm repeatedly, there is no separation between psychological and spiritual growth for women. Our deepest sense of self, an honest understanding of our strengths and weaknesses, is our innate spiritual connection. We can have a relationship to God only in proportion to the relationship we have with ourselves. When some part of us has been wounded and disowned, we are not whole. Part of us is split off and sealed away. And until we heal that wound and reclaim that part of our life, we will be unavailable to God in whatever sphere the wounding was in.

Whether you are a religious loyalist, a returnee, or a dropout, it's a good bet that some part of you believes that sex is an ungodly act. That is the most pervasive societal teaching. Especially for those brought up as Catholics, sex is essentially a religious no-no. Or at least a seriously qualified yes, ideally permissible only to beget children. In addition to exploring our religious baggage about sex, we also have to explore our personal wounds. We live in a sexually exploitative culture in which women are too often portrayed as objects that exist to fulfill the desires of men. Many of us also have experienced the personal humiliation of exploitation, and it may have caused us to lose some of our capacity for sexual intimacy. There is no way to relate to God as a lover, to have holy, passionate sex, if we're disconnected from the process. Then sex will become a chore at best, a sad fact of life for so many women.

In the interest of opening up discussion about the need to heal our sexual wounds before we can experience holy passion, I am going to share a very tender, personal story about the loss of my virginity. Ideally we wouldn't even speak in such terms. Why is it a loss? It might instead be a gain, an initiation into a deeper level of intimacy with the Divine in oneself and in one's partner.

I was only sixteen years old when I lost my virginity and a big chunk of my self-esteem with it. My beau was a suave young man who carried a long, black umbrella rain or shine and was bound for Yale the next fall. He had glued signal flags, which supposedly spelled out my initials, to the door of his Corvette. My mother suspected that he told this to all the girls, and that they were probably his own precious initials. The more she smelled a rat, and urged me to break off the relationship, the more desirable said rat became. I was smitten by the "Umbrella," as my mother called him. A smart and savvy teenager, I was completely devoid of reason when it came to this young man. He was, indeed, the one my parents warned me about.

The Umbrella and I were sitting on my parent's twelve-foot-long 1960s orange sofa one night when they were out. I was in my long-haired, guitar-playing phase. In a romantic reverie, I turned down the lights and played "*Erev shel Shoshanim*," a rather spiritual Hebrew love song that means "Evening of the Roses." At some unconscious level, I knew that love and even the necking I was expecting, were holy. The Umbrella's response was to examine his cuticles. He then executed a well-modulated critique of my performance. It was not positive. I was keenly embarrassed and wanted to crawl into a hole somewhere. Although I felt as if I had been kicked in the gut, I did my best to look interested. After all, who would have wanted to lose such a fabulous catch? Sensing my vulnerability, he gave me the opportunity to return to his good graces. Sex, "going all the way" as we put it in those days, was to be my redemption.

We adjourned to my kelly green bedroom, still decorated with dolls and teddy bears. I was anxious and upset, confused and jittery. Not only was I terrified that my parents might come home and find us, but I was not at all interested in doing the deed. I just didn't want to lose the cool guy whose Corvette was the talk of my friends. I didn't want to lose what, in my misguided childhood fantasies, I actually thought was his love. We disrobed awkwardly, silently, and speedily. There was no foreplay, no tender moments and whispered reassurances. There were no declarations of love, nor even the desire to please one another. Not even a beam of moonlight stole between the slats of the Venetian blinds to bear witness to the botched deflowering of a virgin. The whole thing was pretty much a zero, except for the misery, shame, and confusion I felt when it was over. This was what they write love songs about?

When I saw the Umbrella again the following weekend, he asked with a smug smile how the liaison had been for me. "I didn't feel much," I told him truthfully.

"Your fault," he replied knowingly, "you're obviously frigid."

That was the end of our relationship, but his words stuck in my side like thorns for many years. Not only did I feel sexually inept, I felt stupid and used, worthless and ashamed. My limbic, or emotional, brain forever after categorized sex as something dangerous and unpleasant. That one experience ruined my sex life for years and deprived me of experiencing the act as holy. That is why, ten years later, I thought that the priest who told me to think of my husband as Jesus when we made love was berserk.

Instead of telling us to "just say no" to physical intimacy as we come of age sexually, we ought to be told instead how and when to say yes in the context of interactions that are mature, intimate, and loving. Many unhealthy, disrespectful, and ruinous sexual experiences might then be averted. Sex education is valuable in terms of avoiding sexually transmitted diseases and unwanted pregnancies, but it does little or nothing to educate us about the sacred act of bodies joined in holy communion.

It was years before I began to heal the wounds of loveless sex as part of a course on sacred sexuality, undertaken not because I thought I needed healing—perish the thought—but to round out my credentials as a healer. My ex-husband and I were enjoying time on the lush, feminine Hawaiian island of Maui, participating in a week-long course on tantra, the sacred art of love derived from ancient Hindu and Buddhist practice. Most of the course was devoted to two topics: sexual healing and learning to come back into the body, to the senses. We were told that until we had healed both personal and cultural wounds about sex, there was no possibility of real sexual intimacy or of experiencing sex as a form of communion with God.

Waves breaking on the shore a few hundred yards away provided a constant undertone of peace. Lighted by candles, beautiful images of tantric art on the walls, our little seminar space felt intimate and holy, like an ancient temple. The ten couples in the workshop formed a healing circle one evening. Men were on the outside, women on the inside. "Look into the eyes of this beautiful woman," one of the leaders murmured, his voice floating on a background of tender music.

"You represent all the men who have ever treated her badly, who have failed to see that she is the Goddess herself, and who have used her for their own pleasure or power. You are all the men who have failed to the see beauty in her heart, her mind, and her body. Tell her that you are sorry. Apologize on behalf of all your brothers."

A chorus of murmured voices filled the space. At first I felt mortally embarrassed. I protected myself from my feelings by thinking how hokey this scene was. But the words I heard were honest and real. I had not thought of the Umbrella for thirty years, and suddenly he seemed to be standing right in front of me. I was unexpectedly touched, tears flowing in spite of the unconscious attempt to distance myself from the pain.

"Now, men, move to your right," the leader instructed. We women were each face-to-face with a new man. The ritual of apology was repeated. Ten times different men atoned for the less than skillful, or overtly hurtful, actions of their "brothers." My defenses were completely undone. Intense emotion and physical shaking signaled the triggering of a physiological process through which my limbic system had begun to let go of old memories and to heal. Somewhere in the corridors of time the shame was pouring out of a teenage girl afraid to lose love by saying no, but who ended up losing a precious part of herself by saying yes.

In this week-long course we practiced white tantra—hatha yoga—twice each day. This was hardly new to me. I was a yoga teacher for many years, all part of the grueling process of learning to relax. Somewhere along the way my body had entirely forgotten what it felt like to be undefended. But familiar yoga postures felt different during the course. Breathing in we began a stretch, breathing out we let go and followed the sensations as the body relaxed into the posture. I knew all about this rationally. I was supposed to be an "expert." Yet after a week of sexual healing I seemed to inhabit the body in a new way, to be more intimate with it. I forgot about how far I could get myself to stretch and just enjoyed the postures with the unconcerned languor of a cat. I was actually experiencing what I had been trying to teach my students for years.

Breath became a conscious path back into my healing body. It was so clear that, like many women, I had learned to float away and be elsewhere during sex. In a flash I could mentally go to work, to the supermarket, or play with the dog. I could go anywhere that was not a vulnerable place. I learned to be more mindful and aware of where my mind was in any activity. When it wandered I brought it back to the present with the breath. Daily it became more obvious that vulnerability and trust are prerequisites for any intimate relational act—sex, friendship, and being present to God. Vulnerability is a preliminary that cannot be willed but only relaxed into in situations of great trust and tenderness.

Swimming in the warm ocean that week, the women spoke of being more present to its sensuous touch than we were just a few days before. The feel of the breeze on our skin, the warmth of the sun came like sweet revelations to cave dwellers. The week nearly complete, reentering bodies that were healing from past sexual problems, some of us were finally ready to think about the actual act of intercourse with our mates in the privacy of our rooms. This final step in physical intimacy, we were told, might take weeks or months more to accomplish. But sex—in terms of putting our personal parts together and achieving some sort of release—was no longer the goal. Sacred lovemaking, what the priest had been trying to tell me about years before, was the process we were committed to. When we did make love, it would be to the God and the Goddess within one another.

WOMEN AS LOVERS

Physical love, no matter the sex of our partners, becomes sacred when it is an expression of the deep longing we have to experience the Divine in one another. And the many prohibitions against sex—enjoying it, thinking about, reading about it, having it with a woman instead of a man—are always with us. Some of the religious dropouts I have met are lesbians. They, in particular, carry a heavy load of societal disapproval which creates wounds that can make it especially difficult to experience sex as a divine relationship.

Homosexuality is considered sinful by most religions. Even natural expressions of sensuality between women are suspect. Writer Brenda Peterson, in *Sister Stories*, recounts a slumber party that she and her friends had at a rented beach house. Several women danced the tango together, slow and sultry. "Two women braided another's luxurious black hair; on the deck were languid sighs over head and foot massages; the kitchen sink was transformed into a beauty salon with women rubbing Lady Clairol ash-blond color into their dark roots. In the bedroom four women with faces green from cucumber-clay facials were playing drums and looking downright aboriginal. The easy sensuality, the familiar, female touching, the tender massages we so rarely allow ourselves these days—all those tribal gifts of the sisterhood, just like the sinful foods we declare off-limits, no matter how they delight us."

And beyond sensuality, Peterson comments that many of the women she has asked about whether they've ever made love with another woman report that they have, although this may not be their sexual preference for a lifetime. Furthermore, many of those who have not physically loved another woman have had fantasies about it.

In *Touching Fire*, Audre Lorde speaks of loving a woman on a roof in Morningside Park, New York. "I remember the full moon like white pupils in the center of your wide irises. The moons went out, and your eyes grew dark as you rolled over me, and I felt the moon's silver light mix with the wet of your tongue on my eyelids. . . . The sound of our bodies meeting is the prayer of all strangers and sisters, that the discarded evils, abandoned at the crossroads, will not follow us upon our journeys."

One of the most touching stories of accepting woman-to-woman sexuality is that of a nun, told by Jalaja Bonheim in *Aphrodite's Daughters*. Isabelle was fifty years old when the erotic attraction she felt, but hardly acknowledged, for God as Beloved erupted in a passionate love relationship with a laywoman. She prayed over her predicament, since loving this woman violated two taboos—that of any physical relationship for a religious woman and the taboo against lesbianism. Isabelle was at a retreat during which she felt a strong call to the natural way of life. "I thought about the words of Jesus when he said that not even Solomon, in all his wisdom, could equal the birds of the air. And I thought, 'Yes, they live in harmony with nature.' The night I made the choice to become sexual with my woman lover, the inner Nazi guards were all there in all their array and power and fury, trying to bar my way. But then I thought about what Jesus had said about the birds of the air. I kept asking myself, 'Which path feels more godlike?' And the answer was clearly that it felt more divine to go with my feelings for this woman. So I did."

GOD AS BELOVED

We usually think of sex as an act between two people, two physical bodies, whatever their sexual orientation may be. But sex can also be an act of communion, of intimate loving relationship, with God alone. The fourteenth-century nun Julian of Norwich wrote about a third relationship with God other than Father and Mother—that of spouse—in which she says, God rejoices. While God might rejoice in it, the mainstream Judeo-Christian tradition decidedly does not. There has been endless speculation about how the sexy Song of Solomon, or Song or Songs, ever weaseled its way into canonical scripture. It begins:

> *O that you would kiss me with the*
> *kisses of your mouth!*
> *For your love is better than wine,*
> *your anointing oils are fragrant, . . .*

It continues with pages of sensual imagery, involving not only the lover and the beloved, but all of nature:

> *Awake, O north wind,*
> *and come, O south wind!*
> *Blow upon my garden,*
> *let its fragrance be wafted abroad.*
> *Let my beloved come to his garden,*
> *and eat its choicest fruits.*

That the soul comes awake in love for the Divine Beloved is conveyed in metaphors that are deliciously sexual:

> *I slept, but my heart was awake.*
> *Hark! my beloved is knocking.*

"Open to me, my sister, my love,
my dove, my perfect one;
for my head is wet with dew,
my locks with the drops of the
night." . . .
My beloved put his hand to the latch,
and my heart was thrilled within me.
I arose to open to my beloved,
and my hand dripped with myrrh,
my fingers with liquid myrrh,
upon the handles of the bolt.

While the Song of Songs is the only canonical Judeo-Christian Scripture that is both sensual and sexual, Hinduism and Buddhism are full of such imagery in their art, Scriptures, and poetry. The sixteenth-century Hindu poet-saint Mirabai was an ecstatic lover of God. But rather than seeking the Divine Beloved within a human, she sought it through a direct relationship with God. She composed many poems, probably performed as songs, to the Divine Beloved and persisted in her devotions although her family thought her mad.

She wrote, "This love, Sister, is a love that endures. I have drunk from the cup of nectar and it has set me in a spin. They cannot sober me however they try . . . I have drunk from the cup of the Holy Name, and nothing else pleases me."

I'm not advocating that we give up physical lovers to become ecstatic lovers of God as Mirabai did. But in reading her poetry or, perhaps the most graphic writing on the relationship to God as Beloved, that of the thirteenth-century German mystic Mechtild of Magdeburg, we can get an expanded sense of what a deeply intimate relationship to God might be like.

The great mystical paradox to Mechtild was the fact that God is abstract and impersonal, present everywhere and in everything, and yet at the same time entirely intimate and personal. God to her was a husband, a bridegroom, to be appreciated with the totality of the body and senses. "Listen to me, dear Playmate," she wrote to God in her classic book *The Flowing Light of the Godhead*, "I was pleasantly half-drunk with love; this is why I speak tenderly from the senses." Mechtild is interesting precisely because her relationship to God is intimate in the deepest sense. She discusses everything with her Divine Beloved, and he answers.

Mechtild was a Beguine. This word refers not only to an African dance, as immortalized by the likes of Artie Shaw, Fred Astaire, and then Frank Sinatra in the song "Begin the Beguine," but to a brief women's movement in medieval Europe, centered in the German low country, or north. The Beguines started the first women's lay religious communities in twelfth- and thirteenth-century Europe, free of male influence and unaffiliated with any particular religious order, although they were generally served by parish priests. They tried to live lives similar to the Apostles of Jesus, dispensing with studying the teachings in favor of actually living what they considered exemplary lives. Like Mirabai they gave up earthly love in favor of God the Beloved.

Beguinages were a brief and brilliant flash in the history of women's spirituality. Nothing like them existed before or since. They were secular religious communities in which unmarried urban women came together to pray and live religiously devoted lives, voluntarily practicing poverty and chastity. For one hundred years, from about 1120 to 1318, a large number of such communities flourished. The women supported themselves through simple work like spinning and embroidery, housework for others, preparing the dead for burial, and through gifts from their families. These communities were a hotbed of mysticism for women who sought a personal experience of God as the Divine Bridegroom without the intercession of the Catholic Church.

The mystical Beguine women wrote down their experiences and provided firsthand accounts of divine union for common people, written in the vernacular language of the day rather than in Latin. Women like Mechtild, who wrote seven books of her experiences with God, were faced with the usual questions that women must answer in male-dominated fields like theology and medicine in which direct experience and intuitive wisdom are often discounted as unscholarly and therefore as inherently untrue and unworthy.

Predictably, the mystical Beguine women were eventually silenced by the Catholic Church. They were forced to obey their parish priests or face ex-communication and were warned against preaching false doctrine, which amounted to sharing anything in their experience that deviated from the party line. Eventually the notorious Inquisition came nosing around and, branding them heretical, forced the Beguines to disband communities that were as large as cities of seventeen thousand with their own hospitals, bakeries, and service infrastructure.

Mechtild was born in 1208, and at the age of twelve she had a mystical experience of conscious contact with God that continued daily for over thirty years. In her early twenties she left home to take up residence in the Beguine community of Magdeburg, and in her forties she revealed her experiences to the priest who was her confessor. A Dominican by the name of Heinrich of Halle, he encouraged her to write the experiences in book form. A manuscript of the lost *The Flowing Light of the Godhead* was discovered in 1861, and, since the original was never found, there is no way to know how it may have been altered by her confessor, who was also her editor. There is speculation that he may have added his own thoughts to sections that dealt with theological matters.

The Flowing Light of the Godhead is a melange of Mechtild's visions and some very practical advice about how to live a loving, God-centered life by extending the infinite care and respect of God to other people. Perhaps the most fascinating parts are the dialogues between the soul and God and the soul and Love. Her language is sensual, personal, and intimate. Although Mechtild's writings were censured in her own time, and she was in danger of being branded a heretic, she persisted because she could not and would not contain the inner urge of the Holy Spirit which spoke to her through all her senses. "I cannot nor do I wish to write, except that I see it with the eyes of my soul, and I hear it with the ears of my eternal spirit and feel it in all the members of my body."

Her writings are unabashed mystical testimonies, lovers' trysts. The fact that she is drunk on love gives her courage. Some theologians take Mechtild's more graphic dalliances with God as metaphor. But I imagine her absolutely on fire with fantasies—*experiences*—of God the lover, wet with wild desire and consumed with the delicious physical longing she often compares to a sweet torment. Mechtild isn't thinking about an abstract God. She is involved in a very personal, real, face-to-face relationship.

In Book One, Mechtild writes from the soul to God, "Ah, Lord, love me passionately, love me often, and love me long. For the more passionately you love me, the more beautiful I shall become. The longer you love me, the holier I shall become here on earth." God responds to the soul,

> *When I shine, you shall glow.*
> *When I flow, you shall become wet.*
> *When you sigh, you draw my divine heart into you.*
> *When you weep in longing for me, I take you in my arms.*
> *But when you love, we two become one being.*

And God describes the sweet torment of a lover separated from the beloved,

You are like a new bride
Whose one and only lover has slipped away as she slept.
She had entrusted him with all her love
And simply cannot endure his parting from her for one hour. . . .
Now let me tell you where I shall then be:
I am in myself in all places and in all things,
As I always have been eternally,
And I shall be waiting for you in the orchard of love
And shall pluck for you the flowers of sweet union
And shall make a bed for you out of the soft grass of holy
    knowledge.

Mechtild's experience of God as lover is not unusual, or the province of cloistered mystics. In Jalaja's Bonheim's *Aphrodite's Daughters*, Inès, one of the many women she interviews, tells this story. "A couple of years ago I was walking through the forest, by myself. It was evening, and I was lying on the ground, watching the last rays of sunlight filter through the trees. And suddenly, my whole body was flooded with sweetness, like warm honey flowing through me, so sensual. I don't know how long it lasted; I lost all sense of time. This may sound strange but it really felt as if a divine being had touched me and made love to me. Afterward, I felt a very full, very complete sense of peace and a satisfaction that stayed with me for days."

SENSUALITY, NOT TRANSCENDENCE

Mechtild, Mirabai, and Inès, communing with God as Beloved, must have been radiantly attractive. Lovers glow. Fireflies rise in their wake. They throw off waves of ecstasy like a dog shaking off water after a swim. The eyes of lovers hold an ancient secret that bursts forth in poetry and song. The veil of the ordinary drops away and the world seems new, made especially for them. They have found their true home in their bodies and senses.

Love is not a transcendent activity in which we rise above the flesh to seek an ephemeral, abstract God. It is a divine celebration of incarnation. God the lover told Mechtild where to find Him. "I am in myself in all places and in all things, as I always have been eternally." So the true lover of God is a supremely sensual person, passionately in love with life in every form. Mary Oliver, whom I consider the poet laureate of embodied spirituality, writes of how we bring the world into being through attention and relationship to it.

In her poem "The Summer Day," Oliver muses on who made the world and its creatures—the black bear and the swan, the grasshopper whose every move is a fascination that graces the page. Oliver walks through nature wide-eyed, feeding it back to the reader through every sense. She protests that she doesn't know what a prayer is and then demonstrates that our attention, our sensual intimacy with everything in the world around us, is the purest form of prayer. We become the mirrors through which the Creator can see Creation. Like an intimate friend, we reflect God back to Itself.

The lover brings the beloved to life through attention. This sensual intimacy is how we receive the world and the Mysterious Presence that created and inhabits it. Without appreciation, the world loses its savor. Nature goes to seed. Lovers wander off in search of someone who can see into them, appreciate them. When we fall in love with all creation, with God dwelling in every bush and tree, insect and human, we are worshipping. I enjoy going to new places because I see them with fresh eyes, momentarily overcoming the jadedness that often plagues us in this modern world of shallow, instant pleasures.

Coming upon a mountain pond for the first time one summer, I sat and watched the play of light on the water, felt the earth yield and sigh. Like a fox, I sniffed the complex notes of the wind, and was educated and intoxicated. Walking through a harbor at dawn in the town where I once lived in Massachusetts, I was delighted by melodious tinkling long before I identified the sound as the hardware on the riggings of sailboats swaying rhythmically against aluminum masts. Passing a spring garden in Boulder I was not lifted out of myself but delivered more fully into myself by the clusters of pansies, their bright faces turned to the sun. In those moments I had no illusion that God dwelled apart in a remote heaven. The Divine Presence was palpable in the moment, both within the flower and in the eye that enjoyed its beauty. This kind of attention is an active involvement with life. It is God-ing.

According to the male model of Jacob's ladder, the intimate relationship of God union requires transcendence. It happens when we move out of and above the limited consciousness of our bodies. But in the sensuous world of women, spirituality is an inward movement rather than an outward one. It is an inhabiting of the sensate, wild, and hungry body too often deemed religiously as an impediment to spirituality. We are cheated of our relationship to God by religions that regard the body as a fallen pot of flesh that must be scourged and beaten, whipped and hair-shirted into obedience so that we can transcend its limitations and base desires.

To be sensuous is to be aware that we are part of a larger whole, a circle, a web, that is experiencing itself through us. As different mystics have written, we are the eyes and ears, the hands and heart, of God. God knows Itself through us. We are one, and yet we are also two. The lover becomes one with the beloved, but she doesn't lose herself there. She grows, flowers, and finds herself made new again. Our deep relationship to God, the object of our journey, allows us to live in a world that seems continually fresh and new.

When we consciously seek God in the center of the circle, our insatiable egos quiet down. We feel content, awake, and aware. But when we forget about our relationship to Spirit, we are likely to lose our center. The mind quickly ratchets up its endless list of desires. Getting the things we want and avoiding the things we don't want become a central focus. This is the trap. As soon as we begin to desire something, whether it is a better job, a relationship, or even a cookie, we become discontented. We feel incomplete without the object of our desire. As soon as we get what we want, there is a brief moment of contentment. We are happy. Then the cycle of wanting starts all over again. And even these brief periods of happiness have a gloomy cloud lurking in the wings. "I may be happy now," we think, "but this cookie will make me fat; what if this relationship goes sour or I get cancer or the stock market crashes or my children get into trouble?"

While Jacob's ladder contains the implicit promise that we'll be happy someday, when we've taken the last step into heaven, Sarah's circle promises happiness now. In spite of trials and tragedies, mistakes and hurts, God is always available. We experience that divine relationship through our friends who comfort and guide us, and who help us to become our deepest, truest selves. We can experience that divine relationship through sex, in which God is never closer. And we experience divine relationship through everyday sensuality in which we become more and more present, more and more mindful. It is this quality of attention that allows us to escape the trap of desires, of wants and don't-wants, and enter the kingdom and queendom of heaven here and now.

SPIRITUAL IDENTITY
AND HEALING

The Heroine's Journey

I was in my midtwenties when my auntie Frances lay dying of cancer in the hospital across the street from the medical school where I was teaching. She'd been a beautiful woman, a little red-haired pixie, full of life and mischief. She was a legendary clotheshorse as well, and a hunter. Her specialty was not big game but bargains. It was her favorite pastime, and she had the trophies to show for it.

One of the family myths had to do with Auntie Frances's mother, who I knew only as the "little Mrs. Silverman." A slight woman, she was renowned for disappearing under the pile of clothing her daughter would collect while rummaging through the designer racks in Filene's Basement when it was the only decent bargain outlet in Boston. I saw this scene with my own eyes. Little Mrs. Silverman resembled a large turtle carrying a week's worth of laundry on its back as she trailed around patiently after Frances.

There was an entire room in Auntie Frances's house filled with racks of dresses, tags still in place. Although she wore a size 4, some of the dresses were as large as size 20. Who could pass up such beautiful fabric, such elegance? Maybe someday she would have the dresses cut down to size. In a contest with Imelda Marcos, my aunt would have claimed more pairs of shoes. It was hard to see her diminutive figure so thin that she hardly made a bump under the sheets of her hospital bed, pale skin as thin as parchment, and the mischief gone from her eyes. It was hard to recognize her but for the raspy, nasal voice, which had served to make her an even more colorful character. The last words she spoke to me have been a source of guidance and inquiry for thirty years.

"Life passes by so fast, Joanie. Believe me, in the end the shoes and clothes don't matter. Beauty doesn't either. They all just pass away. I feel like there were other things I could have done, more important things, and I don't even know what they were. You're young. It's your time now. Don't let life pass by without figuring out who you are and why you're here."

Reflecting on her words, my first thought was that the two of us came from different generations. Daughters born in the forties and fifties stood with their mothers on some kind of symbolic Continental Divide. The traditional waters that flowed east from the hearts of the mothers sought home and family as their destination. The awakening waters that flowed west from the hearts of their daughters sought a new world of equality in work, politics, and wages. My generation dreamed of a fair and visible place in a culture where women had been largely invisible, carrying around the burdens and trophies of the powerful like little Mrs. Silverman.

But I didn't really think that Auntie Frances was speaking about women's liberation on her deathbed. It felt more like spiritual liberation was on her mind. She was having an identity crisis, wondering who she really was and whether her chosen role had limited her, preventing her from plunging into deeper and more meaningful waters. The most remarkable thing about death is its insistence on harvesting life's meaning, even in those not prone to introspection.

Her generation of women, and so many before it, were acculturated to the role of helpmate to men. As I thought about her words, I began to wonder if my own generation was really substantially different. Rather than being helpmates to men, some of us just wanted to be like men ourselves. So much of our energy went into dismantling the fences that traditionally kept women off male turf. My female academic colleagues and I were forever joking about how what we really needed was a wife. Perhaps in the end we were not so different, Auntie Frances and I. We had both chosen a role to play and sought safety and pleasure in our identities. She had chosen a woman's world. I had chosen to fight for a world where men and women were equals. But was there some deeper identity, a spiritual identity, that we were both missing?

There certainly weren't any role models in my life for asking this important question. My mother stood by and wrung her hands ceaselessly about the fact that I'd chosen a hard road. I should have found a man to take care of me instead of becoming self-reliant. Spiritual concerns were the furthest thing from her mind. In the 1990s, Teilhard de Chardin's famous old quote about the fact that we are spiritual beings having a human experience, rather than human beings seeking a spiritual experience, was revived and hit the mainstream. My mother didn't have the vocabulary for such thoughts, or much interest in them. And although spirituality is popular now, I don't think that most women have really internalized what having a spiritual identity means, an issue that we are about to explore.

Thirty years after Auntie Frances's death I am still looking for spiritual role models. Princess Di, although I greatly admired her strength and her struggles, didn't do it for me. Mother Teresa doesn't work well, either. I admired her enormously, but I can relate more easily to a woman who is life-size rather than one who is about to undergo initiation into sainthood. Women celebrities, for the most part, are caught up in glamour roles. Although people like Shirley Maclaine did significant service in getting women to think about spirituality, I don't know if many of us really learned about being spiritual from her books.

My friend Janet, whom you met in the last chapter, is one of the best role models I've come across for what a woman's spiritual identity might be, and how it is lived. She is honest and authentic, funny and bright. Although a former star in academic medicine, a speaker, and an author, she doesn't for one moment confuse these roles with who she is. Her commitment never wavers. It is to absolute honesty and intimacy in relationship as part of the journey to God. About this she is meticulous and spectacularly present. Short on dogma, she doesn't waste a lot of energy on wondering where our souls go when we die or if they get recycled in human form. She knows her weaknesses and accepts herself as she is, although a strong commitment to psychological growth is always evident. Just as important, she accepts other people as they are. God is solidly in the center of her circle. He is the North Star by which she sets her compass. Whatever she does, she does for God and with God. That, I believe, is her spiritual identity.

Soon after Auntie Frances died, I started working with AIDS patients. It was like winning a season's pass to the thresher, a heart-wrenching season of harvest. The year was 1980, the very beginning of the AIDS epidemic, before any of the life-prolonging "drug cocktails" were available. The grim reaper was working overtime and so was the meaning-extracting machinery of many of us who worked with the dying. I learned to do a little "harvesting" exercise then, both because it was helpful to patients in retrospecting their lives and preparing for death and also because Auntie Frances's words were still alive and questing inside me.

In the sleepy recesses of reverie I float out of the body and stand in the Divine Light before God, who wants to know why I haven't used the gift of this human life to become fully myself. In this state of clear consciousness, Selfhood transcends a sense of specialness or ego. It's not about beauty or work, being invisible or seen, powerful or compliant. It carries within it the reality that one's true Self is a spark of divinity that shines unobstructed only in the moments of unself-conscious being when we meet life with the full and open measure of our attention.

An image that seems to capture this selfless Selfhood floats by unbidden. I am with an AIDS patient named Sam in the hospital. He knows that he will die from this illness, but at the moment he is all eyes and ears and heart. We talk of love and how strange it is that something so easy and natural seems to be so hard to give and receive. We trade stories of the times that love has broken through, stringing them like precious gems on the gossamer thread of memory. We speak of fishing trips with a father usually remote, the wet tongue of a puppy, making up after an argument, looking into a microscope and seeing something uncommonly beautiful, serving turkey at a homeless shelter on Thanksgiving. Sam looks into my eyes, "I have never felt more peaceful, more safe."

I am weeping, safe also in this larger sense of Self, the spiritual self. Sam holds my hand, says something to the effect of how my children must love me, how lucky they are. I stumble over words, know that he has caught a glimpse of something inside me that is not usually available, even to the people I love the most. It is the relationship between us that has lifted the bushel off the Light. I am my Self only because he is his own Self in this moment. The chatter and doubts and ruminations of ego are gone. We have seen the God in one another. Neither of us cares how we look, how clever our words are. We don't even care if the world ends here and now. We are whole and the story is told. Our lives have had purpose and meaning in this one precious moment.

The memory floats by in an instant, leaving the bittersweet taste of longing in my mouth. I understand what God has asked me. It wasn't about my achievements but about the very lightness of being that is the divine nectar in the center of the heart. It is clear that I have traveled through life thirsting for what was inside all along, while focused externally on the ever-changing horizon of achievement and opportunity. I have identified with my changing roles more than with the Inner Light which is immortal. I have suffered from a case of mistaken identity.

"Gee," I say, looking down at my feet and feeling foolish as the reality of life washes over me. "I meant to use the gifts you gave me. But I confused the big Self with the little self. I wanted to be perfect so that I could be loved. But my thighs were too fat, my feet were too big, and my breasts were too small. That just consumed me. I knew I'd never look like Cindy Crawford no matter how much I exercised or watched my diet. But I could never let go of the desire."

God shines the penetrating lamp of wisdom and compassion upon me, and my body—now made of the stuff of rainbows and stardust—temporarily dons its former coat of flesh. It is absolutely perfect, a miracle of beauty and divine engineering. I can't imagine why I didn't always love and appreciate it for what it was, the agency of love in physical form.

My work life flashes before us in a panoramic review. I was a pretty good scientist, I think, but not nearly as clever or dedicated as Marie Curie. With that thought, the light dims as if a rheostat has been turned down. I was a pretty fair writer, I think, and suddenly feel the power of the words in my books as they were experienced by those who read them and by others that the readers touched. My heart flies open and I am flooded with joy.

Then I think of the books never written, of how I lacked the imagination and gift for metaphor of a Barbara Kingsolver or a Louise Erdrich. The sparks of love dim once again. The image of a face, peering out from a book jacket appears in the darkness. My stomach does a flip-flop. I was a much better writer than that vapid so-and-so who had three best-sellers. The light dims entirely, and I stand in a crystalline, cold darkness. Alone with jealousy and feelings of failure, I am in hell.

Scenes from my life continue to pass by, but they are no longer illuminated with the Light of compassion and understanding. All the guilt I have ever felt rains down like sleet in the black belly of a cold night. I was a pretty good mother, but not nearly as good as my friend Chris. She really knows how to nurture—not only her family but her friends as well.

"You would have done better assigning my sons, Justin and Andrei, to a more evolved soul," I shout at God. "What does a twenty-three-year-old girl know about being a mother anyway? How did you expect me to raise children and cure cancer at the same time?"

I begin to swirl and float through the oppressive, frigid darkness. Eons seem to pass. Then gradually a sound begins to swell in the distance. Is there at least the company of a far-off nebula to ease the loneliness of eternal night? I slowly realize that the music is the laughter of angels. My performance has been highly amusing. They gather around, a circle of friends I have known and loved. Each one is a mirror for the Light, the Self, that has always burned inside, visible or not. As I turn to face each one, a new part of my wholeness is revealed and the inner Light dispels the illusion of darkness. The scene fades and a deep peace overtakes me.

As often as I do an exercise like this, the ego and its desires can still exert a hypnotic spell over everyday life. I still routinely forget my spiritual identity and get overinvolved with my roles. On occasion I remember Auntie Frances and say a prayer for her. I thank her for the gift of a vivid memory that resurfaces when the world is too much with me, asking the gentle question, "What needs to be healed so that you can remember who you really are?"

HEALING THE WOMAN'S SELF-IDENTITY

The issue of women's healing is somewhat different today than it was in my auntie Frances's time. The women who were her peers generally stayed home, tending their families. Today most women work, even if they also have children. We have economic and political power that was undreamed of only a generation ago. Yet old stereotypes still remain. To be a powerful woman in white Western culture is to be labeled unnatural and unwomanly. To feel deeply, empathizing with the joy and pain of others, is to be overemotional. To be intuitive is to be antiscientific—a denial of rationality. To be pretty is to be a bimbo. To be muscular is to be a dyke. To be round and yielding is to be fat. How can we be sensual, in our bodies, if we perpetually deny their beauty? How can we enjoy the feminine roundness of our forms if our image of a good body is that of a preadolescent boy, all angles instead of curves?

"How blind I have been to myself," I thought one morning, standing in front of the mirror naked. "What a traitor. How strong the thighs that carry me. How round the hips, warm and full. How sensuous the buttocks. How beautiful these small breasts that nourished my babies. What was I thinking all those years when I struggled to be twenty pounds thinner? I was a wraith."

I apologized to myself, and ran my hands again over the lush nakedness. I caressed and loved even the cellulite. I thought of a boyfriend in college. I was five feet four and a hundred eighteen pounds, the same weight I am today. He told me that I looked like a truck from the rear. I was too fat for him. The expanse of me was too much to love. The shame of it burned me, incinerated any love for this body. I stopped eating and dropped to ninety-nine pounds. I stayed there, more or less, for a decade. I bought my blue jeans in the boy's department and cherished hip bones that stuck out like cleavers.

For years I dreamed of that tiny girl and missed her. I felt fat and undesirable, even in size 6 or 8 clothes. I denied and hated myself, made an enemy of my flesh, and desecrated the holy temple of this body. I smiled and forgave the boy who loved bones. After all, he was just a child. I was fifty-three years old now, beautiful in this strong woman's body with its wide and welcoming hindquarters that sit with authority and strength upon the earth. It was time to let go of childish things. It was time to heal.

Sometimes I joke at our retreats that if we could collectively reclaim all the energy we have wasted yearning for different bodies, women could have changed the world by now. Until we heal, taking back the power we have given away to others, we will remain hobbled and inauthentic. If we are inauthentic, our relationships can't be authentic either, and walking Sarah's circle becomes like hiking through a marsh.

Unfortunately, women's body identity is likely to remain a major issue in American culture. Most of us will never live up to the retouched images of the perfect bodies and faces that gaze out from magazines. We know this, but knowledge isn't always freeing, even if we've spent some time healing the wounds that underlie our problems with self-image. And it isn't getting any easier for our daughters and granddaughters, nieces and students. Today's teens are a thousand times more depressed than their counterparts from the 1950s. It is harder and harder for young girls to find their own style and to like themselves. They are starving, literally and figuratively, in a society of plenty.

The weight of constant cultural icons—perfect young bodies—can overwhelm us. That's one of the reasons why it is so hard for many women to age gracefully. One of the best ways to loosen the teeth of the ego, and its desire for the perfection that it believes will guarantee love, is through humor. When we laugh the ego lets go. And when we laugh together, we bond over common foibles.

There's a story about a woman who went to the doctor for a consult on a facelift. He recommended a new procedure in which a small knob is installed just under the hairline. As new sags show up, you just turn the knob. A few years after the surgery, the woman appeared in the doctor's office, concerned about the big bags beneath her eyes. The doctor nodded his head sagely. "You've been overzealous with that knob," he lamented. "Those aren't bags, those are your breasts." "Oh"—the light of understanding dawned on the woman—"then that explains the goatee."

But the self-esteem issues women face are more than skin-deep. They have to do with judgment and comparison that can lead to bitterness, loneliness, isolation, and jealousy. We may never match up to the accomplishments of Marie Curie or our ex-husband's new wife. The coveted teaching job or best-seller may go to someone we consider far less qualified. These are issues of the small self, the ego. The journey home to God is a journey home to our deepest Self, to the ability to connect deeply and intimately and lovingly with other people and ourselves.

When our most primary relationship, the one we have to ourselves, is afflicted or hateful, it is not possible to be authentically present to relationship with others or to have a meaningful relationship to God. Too much judgment clouds our vision. Jesus spoke of this transference of self-hatred onto others with a simple analogy. We see the motes in other people's eyes because we have not removed the motes in our own. Psychologists call this projection. Whatever we despise in our own self we see in someone else. If we cannot tolerate our own anger or gossiping, we criticize someone else for the same behavior.

To walk Sarah's circle, we have to forgive and to heal so that we will be available for intimate relationship. Love can only flow when there is respect and trust for ourselves. Otherwise we will relate from our roles, from our egos and our fears, rather than from an authentically developed sense of self. Our gifts may not be those that destine us for the kind of greatness where the world beats a path to our door. But it is more how we do, in the end, than what we do, that counts.

AUTHENTICITY AND WHOLENESS

The word *healing* comes from the old Anglo-Saxon word *haelan*, which means "wholeness." Spirituality and healing, really, are one and the same thing. The Cherokee talk of being one hearted, rather than two hearted, as a metaphor for spirituality and healing. I think they mean being whole through and through so that our actions match our beliefs. When we are one hearted there is no mask for the outer world under which a secret person lurks. We feel at home in our own skin, comfortable in our self. What you see is what you get.

Authenticity, in which we create outer lives that match our innermost values, has never been an easy task for us women. Assaulted by a society that trains us to adopt false identities of beauty and power, self-importance and place in the pecking order, most women accumulate a thick covering of false selves, like barnacles that cover the bottom of a boat left too long at sea. The encrustation serves a purpose. It covers vulnerability and seals off fear. "I must be okay," we reason. "After all, I'm pretty, or I'm good at my work, or I married a doctor, or I raised successful children." But if the children get into trouble, we divorce the doctor, we're fired from our job, or we start to age and beauty fades, the facade falls off and we find that none of these roles was our true identity. Then we come face-to-face with the question that Auntie Frances asked at the end of her life: "Who am I, really?"

In the modern world, women's authentic selves are particularly challenged because ground that has been stable for generations is shifting beneath our feet. How can we work in what has traditionally been a man's world and still maintain our feminine values of relationality? If we choose to mother children and also work, where will we find the balance? If we succeed, will we be branded unfeminine and aggressive as in the days of Elizabeth Cady Stanton when the writers of the Declaration of Sentiments were compared to hens that crow?

I was being interviewed by a magazine reporter in the mid-1980s about a research study I was involved in. He had interviewed several male colleagues as well, and one had labeled me aggressive. The reporter hung on to this label like a starving dog worrying a bone. I was embarrassed, and I felt betrayed. Why aggressive? This conjured up an image of self-centeredness, of power over, rather than of the teamwork I thought we shared. Every member of the team was consumed with the research, working long hours to get it done. We were all faced with the reality of "publish or perish" which, for a time, was even a government postmark on university mail. We were all trying to help others with our research, keep our jobs, and get more funding.

Single-minded strength of purpose was apparently an acceptable characteristic for men, but for women it was called aggressiveness. I could just imagine the self-satisfied reporter talking with friends over a few beers that night. "You should have seen that ball-biting bitch I interviewed today. The guys she works with say she never gives an inch. I'll bet her husband is a wimpy little guy. Probably nothing left between his legs."

Since I spent most of my work time with patients in a healing-as-caring model of practice, the idea of myself as an aggressive bitch was at odds with my own self-image. I felt cheap and inauthentic. But as the urge to smack the smug reporter and the guy who had called me aggressive welled up, I thought, "Well, here's aggression. It's not so bad. It comes from the urge to protect what is valuable, whether it's a research project or my self-respect." If I am aggressive, it is the power of the she-bear rising, the power that protects what is precious.

In the end I was grateful for the incident with the reporter. It helped me reclaim and heal a part of my power that I had buried in the shadow, a term Carl Jung used for the dismembered parts of ourselves that we feel ashamed of because someone has said they were bad. Women have big shadows since we have been expected to conform to certain specific roles, behaviors, and even body types. The material in the shadow tends to come to light at midlife, as the body's hormonal milieu changes. In preparation for the increasing gift of intuition, and the power of the she-bear that makes us feisty and protective at midlife, there is a natural cycle of healing. Without it, we stay bonded to the ego. As we progress through it, we become more transparent, more authentic, more in touch with who we are rather than with what we do.

The period of midlife healing often leads women to deconstruct their lives when it becomes obvious that careers or relationships are no longer nurturing, and that they don't serve the higher ideals of the spiritual Self and its interest in relational connectedness. Many women report that the journey to authenticity is a dark night of the soul, a period of "don't know." Don't know what I'm doing, don't know where I'm going, don't know what comes next.

"Am I crazy?" a close friend asked me during this passage. "Is this just garden-variety self-destructiveness? I've given up everything, my job and my relationship, and nothing else has come yet—two years later—to fill its place."

Not to worry. Periods of "don't know" are part of the landscape of becoming authentically whole, in touch with inner power and authority. The process we go through is contemplative, much like the one my auntie Frances went through before her death. What is most valuable? What is most precious? Does my life reflect what I value most? If not, deconstruction follows as we make room for something new to be born.

In this culture, we are told to set goals. We are supposed to know where we are going and then take specific steps to get there. But this is not always possible, or even wise. It is the male model of linear, rational thinking. But the life process of women, as we discussed in Chapter Three, is more chaotic and disorderly, more circular and intuitive. Sometimes we can't see the next horizon until we step out of the old life. We don't yet know where we are going. We may not know the place until we arrive.

Ideally, as we learn to walk Sarah's circle, we come to trust that a greater Spirit will lead us. But it is a characteristic of the initiation into wholeness and authenticity to lose that trust, that faith. There is a special grace during these periods of doubt that may not be apparent until later. Our souls are so bare during this time, so open, that the things we learn become etched upon our minds and hearts in bold relief. Sometimes we have revelations that are thrilling, but they get lost in the subsequent busyness of life. But the revelations on the road to authenticity—when we slowly but surely find our spiritual vision and arrange our outside life to match our inside one—are seals upon the soul. We remember the people and the teachings in this passage that open us to a deeper level of who we are.

Women's dark nights of initiation can be fierce. They tear the inauthentic, false self to shreds. There is nothing to hang on to in our old way of being that will save us. Left adrift in strange waters, we must find the true, authentic Self or die. The death may be one of depression in which we lose the ability to relate. Lacking mirroring from others, we seem to disappear. We cannot find ourselves anywhere. It may even be physical death from despair and suicide or from an illness that has sneaked into our body like a burglar when no one was home.

During these frightening initiatory periods of becoming more wholly and holy ourselves, the stories of other women who have weathered similar storms can be life rafts. Personal stories provide wisdom that can sustain and inspire us. We may find ourselves saying, "If she lived through that, so can I." Truly archetypal stories are like blueprints for soul growth. We hear them and some part of our being clicks in and locks on, like a homing device. We were lost, but a signal just came from God that will guide us home. The descent of Inanna is such an archetypal story, a guidance system for becoming authentically whole. As you will see from the accompanying story of my friend Susan, it has the power to heal.

THE DESCENT OF INANNA: THE SECRET OF LOVE'S TRUE POWER

A friend of mine arrived home from a conference to find new locks on her house and all her belongings and those of her daughters' from a previous marriage neatly packed up and loaded into a moving van headed for a storage facility. There was a note on the front door from her husband. It read something to the effect of: "Susan, I know this may come as a shock, but I've felt that our marriage has been over for years. It's hard to say good-bye, so I thought I would spare all of us the pain and pack up your things while the girls are visiting their father for the summer. I'll pay to store everything until you've found a new place. Meanwhile I trust that you and the girls will be comfortable in the apartment we keep downtown. I had my lawyer draw up a divorce agreement and deliver it to your office. Please review the documents at your earliest convenience so that we can expedite this matter and come to an equitable settlement."

There are times in life when we initiate the move to authenticity. At other times we are propelled into a new life when the roof caves in. Susan, a level-headed psychiatrist, read the bizarre and cruel note from her husband and promptly hurled her purse at the large picture window next to the front door. When it bounced off harmlessly, she went to the driveway and pried up a heavy paving stone from under a lush patch of the variegated hosta she had been nurturing for years. Positioning herself several feet from the window she raised the stone over her head and launched it with a great roar. The enormous window shattered and the burglar alarm began to wail as Susan got back into her car and drove across town to her office.

By the time she arrived the wind had gone out of her sails. The urge to fight back—her usual mode of coping—had mysteriously evaporated and she began a descent into the darkness of her psyche marked by passivity, depression, unabated grief, and obsessive guilty rumination. "What is it about me," she pondered, "that wasn't good enough to keep my husband? I'm a psychiatrist and I didn't see it coming. Am I that blind? That unaware? If so, I'm a failure at everything, not just marriage. I don't know myself at all. I don't know anything."

"Where has Susan gone?" her friends wondered. "Who is this person who looks like her, but isn't?" We began to fear for her life. And for a year it did seem that she was effectively dead—caught in a state of suspended animation in which her body approximated the motions of living but her soul was someplace far away. As long as Susan felt isolated, as if the passage she was undergoing were solitary and related to some individual failing, she could not heal. Several friends got together, in the hopes of creating a space where the ever-self-possessed Susan might tell her story and share her feelings. Central to the ritual we planned for her was a reenactment of the ancient story of Inanna. It speaks not only of resurrection through dark nights of the soul but also of the importance of surrender and friendship.

The earliest writer in history whose name is known was a woman, Princess Enheduanna of Akkad in Sumeria. She was born about 2300 B.C.E. and composed songs in honor of the goddess Inanna, which she inscribed on signed clay tablets. A considerable amount is known about the history and stories of women from this period, when simple symbols were pressed on wet clay with folded reeds, because the tablets withstood the ravages of time, flood, and fire. Household accounts, school lessons, stories, and a whole treasure trove of information about daily life were recorded. The stories of women from later biblical times, in contrast, ironically were lost because, with the advent of more modern schemes of writing based on complex alphabets too elaborate to be pressed into clay, the bulky tablets were no longer used. Parchment and papyrus scrolls didn't withstand the rigors of time as well as clay, so the story of Inanna is truly an ancient treasure of women's spiritual wisdom.

From the Great Above she opened her ears to the Great Below.
From the Great Above the goddess opened her ears to the Great Below.

*From the Great Above Inanna opened her ears to the Great
Below.*

*My lady abandoned heaven and earth to descend to the
Underworld.
Inanna abandoned heaven and earth to descend to the
Underworld.
She abandoned her office of holy priestess to descend to the
Underworld.*

As a prelude to the story, Inanna the queen of earth and heaven, goddess of love, receives fourteen *me,* or blessings of power, from Enki, the god of wisdom and waters. Enki is both a mentor and a prophet. He is that force of growth, healing, and transformation that often arranges for our lives to fall apart dramatically so that in discovering and using the *me,* the blessings, with which we have already been gifted, we can own our true power. Enki prophesies that Inanna will come into mastery of Truth and the Art of Lovemaking, two of the *me* that he has blessed her with. In essence, he has promised that she will find her true spiritual identity, and that will allow her to follow the feminine path of authentic relationality.

Implicit in the story is a warning. To be blessed is to be challenged. It implies a process of growth, and growth often means initiation. The old must die so that room for something new can be created. Whether we are abandoned ruthlessly like Susan or decide to deconstruct our lives as an answer to some deeper calling, we are taken to the Underworld. Through a process of surrender, during which our souls go into suspended animation and the life seems to leave us, we find that we cannot make the ascent alone. We need friends and helpmates to guard us during this vulnerable time. When we emerge and begin the ascent back out into the world, we own the *me* that were given to us as blessings.

The story of Inanna is an archetype for women's psychospiritual growth. It is the best story I know to illustrate what walking Sarah's circle looks like. It is a pattern for the heroine's journey that is quite distinct from the kind of stories that portray the "hero's journey." In Jason and the Golden Fleece, for example, the man who aspires to grow must set out on a journey where he vanquishes the dragon and overcomes the obstacles alone. He is the prototypical warrior, journeying beyond the known world to bring back something of value for himself and its other inhabitants. But Inanna cannot make the journey of transformation alone. Her path to wisdom and her divine birthright as the goddess of love is one in which friends are the key components. Without them she would not survive.

Inanna prepares to descend to hell to visit her sister Erishkegal, queen of the Underworld. In various versions of the story, translated from tablets discovered as recently as the 1940s, Inanna's descent has different motivations. In one version Inanna requests entrance to hell to attend the funeral of her sister's husband. But Erishkegal fears that she has really come to conquer the Underworld, for what else could truly have brought her on such a dangerous journey to the land of the dead?

In case of trouble, Inanna instructs her loyal friend and servant Ninshubur to wait for three days at the entrance to the Underworld, and then to call upon the gods for help if she has not returned. Inanna then girds herself with all her powers—a crown upon her head, a circlet of lapis beads around her neck, two strands of precious gems over her heart, a wondrous breastplate, a gold ring for a bracelet, her royal robes, and a lapis measuring rod and line. The gatekeeper Beti sees her coming, arrayed like the stars of heaven in all their glory. He calls worriedly to his mistress Erishkegal. A great goddess, as large as the earth and sky, is waiting at the gates, demanding entrance.

Erishkegal instructs Beti to open each of the seven doors to the netherworld just a crack, so that in squeezing through, Inanna will have to divest herself of one power at each gate and arrive bowed low and powerless before her. At the first gate Beti removes the crown of Inanna's intellect. When she questions him about removing her powers at the first and subsequent gates he replies, "Quiet, Inanna, the ways of the Underworld are perfect, they may not be questioned."

At the second gate Beti removes her lapis necklace, and with it the power to defend herself through speech. At the third gate he removes the double strand of beads over her heart, the twin flames of wisdom and compassion. At the fourth gate he removes the breastplate called "come, man, come" through which she can summon the help of men through her charisma. At the fifth gate he removes the golden ring from her wrist, curtailing her power to strike back. At the sixth gate the lapis measuring rod and line are taken away, so that she cannot find her bearings. At the seventh gate her royal robes are stripped away, and with it her outer personality, her ego. Inanna, as naked and defenseless as a newborn, is ushered into the throne room before Erishkegal.

Suddenly, quickly, the seven fierce Annuna—the judges of the Underworld—surround Inanna and pass judgment against her. "Then Erishkegal fastened on Inanna the eye of death. She spoke against her the word of wrath. She uttered against her the cry of guilt. She struck her. Inanna was turned into a corpse, a piece of rotting meat, and was hung from a hook on the wall."

Meanwhile, the faithful Ninshubur has waited for three days and three nights for her mistress to return. She suspects foul play and begins a loud lament, accompanied by the beating of drums. She dons a simple mourning dress and hurries off to the gods to ask for help in saving the queen of earth and heaven. Father Enlil, god of air, refuses aid. "She asked for it," he grumbles. "Whoever receives the powers of the Underworld has to stay there."

Then she goes to Father Nanna, god of the moon, and begs him to save Inanna. He is as grumbly as Enlil, and will not lift a finger for his daughter, for she has chosen her destiny. Finally Ninshubur visits Enki, the god of wisdom who had gifted Inanna with the fourteen *me*, the blessings of power, to begin with. Enki is distraught, filled with love and concern for his beautiful daughter, the holy priestess of heaven.

Enki scrapes dirt from beneath his fingernails and fashions two odd and wonderful creatures, neither male nor female. To the *kurgarra* he gives the food of life, to the *galatur* the water of life. He instructs them to sneak into the Underworld like flies, through the cracks in the gates, and then gifts them with the secret of love's true power.

It seems that Queen Erishkegal is in great pain and giving birth, writhing around naked and uncovered. He tells the creatures to mirror her pain. If she cries, "Oh! Oh! My insides," they are to reply "Oh! Oh! Your insides." If she cries, "Oh! Oh! My outsides," they are to cry "Oh! Oh! Your outsides." If she screams, "Oh! Oh! My belly," they are to scream "Oh! Oh! Your belly!" And this they do.

The queen is so touched at being seen, acknowledged, and received so deeply that she is willing to grant these two creatures whatever they want. She is willing to gift them with the rivers or the grains of the fields, but they request only Inanna's corpse, hanging from the hook on the wall. As Enki has instructed them, the *kurgarra* sprinkles the food of life on the corpse, and the *galatur* sprinkles it with the water of life.

Inanna rises up out of death and prepares to ascend from the Underworld when the Annuna, those seven quick-on-the-trigger judges, grab her and inform her of one more of those rules that must be obeyed without question, a special quirk of the Underworld. You can't leave unless you deliver someone else to take your place.

So up Inanna goes, accompanied by a nasty little pack of *galla*, demons from hell who are pledged to keep an eye on her until she offers up a replacement. The *galla* think that Ninshubur would do nicely. But Inanna refuses to give up the friend who has, after all, just rescued her from hell. Next they try to claim Shara, Inanna's son who, thinking her dead, is dressed in sackcloth and grieving. When Shara sees his mother, he throws himself at her feet in joy and she shoos the *galla* away from him. They walk on a while toward the city where she lives and soon come upon her other son, Lulah, who is also dressed in soiled sackcloth, mourning for his mother. He, too, throws himself into the dust at her feet and she waves the *galla* away from him.

Finally, Inanna and the honor guard from hell walk into the queen's home city and there, sitting on his fabulous throne, resplendent in garments of *me*, is her lounge lizard husband, Dumuzi. He is reveling in splendor, enjoying urns of milk and the music of the reed pipe, not in mourning at all, forgetful of his supposedly dead queen. Seeing that he is careless of her death, forgetful of the rituals of remembrance, Inanna is infuriated. She is dishonored, feeling unseen and unloved. So it is written that Inanna "fastened her gaze upon him: the gaze of death: she said against him the word of wrath, and cried at him the cry of damnation: guilty!"

Inanna utters exactly the same words of condemnation to Dumuzi that Erishkegal had spoken to her. The *galla* promptly set upon the lax and careless husband with axes, and he begins to wail hideously and cry out to the gods for help. One of them, the merciful sun god Utu, changes Dumuzi into a snake, and he slithers out of the clutches of the *galla* and hides for a short while at his sister's house. But the *galla* soon find him. So Dumuzi's sister prays that she might be taken to hell instead of her brother, and Inanna agrees to a compromise. Dumuzi will stay in hell for six months a year and his sister for the other six. This story of alternation between darkness and light prefigures many of the myths of agrarian cultures in which the land lies barren while a god or goddess is in the Underworld, coming to life again in the six months when they emerge.

The story of Inanna is rife with layers of meaning. Enki prophesied that Inanna's descent would actualize the *me* of truth and the art of lovemaking, so let's take a closer look at both of these. Oftentimes, the hardest person to love is ourselves. Most of us have an inner litany, a jingle, a mantra of self-hatred that we recite regularly. "I'm too fat, I'm too thin, I'm not as beautiful as Elizabeth Taylor, as talented as Alice Walker, as kind as Mother Teresa." Like the seven Annuna of hell, we are quick to pass judgment and condemn ourselves.

It is an interesting exercise to write down the seven judgments that you think the Annuna would pass on you—yelling Guilty! Guilty! The judges of hell are the shrillest rendition of our own ego, the truth of what keeps us separated from our authentic Selves. Inanna's descent to the Underworld allowed her to meet her ego in the form of her sister, Erishkegal, whose judging minions condemned her. But there is a greater power than that of judgment. It is the power of wisdom and love, represented by Enki who sent Inanna on the quest to meet her shadow and the judgments it held so that she could claim the true power she had been gifted with.

When wisdom and love are present Truth can emerge because we dare to look at ourselves, knowing that the greatest truth is not about our failures but about the ability to transform and be transformed by acts of kindness, care, and help.

SUSAN'S HEALING: THE ARTS OF
TRUTH AND LOVEMAKING

The usual definition of lovemaking has to do with sexual pleasure, a special kind of giving and receiving. In a more general sense, giving and receiving in any situation is part of the Art of Lovemaking, the special kind of relatedness that is a woman's spiritual path. Inanna's moment of being naked and on the hook, completely vulnerable, contains within it the blessing of surrender. Erishkegal, too, the lonely queen of darkness, is redeemed by the mirroring of the *galatur* and the *kurgarra*, who feed back her pain to her. Many women, like my friend Susan, are better at giving than receiving. It takes strength to be "the healer," but without the gift of vulnerability—the handmaiden of intimacy—it is hard to face the truth of our lives and the healing that can emerge from times of pain and darkness.

Before Susan's husband left her, she was a powerful, independent woman. Successful in her work as a psychiatrist, confident in her abilities, she prided herself on what she could do for other people. Unused to receiving help, Susan repelled her friends with stock answers to our questions about her well-being: "I'm coping. I'm healing. I'll be all right. No, I don't need to talk about anything. Tincture of time. That's all I require." Susan didn't know how to ask for help or how to receive it. She looked half-dead to us, but her strong facade of invulnerability prevented her from taking an honest look at her own reflection.

Susan's friends met. I told them the story of Inanna and how it was archetypal of the experience that Susan was having. We conceived a wild idea. Perhaps enacting it would help Susan put her problems in a larger perspective. Our greatest hope was that the story could provide an emotional breakthrough or, at the very least, a tangible sign that we cared deeply for our friend. When we told Susan that we wanted to arrange a healing circle for her, on the anniversary of the day that her husband kicked her out, she almost didn't come. She finally relented grudgingly. We told her to bring bagels and cream cheese for an 11:00 A.M. brunch and meeting. She liked to be useful.

Eleven of us gathered in my sun-soaked living room at ten in the morning to prepare for the ritual that we had planned and practiced the day before. Emily and Bobbie, Susan's sixteen- and fourteen-year-old daughters from her first marriage, were among us, sporting black robes and mustaches made of eyebrow pencil. They were to play several different roles ranging from the Annuna, the judges of hell, to Innana's sons. Susan's oldest daughter would also play the role of Dumuzi's sister, who agreed to take his place in the Underworld for six months each year.

When I first explained the story to our circle, Bobbie and Emily wanted to be the *gallas*—the hounds from hell—who tried to cut up the faithless husband Dumuzi, whom they immediately identified as their former stepfather. The girls were open, both about their anger toward him as well as their anger at their mother, whose stony silence had prevented them, as well as herself, from moving through grief into healing. They are great kids and had been a tremendous support to each another. Anxious to support their mother as well, they threw themselves into their roles, body and soul.

I took the part of Inanna, and other friends signed on as Enki, Beti, Ninshubur, the *kurgarra*, the *galatur*, the *galla*, and Dumuzi. Her daughters would dress Susan in a splendid red robe and a black veil, befitting the queen of the Underworld, and her sixteen-year-old daughter, Emily, would coach her in the part, whispering the lines as we put on the play.

Susan arrived at the door impeccably dressed in a navy business suit and a pair of Ferragamo pumps, a sack of warm bagels in hand. Her eyes were wide with surprise at the sight of me barefoot in a long, green sequined dress I borrowed from a friend, and a blue cape constructed of cotton cloth, adorned with yellow stars and a crescent moon. I sported a garland of daisies, a gold belt and bracelet, a long, blue stone necklace, a breastplate made of aluminum foil, and a long rod with dangling feathers as befits the goddess of earth and heaven. She must have been wondering what conference I picked this outfit up at. Just as Susan was about to balk, her two daughters appeared dressed as the Annuna. They led her into the living room, where the friends were gathered.

Emily, star of several school plays, addressed her mother with professional aplomb and told her that we had planned a healing psychodrama. Several of us helped to explain the ritual and gave Susan the choice of whether or not to go through with it. Relief permeated the room when she consented. We all hugged her. With the help of Bobbie, Emily led Susan into the guest bedroom where the two girls dressed their mother as Erishkegal and filled her in on her part. The girls were our secret weapon. It is hard for a mother to deny her children.

Our friend Charlotte blew a trumpet blast and the play began. Enki gifted me with the *me* of Truth and Lovemaking, and I went off muttering about what kind of price I was likely to have to pay to learn such valuable lessons. I soon found out as, descending to the Underworld, I was stripped of cape and garland, bracelet and belt, necklace and breastplate, wand, and finally the green dress. I knelt before the veiled Erishkegal in bra and slip, cowering. She was not in much better shape than I was. Each time I was stripped of a power on my way to meet her, she flinched. By the time my dress was ripped off, she was weeping. Emily nudged Susan in the ribs. "Condemn her to death now, Mom."

Susan's first attempt at the death sentence was wimpish at best. Emily persevered in her coaching. Susan finally belted it out. "Death, death to the upstart Inanna, who is trying to steal my power. I condemn you to death." She wept as I was hung from a hook by the fireplace by my bra strap. Ninshubur—our friend Jackie—leaped into action and got instructions from Enki on how to save her friend. In no time flat the *galatur* and the *kurgarra* he created sneaked into the Underworld bearing the food and water of life. Emily coached her mother, who was now off her throne and laying on the floor in labor. "Writhe around, Mom, you're giving birth. Tell us where it hurts."

"Oh, my God, my back is killing me," moaned Susan. Kate and Leigh, the *kurgarra* and *galatur*, stroked her brow and looked into her eyes. "Oh, my God, your back is killing you," they moaned. "Oh, my God, my belly is about to burst." Four hands descended upon Susan's belly. Kate's and Leigh's eyes had not left Susan's. "Oh, my God, your belly is about to burst." Susan's whimpering crossed the line between fantasy and reality. "Help me, my womb is ripping open." Their eyes stayed riveted on hers. "Help her, her womb is ripping open," Leigh and Kate shouted.

Susan lost it altogether and began to ad-lib. "Help me, my heart is broken." I nodded to the group. We all responded, "Help her, her heart is broken." "Help me, I'm dying inside." The chorus of grief escalated. Kate and Leigh continued to hold Susan, to look directly into her eyes. "Please, I don't want to be alone," Susan finally gasped. "You were never alone," we replied.

We moved closer, allowed Susan to cry it out. Kate and Leigh helped her sit up. "You were never alone," they repeated. Susan let them support her, and back in her role as Erishkegal, rewarded their compassion with an offer of anything they wanted. They pointed to my body, hanging from the hook. Tenderly they laid me on the floor at Susan's feet. I was sprinkled with water and little golden stars.

Inanna was brought back to life, and the play went on. I ascended from the Underworld with the *galla*. To Susan's delight, we chastised the faithless Dumuzi, whose sister—dear Emily—finally talked me into letting her spend half of every year in the Underworld in her brother's place. Emily sat down next to her mother in the Underworld, resting her head in Susan's lap.

"I bet it's lonely down here all by yourself, Erishkegal," Emily sympathized.

"Very lonely," Susan replied in a shaky voice. She was stroking Emily's hair.

"How have you lived alone here for so long?" Her daughter's voice was filled with concern. She sat up and looked at her mother.

"Being queen of the Underworld keeps you pretty busy, you know. You have to keep everybody's secrets. Guard them from the light of day." Susan's professional demeanor was reasserting itself. She sat up straighter.

"Do you want to know my secrets?" Emily's smile was filled with pain. "I've missed you. You've been gone all year. I've been scared for you, and angry. You haven't been there for us, Mom." The sound of blowing noses created a stirring soundtrack for the ritual.

Bobbie joined her mother and sister in the circle. "We're not babies, Mom. We know that you've been hurting, and we love you. Please let us love you. Please let us in. The Underworld isn't so bad as long as we're together." The three women hugged. We all moved around them and the hugging continued. With runny mascara, in full Thespian regalia, we poured the coffee and sliced the bagels. We welcomed Susan back. Inanna's descent was Erishkegal's awakening.

THE SPIRITUAL SELF

Susan's initiation by darkness might have ended differently had not a caring group of friends come to rescue her from the Underworld. In the months that followed, Susan began to open up in a new way. Her professional veneer stayed intact as a therapist, but she became increasingly more vulnerable and real as a friend. Now she could not only listen well, she could also speak from her heart about the things that were bothering her. As she did this she was rewarded with a series of revelations about herself and her marriage.

Susan's husband may have appeared a cold-hearted villain, but she was slowly able to tell us of her own role in the demise of the marriage. Susan's mask, her inauthentic self, had prevented deep intimacy from growing. She simply didn't know how to share her feelings and retain a sense of control at the same time. The daughter of two alcoholic parents, she had effectively raised two younger siblings. She was their rock. Efficient and effective, Susan had never really had a childhood. She was the one who hid her parents' bottles so that the trash collector wouldn't see them and let out the family secret. She was the one who answered the telephone at night when they were drinking. She kept the situation as tightly under wraps as she could.

Susan's fear of losing control to anyone or to any situation kept the old patterns of secrecy and efficiency firmly in place. She had so much fear and shame hidden inside that she had never even told her own therapist the truth about her childhood. A dauntingly powerful person, she had somehow bamboozled her therapist during training, inventing an idealized childhood. The core of her false identity never came to light. She conducted her marriage the way she had run the house as a child. She was brusque and efficient, thoroughly unavailable to her own emotions. They frightened her too much.

Susan's first marriage recapitulated her childhood. She chose an alcoholic. After she divorced him it never occurred to her to get help, to go to a program like Al-Anon. With characteristic control, she simply decided to marry a successful, powerful businessman who was also emotionally unavailable. Eventually frustrated at the distance between them, and blaming her husband for their problems, Susan had a series of affairs. True to his own personality, her husband took back control in a very blunt way. He unceremoniously kicked her out, without even discussing what had happened between them.

Sometimes pain is the prelude to growth. Susan had told many clients just that. But it was a very different thing to confront her own pain. Perhaps the most agonizing secret Susan shared was that she, who had been a teetotaler, had begun to drink heavily after being kicked out of her house. Her life was rapidly spiraling out of control, and without the help of friends she may have ended up as an alcoholic, succumbed to her depression, or even committed suicide. A few months after our ritual she went into therapy and started to attend Al-Anon meetings. There they spoke of surrendering your addictions, whether to alcohol or to control, to a Higher Power. Surrender and vulnerability, and the people in her Al-Anon program, became Susan's teachers.

Very slowly, over a period of many months, Susan was able to own her grief, her aggressiveness, her tendency to stonewall and intimidate people, and her need for control. Rather than feeling ashamed of these qualities, she came to realize that they were a part of her character that had kept her alive and sane in an insane world. Owning these qualities, she was able to reclaim her wholeness. Her "bad traits" had once served her passably well. While committed to finding better ways of relating to herself and her family, her friends and her clients, Susan came to accept herself the way she was.

We were sitting in the kitchen of her home one Saturday morning about a year after the Inanna ritual. I was kidding her about the dishes in the sink, a sign of "disorder" that the old Susan would never have tolerated. She took me into her home office, which was a mess. I might have said an unholy mess, but the chaos was absolutely holy. "God loves me the way I am," Susan offered with a smile, "mess and all. It's not worth the energy to try and be perfect. No one is. All we can do is to be honest, to tell the truth, and to show up in our relationships. I used to repeat a slogan to myself all the time from this positive-thinking guy Coué who was popular in the 1920s. It was my mother's favorite affirmation. 'Every day in every way I get better and better.' The funny thing is, since I've stopped saying it, I really am getting better. I do like some of the Al-Anon slogans. 'Easy does it,' and especially, 'Let go and let God.'"

Susan's insight that God loves us just the way we are sounds like a Sunday school ditty. But sometimes the truth is very simple. We are loved. But since love is a transitive verb, we have to be open to receive it. That's the lesson Susan learned. And that's the lesson many other women have to learn to find our spiritual Selves, the Inner Light, the center of the circle. We live in a society that touts perfection. Self-help books and magazines trumpet the possibility of ten days to firmer thighs, buns of steel, eternal youth, fabulous wealth, and the promise that we will never be one of those unfortunate women who keep doing unspeakably stupid things. Susan's false identity, her role as the perfect psychiatrist, left no room for love to flow. Her flawed but authentic self drank love in with the gentleness and beauty of morning dew sipped by a grateful earth. In authentic relationship with ourselves we create the possibility of loving relationship with God and with the entirety of creation.

VOICES OF OUR ANCESTORS

Reclaiming Women's Religious Stories

S tory has the power to inspire and heal, to create archetypes of growth, and to illumine the path before us. Women who read the story of Inanna often report being deeply touched by it, dreaming about it, reflecting on it, and retelling it. Many say that it has not only given them a new understanding but also may have been a catalyst for change and transformation as it was for Susan. Through the story, they have been touched by a living Spirit.

The metaphor of story is the language of the soul. It renews us, and is renewed by us, from generation to generation. A good story is timeless and multilayered. Like a nest of Russian dolls, once opened, a new image is revealed. Every time we hear a story, after all, we are a different person, and the story resonates in another part of our being. The retellings become even richer when villains or incidental characters are given lives of their own. Did you ever wonder about the wicked queen who fed Snow White the poisoned apple? What sadness turned her own love and beauty to ashes? Is there an understanding of her life that might be healing for us?

From a neurological perspective, story touches the limbic system. This is the emotional brain, the heart of the mind. The limbic system is where we store the memory of old traumas. A part of any successful therapy is the creation of new stories, using fragments of the old, that provide an expanded frame of reference with a different emotional valence. If a dark night of the soul is reclaimed as an initiation, for example, rather than a terrifying threat to the status quo, the limbic memories take on a positive new meaning. Rather than beating ourselves up, confident that we've made a mess out of our life through some inherent stupidity, we think of our trial as a gift of Spirit, a call to a more authentic spiritual Self.

The power to guide, transform, and heal is supposed to be a characteristic of scriptural stories from all traditions. They are, in their ideal sense, stories about God inspired by God. A concrete form of grace, they can be gifts of guidance that endure through the ages. The heros and heroines of these stories are offered as templates for our lives, providing role models that we can internalize and call upon when we need help and inspiration.

Spiritual role models for women in the Old and New Testament are scarce and we are starving for them. Millions of women, particularly religious dropouts who don't buy the moral of most women's Bible stories—that we should be the subservient helpmates of men—are looking elsewhere for guidance. Clarissa Pinkola Estés's book, *Women Who Run with the Wolves*, is popular because it contains archetypal stories relevant to women's inner lives and the development of a sense of self, power, and inner authority.

Millions of women savored every detail of the life and death of Princess Di, hoping to find an archetypally redemptive story. In the beautiful but vulnerable princess, the timeless stuff of fairy tales, we hoped to find some pattern that would help us make sense of our own lives. Perhaps we were so fascinated by Princess Di because of the failure of the Judeo-Christian religious tradition to provide inspiration for women. Who are the spiritual role models we might relate to? Do we want to be like Eve, the prototype of an easily duped woman who can't follow God's directions and is responsible for bringing pain and death to the entire human race? What about Jezebel, the betrayer? Even her name has become a synonym for a treacherous woman.

When I renewed my interest in Judaism I began reading about the Sabbath. One of the traditional Sabbath blessings for the girls of the household is that they might grow up to be like Leah, Rachel, and Rebekah. Leah and Rachel were both married to Jacob. Shrill, scheming, and backbiting, their major interest was in who could bear more sons. If there was some redemptive aspect to their characters, the biblical storytellers left it out. Why would being like them be any kind of blessing? Unless, of course, the desire to mother sons at any cost was considered the highest pinnacle of women's virtue.

Even when women figure prominently in a biblical story, their point of view is generally lacking. The relational parts of the story most relevant to women aren't told. Where, for example, was Sarah when Abraham set out to sacrifice Isaac, the miracle son of her old age? How did she feel, think, and act? What did it mean to her that her husband was going to murder their son on God's orders, and how can it help us, thousands of years later? My friend Eve Ilsen, a storyteller and keeper of the Jewish wisdom heritage, believes that there was once a women's oral tradition that was never written down and that finally disappeared in the mists of time.

Some of today's women theologians are trying to re-create a women's oral tradition, exploring and reimagining biblical stories from a woman's perspective. Since women were hardly more than chattel in biblical times, we were typically minor, incidental characters in the old stories. Our inherent spirituality was neither understand nor honored.

Carol Christ and Judith Plaskow were graduate students together in religious studies at Yale in the late 1960s and early 1970s. The field of women's studies was in its infancy, and religious studies was a male-dominated field. The story of these two women's support for each another is a touching reminder of how far we have come in thirty years. "Judith encouraged Carol to write her thesis on Elie Wiesel and the Holocaust even after the man who had been Carol's advisor dismissed the subject with, 'Why would you want to write about a depressing topic like that?' Carol encouraged Judith to stick with her thesis on theology and women's experience when the director of graduate studies told Judith she had a good subject if only she would drop the references to women!"

These two friends organized an alliance at Yale for women's studies and religion and later became involved in establishing the nationwide women's Religious Caucus. Out of this rich milieu came Plaskow's much-quoted retelling of the central religious myth of Judeo-Christian theology—that of Adam and Eve.

She and three other women were attempting to create a myth, a powerful event and symbol, of women's religious experience with the power to neutralize and redeem patriarchal, degrading views about women. We are not, and never were, the confused, weak, manipulative creatures that women were generally cast as in biblical stories. Many women have dropped out of religion because they feel degraded by these stories and by their continuing effect on the oppression of women worldwide. This is precisely why Elizabeth Cady Stanton worked for twenty years to create *The Woman's Bible.*

We need a new *Woman's Bible,* more accessible than the valuable, lengthy, annotated tome that Stanton and her colleagues published. This bible would make the way that we walk Sarah's circle explicit and provide powerful archetypes for the journey. It would heal the anger of some dropouts as well as provide inspiration to returnees and liberal loyalists. Christ and Plaskow have made a start on retelling and redeeming some of the biblical stories involving women. They recognized that they could build a new myth on the old, reclaiming it through the eyes and hearts of the women involved. The story they chose to begin with was not only of Adam and Eve but of Lilith, a frightening she-demon who, according to Jewish rabbinical tradition, was Adam's first wife.

OF LILITH AND EVE:
THE FIRST STORYTELLERS

Lilith is an alluring enigma about whom there is scanty but conflicting literature. Referred to in ancient texts dating back to the Sumerian epic of Gilgamesh written in 2300 B.C.E., the Talmud, Kabbalah, Hebrew Midrash or commentary on the Torah, and the apocryphal Alphabet of Ben Sira, Lilith is a much-maligned she-demon, a wild-haired, winged nymphomaniac, seducer of men and baby killer who, in some accounts, was also Adam's first wife. In recent feminist literature inspired by Plaskow and picked up on by others, Lilith has captured the imagination of women as an archetype of the rebel. She questions outer authority—even apparently divine authority—and walks on a path of her own, exploring life through the agency of her own inner authority. A casual search for Lilith on the Internet revealed close to 3 million sites on one search engine alone, so it is obvious that she is experiencing a tremendous revival.

According to the Alphabet of Ben Sira, God created Adam and then saw that it wasn't good for him to be alone. So He took the same earth out of which He had created the first man and fashioned Lilith, the first woman. Almost immediately, the couple started to fight about sexual position as a metaphor for power.

"She said, 'I will not lie below,' and he said, 'I will not lie beneath you, but only on top. For you are fit only to be in the bottom position, while I am to be the superior one.' Lilith responded, 'We are equal to one another inasmuch as we were both created from the earth.' But Adam would not relent. When Lilith understood this, she pronounced the Ineffable Name and flew away into the air. Adam stood before his Creator: 'Sovereign of the Universe!' he said, 'the woman you gave me ran away.'"

When I tell this story in workshops and retreats, women laugh and cheer Lilith on. But things didn't go smoothly after Lilith defied Adam and flew off over the Red Sea. God dispatched three angels to make a deal. If she came back all would be forgiven. "If not, she must permit one hundred of her children to die every day." When Lilith refused to return to Adam no matter the consequences, the angels threatened to drown her, but she stood firm and made her own bargain. She said that she was created to cause sickness in infants, but when she saw the names or form of the three angels on an amulet, she would leave the infant alone. Trying to tease out the "real Lilith" from the ancient tradition of demonizing any woman who stands up for herself is not possible, but nonetheless her story captures the imagination.

So, if Lilith was Adam's first wife, how did Eve get into the picture? According to ancient texts, when Lilith decided that she would prefer any fate to having to live with Adam, God caused him to fall into a deep sleep and took one of his ribs to create Eve. Lilith and Eve were both first ladies in their own way, and each was alone. There were no luncheons, no sleepovers, not even a casual conversation in the corner deli.

The central aspect of the myth that Plaskow's group developed was sisterhood. Eve and Lilith, like all of us walking Sarah's circle of relational growth, can develop only through each other, through sharing our lives. Lilith, according to their retelling of the myth, is kept out of Eden by Adam, who builds high sloping walls to repel the demon. He frightens Eve with stories of Lilith's baby-killing exploits, although one wonders what babies are being referred to in this or the original myth of Lilith, since Adam and Eve have as yet produced no offspring.

Lilith, Plaskow imagines, comes around the walls of Eden, hoping for some company. Adam does battle with her, sending her away. For her part, Eve wonders about this woman whom she occasionally glimpses on the other side of the wall, secretly admiring her bravery. Is she a demon, or simply another woman like herself? How fascinating Lilith must have seemed, since Eve has never met another woman. Eventually, curiosity prevails. Climbing out on the limb of an apple tree, Eve swings out over the wall and drops in on Lilith for a visit. Like any two women, they tell each other their stories. They speak of the past and the future many times, until the bond of sisterhood grows strong between them. And Plaskow's myth ends, "And God and Adam were expectant and afraid of the day Eve and Lilith returned to the garden, bursting with possibilities, ready to rebuild it together."

Rabbi Lynn Gottlieb has also written and performed a new Lilith/Eve myth in which Lilith is made of the stuff of the stars. Gottlieb calls her Fiery Night Woman and speaks of her in terms of how women use power. Lilith, she maintains, "is the shadowy side of our power, the power that has not yet been tamed and put to use in the service of our greatest personal gifts, whatever they may be. Lilith is a side of feminine power with which we must reckon. When she is repressed or dominated, she becomes desperate, enraged and insane. When she is acknowledged and loved for her fire, she becomes a source for positive creation. Tracking our Lilith nature is the key to our spiritual awakening."

TAKING LILITH PERSONALLY

So what does it mean to be unconscious of our Lilith nature? A friend of mine named Sandy had a husband who couldn't tolerate her hugging or kissing another man in greeting. A warm, cuddly person, Sandy naturally gave all her friends an exuberant, heart-filled, snugly hello. It was against her nature not to do this, and I watched her struggle to honor her husband's preferences. With growing resentment, she gave in to "no man hugging" and other of her husband's idiosyncratic demands, including his idea of how to get tasks accomplished.

Sandy is one of the most efficient people you will ever meet. Like many women, she multitasks. She picks up a pile over here and folds the laundry over there, stops to scrub the toilet and then remembers to call the dog groomer, but everything gets done—and fast. This multitasking drove her husband Max mad. Mad Max was the sort of person who eats all his peas before going on to eat all the chicken, wrapping up his meal with the mashed potatoes. Sandy's "a bite of this, a bite of that" way of working was apparently more than he could stand. So Sandy, who continued her multitasking ways, always kept an eye out for Max. When he came around, she'd instantly convert to an "eat all the peas together" approach to whatever she was doing. Otherwise he would give her pointed instructions on how to do the job better. After a few years of this, Sandy began a series of wild affairs. She was tired of being repressed, but, instead of dealing with it consciously, her Lilith nature stepped out of the shadow and exerted power in a way guaranteed to be most hurtful to Max.

If we are conscious of Lilith we take the bull by the horns, or by an even lower and more sensitive part of his anatomy. Instead of having a series of affairs, Sandy might have consciously called upon the power of Fiery Night Woman and, like Lilith, told her mate, "We are equals. You have your way of doing things and I have mine. I'll respect yours, and I expect you to respect mine, or I'm out of here." With that, either she and Max might have reached a new understanding and a better balance of the male and female within themselves and between each other, or she could have flown off like Lilith across the Red Sea—a symbol of freedom from bondage—and made a new life in a way that was much less hurtful to Max and herself.

Archetypally, Eve and Lilith are the two sides of the growing feminine personality. The Eve archetype is creative and filled with possibility yet subliminally bothered by the sense that there is more to life than she sees. Eventually she summons the courage to explore creative possibilities outside her normal experience. Lilith, the archetype of independence and courage, is always reaching across the veil that hangs between our conscious mind and unconscious longings, beckoning us out of the box in which we live. When these two interior women come together, unprecedented creativity is the result, but it is likely to shake up the status quo and pose a threat to existing structures.

How well I remember Sheila, a women in her thirties who was a client of mine for several years. She worked as a secretary in her father's business, raised four children, and maintained a home that was a center for every family activity and the site of protracted visits from great hordes of freeloading relatives. No matter what her own needs or desires might be, she was expected to be the unstinting lifegiver to all, and as a result was suffering from severe anxiety and chronic stomach problems.

In the three years that we worked together Sheila became much more aware of her own needs for a life in which there was room for herself, and for a career in graphic design. But as she tried to exit the old garden and create a new one, her father and husband—

like the archetypes of God and Adam—got progressively more upset. They blamed me, the Lilith in her life, for upsetting the apple cart. But her interior Lilith was already active. I was simply an outer manifestation of the energies she had already connected with.

Sheila's story has a happier ending than that of Sandy and Mad Max. Because Sheila was conscious of the Lilith energy in herself, she didn't invest it in me and give away her power or deny it and act out. She was able to relate to her husband and father in a respectful but firm way that eventually allowed her to expand the walls of the garden and to redesign its interior spaces, without having to fly the coop. She is now a graphic designer who still entertains a lot but on terms that balance her own needs and those of her husband and children with the throng of entitled relatives and her demanding father.

I, too, like to reimagine the story of Eve and Lilith. In my version Adam initially succeeds in keeping Lilith and Eve apart. But Lilith is a shape-shifter. When she can't fly over the high walls of Eden, she crawls under them. When Eve meets Lilith in the form of a serpent—long a symbol of rejuvenation and rebirth since it sheds its skin—she accepts the fruit of new life even though God has told her not to eat of the tree of knowledge of good and evil. Empowered by Lilith to expand her understanding and find her own inner authority, she shares the knowledge with Adam, whose eyes are also opened to new possibilities. It is my hope that when Sheila's inner Lilith met her Eve, the males in her own family also learned something of importance that opened their eyes to a new understanding.

THE PRIMORDIAL BATTLE OF THE SEXES

If the Old Testament deity had been a Goddess, we can bet that the scriptural stories about women would have taken a very dif-

ferent tack. In order to reimagine biblical stories and understand hidden symbolism like that of the snake, we need to review a few facts about the civilization out of which the Old Testament grew, and what the culture's previous creation stories
were about.

The Mesopotamian creation story, the Enûma Elish, tells about
the destruction of Tiamat, the dragon-mother of creation. This ancient Goddess was the personification of the formless deep, the
void out of which creation came. Her womb, and the menstrual
blood that flowed from it, was considered the primordial stuff of
creation. Tiamat's upstart son, Marduk, killed his mother and then
claimed to have split her carcass into the upper and lower waters,
separating the earth from the firmament as God did in Genesis. According to one of the world's best mythologists of women's wisdom, Barbara Walker, the original division had previously been
made by the Goddess Herself. Her son was a malicious usurper,
jealous of the fact that his brother was chosen as Tiamat's consort
and king of the universe.

Marduk came to be worshipped as the Creator by the Babylonians and is a likely model for the Creator God in Genesis, which
is a thinly veiled retelling of the Marduk myth leaving out the juicy
parts about matricide and usurpation. In Genesis, matter is created
from the emptiness and void, in Hebrew *tohu v' bohu*. *Tohu* is related to the Hebrew word *tehom*, which comes from the same root
as Tiamat, the formless feminine darkness of the dragon-mother.

In both Old and New Testament, God perpetually struggles with
the forces of evil identified with the feminine powers of Tiamat,
Rahab, and the Leviathan, which are all names for the dragon of
chaos and creation in Mesopotamian and Babylonian mythology.
The male God, Elohim, is locked in perpetual combat with the ancient Goddess, a reflection of the patriarchal culture of ancient
times and its attendant fear of the power of women. The ancient

question about who created the universe, God or Goddess, is the most primal form of the battle between the sexes.

The snake and the dragon are interchangeable characters representing the feminine. If you had just stolen the universe, it is a good bet that you would be terrified that the rightful regent, or some force allied with the deposed regime, might come back and try to recapture the loyalty of the subjects. Probably the best way to undermine such a possibility would be slander. Why pay attention to the feminine? Women are what caused all the trouble in the world to begin with. And if women are dangerous witches, beware, too, of their animal familiar, the snake.

The snake is Eve's ally in the garden representing the feminine force of creation and renewal. While the serpent is perhaps the oldest symbol of feminine rejuvenation, shedding its skin periodically just as we shed the lining of our uterus, the noble serpent got demoted to the role of the devil. It has become a symbol of evil and revulsion. The reason for this serpentine slander had everything to do with the change of the guard from the ancient Middle Eastern Goddess cultures to belief in a male deity. And if the snake came to symbolize the devil, then woman came to symbolize the devil's handmaiden. Our only hope for salvation was to subjugate our unruly natures by following the directives of men.

The ancient historian Philo Judaeus summarized the woman-hating worldview of biblical times in this commentary on the Essenes, an ascetic sect of Jews responsible for writing the Dead Sea Scrolls: "No Essene takes a wife, because a wife is a selfish creature, excessively jealous and an adept in beguiling the morals of her husband and seducing him by her continued impostures. For by the fawning talk which she practices and the other ways in which she plays her part like an actress on the stage, she first ensnares the sight and hearing and then, when these victims have, as it were, been duped, she cajoles the sovereign mind."

TAKING EVE AND THE SNAKE PERSONALLY

I often dream of snakes in times of transformation, taking such dreams as signs that the feminine force of creation is calling me to deconstruct some aspect of my life and to enter the fertile darkness so that something new can blossom.

Carl Jung wrote of synchronicity, the appearance of inner archetypes in the outer world, as a manifestation of Spirit and guidance. He was referring to situations in which you are thinking about something internally, and a concrete manifestation of your thoughts appears externally. For example, you want to join a new church but don't know where to go. The mailman comes, and to your surprise there is a brochure from a church you have never heard of that speaks directly to your soul. Obsessed with whether you should give up your job and take another working for world peace, doves appear everywhere. They fly by. They roost in your bushes and sing their mournful songs. They peek out of advertisements, their soulful eyes seeming to follow you.

Jan Maier, the music weaver at most of our *Gathering of Women* retreats, had a stunning experience of synchronicity with a snake during a retreat where I had told the story of Eve and Lilith. It occurred on a highly symbolic day, although neither of us appreciated the full significance of the timing, or indeed the power of the synchronicity, until a few days later. Not only was it the Sabbath of a full moon, it was also the fall equinox. This most auspicious day fell during the Days of Awe between Rosh Hashanah, the Jewish New Year, and Yom Kippur, the Day of Atonement. This ten-day period is a time of deep introspection and reflection, undertaken so that one can heal personally and be a part of *tikkun olam*, the healing of the world.

On the day of our snake walk the hours of daylight and darkness were exactly equal. Grandmother Earth was about to draw down her energy for winter. The solstices, the longest and shortest days of the year, and the equinoxes, those times during spring and fall when the hours of light and dark are balanced, have been sacred to most Goddess-centered, earth-centered, and indigenous cultures, who view them as gateways between the worlds where the human and divine can most easily touch. Dreams and reality interpenetrate on these sacred days, myths work their magic, and the snake can most easily enter our innermost garden.

Jan and I were both going through changes in our lives that required us to step more firmly into our inner authority. This burning need to re-create ourselves was the subject of conversation. Ready to leave a career in nursing to devote herself to creating community through music, Jan had to overcome a major roadblock. Although she could sing like an angel, was gifted in getting others to sing, and was producing a fabulous CD called *Mountain Skyes*, Jan suffered from performance anxiety. She had to overcome fear, find her voice in order to use it. At the moment of our walk she felt stuck, ready to break loose, but still held back. I was also caged by fear. Although I loved my work, the women's retreats in particular, I was burning out. Women were saying things to me like, "I looked at your schedule. How do you keep doing this? Aren't you exhausted? I'm praying for you."

I used to shake off those kinds of comments. "Tired, me? Heck no, I'm superwoman. I love this." But I told Jan that I was starting to sound like a broken record. I didn't believe myself anymore, and had taken to hiding my pain. I needed to find the courage to cut back my entire travel schedule and the number of our women's retreats as well. It was hard to say this. The retreats were precious to Jan, to Beth Lawrence, and to me. We had become a mobile spiritual community. But I was tired physically, tired of missing my friends at home, tired of trying to create intimacy with my husband Kurt on a cell phone from convents somewhere in Minnesota, Pennsylvania, California, Texas, Boston, New York, Nebraska, and points between. I feared that in cutting down my schedule I would drop out of sight on the speaking circuit and end up financially strapped. I also feared that in cutting down the retreats I might cut myself off from the only spiritual community I had at the time.

Deep in conversation about our fears and hopes, Jan and I meandered down an Appalachian country road, refreshed by that wondrous combination of warm sun and cool breeze. The boughs of apple trees, heavy with ripe fruit, swayed above us. We found a long stick and stopped to knock some of the sweet apples off a high branch, savoring their tartness as we continued down the road on our first intimate walk together. While we'd known each other for a long time, it was in a professional capacity. This was the first time we'd experienced personal intimacy with each other, woman to woman.

Not far from the apple tree, we were puzzled to find a snake laying motionless, in a strange, nearly jagged configuration in the middle of the dusty road. It looked like a lightning bolt. The poor snake seemed dead and wouldn't move even when touched with a stick, yet its unusual lightninglike contour had us glued to the spot. We waited and watched, then finally began to walk away. Drawn to the serpent, we kept pausing to look back. To our amazement, sister snake slowly revived and slithered off into the brush. Neither Jan nor I immediately recognized the mythic symbolism of the snake beneath the apple tree.

During the retreat, Jan had been especially moved by the story of Eve and Lilith, of how Eve had been changed radically by eating the apple of freedom. A few days after the retreat, Jan awakened slowly in the middle of the night and lay very still in bed. She recognized that she was in an altered state of consciousness, one of intense creativity and clarity. A series of sudden and penetrating images and insights came together like pieces of a puzzle.

On the walk we had to work hard to get the apples, reaching for them with a stick. This got our attention. The snake further riveted us. Rather than simply passing by, it lay in wait in a posture so bizarre as to be unforgettable. Finally, the walk occurred at an especially propitious time of year for change. A full-moon Sabbath, an equinox during the Days of Awe, this is the stuff of myths and transformation.

Jan was particularly struck with the symbolism of the snake. Although her childhood religious upbringing considered it evil, she realized that it had helped Eve jump to an expanded level of consciousness, rather than some kind of fall. When Eve ate the apple she was suddenly and irrevocably changed. Her eyes were opened. She reached a new level of self-knowledge and world awareness, which required great courage.

Jan continued to lie still, afraid to break the spell, fascinated by what her intuition was telling her. In the altered state, the apple continued to reveal its transformative powers. She had a strong physical sensation of an energy change within her body, as if something were leaving her from head to toe. By relaxing and trying to be exquisitely receptive to the meaning of this unusual experience, she was able to name the energy that left her. It was fear. She had no idea what kind of fear but felt sure that she was at a major turning point, touched by a moment of grace.

"Synchronicity or coincidence, these snakes and apples, the story of Eve and Lilith and the disappearance of fear?" Jan wondered. When it comes to miracles, Jan is a fairly skeptical person. But she realized that however she interpreted this event, it was extraordinary. Explanations and beliefs didn't matter. Something wonderfully significant had happened, and that was enough.

Jan discovered the meaning of the miracle shortly thereafter. Her stage fright simply disappeared. She is certain that this fear and self-consciousness about singing were what had drained out of her toes in the moment of revelation. Touched by Lilith, the spirit of the snake, and at long last free of severe self-doubt, she could begin her metamorphosis, bringing healing and community into the world through song. She now does exactly that, giving sermons and performances at churches, facilitating retreats, leading workshops across the country, and teaching people how joining our voices in song can be a way to bring about relational connection. Jan was so intrigued with the snake we had seen, lying in that peculiar, jagged form like a lightning bolt, that she consulted an expert in herpetology. She found out that snakes do sometimes suspend animation in that singularly odd posture, and that it is exceedingly rare.

I also experienced a miracle after our walk. It was far less immediate and stunning than Jan's, but powerful nonetheless. I cut back my schedule, something I had been threatening to do unsuccessfully for years. With time to go to India, my faith was renewed in our pilgrimage. With time to create intimacy with my husband, our love was renewed. With time for friends, I began to feel alive again.

The experiences of women like Jan demonstrate that the power of story is more than metaphoric. Archetypal stories, like that of Eve, Lilith, and Inanna, are like phone lines that connect us to the living Presence of ancient beings who can help us on the spiritual journey. When we are ready for change, stories can also pull the bushel off our Inner Light. Our intuition becomes clear and insistent. When we allow ourselves to be receptive, the voice of God and the help that is always available become potent realities.

MARY MAGDALENE:
THE MOST BELOVED DISCIPLE

There are two kinds of ancient story. The first type is mythical and archetypal, like those of Inanna, Eve, and Lilith. The second type is more homely and down-to-earth. They are stories of real women who once lived in the flesh. We can enter their world meaningfully to the extent that historical background makes them, and the circumstances of their lives, accessible to us. We can imagine the heroines as if they were contemporary women like us. We can inhabit their lives. If the heroine of such a story continues to live on in us, whispering guidance that helps us to walk our path, then we call her a role model. Mary Magdalene is such a role model for me.

During a yearlong course in the New Testament that I took in my late twenties, the importance of Mary's story evaded both my own radar and that of the instructor. I put the Magdalen, as she is often called, aside in a ho-hum sort of way. She was just a repentant whore, exorcised of her demons, who developed a devotion to Jesus, her healer. A very different Mary is going to emerge here. The Mary who comes alive by considering an amalgam of sources, both biblical and historical, is a powerful priestess. Her relationship to Jesus is a two-way street. She is his healer as much as he is hers, and they are the loves of one another's lives.

Mary was the person closest to Jesus. She was the one who comforted him and understood the conflicts that arose during the years of his teaching. She was skilled at the art of listening, the Art of Lovemaking that we learned about from Inanna's story. Jesus the godman was no different from the goddess Erishkegal. He needed to be mirrored in order to be whole. He could enter himself fully, his humanity as well as his divinity, only when another human being came into deep and holy relationship with him.

I have always thought of Jesus as a perfect balance of male and female aspects. He was assertive and direct, rational and straight-forward. Yet he was a master of subtlety and metaphor. He taught by example as well as by allegory. Let she who has the ears to hear, hear. When I was in grammar school my favorite television program was *Mr. Wizard*, the science teacher. He took a beaker of plain white sugar and poured a clear liquid into it, sulfuric acid. There was an immediate and impressive chemical reaction. The sugar and the liquid began to boil and steam and then to grow out of the flask like a giant cupcake. After a few moments, the two chemicals had combined to form something startling and new, a tall spire of jet black carbon. I think that Mary and Jesus were like that. They combined in a way that created something utterly unique and wonderful, something that neither could have been alone. Their story, as I imagine it, exemplifies growth through self-in-relation.

The New Testament is not the only source for Mary Magdalene's story. In the town of Nag Hammadi in upper Egypt, a clay urn was accidentally unearthed in 1945. It was on a site that had once housed a Coptic monastery. In it were ancient papyrus texts, estimated to be at least eighteen hundred years old, written about the same time as the Gospels that were included in the New Testament. The early Church was responsible for sifting through all the writings about Jesus and then choosing which ones to compile into Scripture. The rest were destroyed. Apparently the Coptic monks, realizing the value of these other Gospels, buried them to ensure their safety. They are now, by definition, apocryphal texts, meaning simply that they wound up on the cutting-room floor.

In the Gospel of Philip, one of the texts included in the fifty-two tractates from the Nag Hammadi Library, it is written: "And the companion of the (Savior is) Mary Magdalene. (Christ) loved her more than (all) the disciples (and used to) kiss her (often) on her (mouth). They said to him, 'Why do you love her more than all of us?' The Savior answered and said to them, 'Why do I not love you like her? When a blind man and one who sees are both together in darkness, they are no different from one another. When the light comes, then he who sees will see the light, and he who is blind will remain in darkness."

Another of the tractates from these lost Gospels is entitled the Gospel of Mary. In it Jesus' favorite disciple speaks for herself, revealing some of the tension that existed between her and some of the male disciples. The cultural distrust and devaluation of women in general, coupled with Mary's favored position with Jesus, are probably part of the reason why the early Church tried to destroy these documents.

The Gospel of Mary begins with a discussion that the disciples have with the risen Savior in which he explains the nature of sin. He also gives them a good mental-health tip before sending them out on their mission to spread his message of love. When feeling discouraged, he suggests that they find encouragement in the different forms of nature. The male disciples collapse into fear and rumination the moment that Jesus leaves. They begin to weep. If the Gentiles killed Jesus, what's to stop them from meeting the same end?

Mary steps forward in the role of comforter and guide, turning their hearts to the "Good." She tells them, "Do not weep and do not grieve nor be irresolute, for his grace will be entirely with you and protect you." Peter then tells Mary that "we know the Savior loved you more than the rest of women. Tell us the words of the Savior which you remember—which you know, (but) we do not, nor have we heard them."

She agrees to reveal what Jesus has told her in a vision. The first question Mary asked Jesus is how one sees a vision, whether through the soul or through the spirit. He responded that the vision comes through neither, but through the mind, which is between the two. Unfortunately, the pages containing most of the rest of the vision are lost, but the little that remains concerns the soul's journey through the four "powers" that try to block its way after death. When the soul gets to the fourth power, which is a composite of seven forms including desire and ignorance, that power asks where it is going. "The soul answered and said, 'What binds me has been slain, and what surrounds me has been overcome, and my desire has been ended and ignorance has died.'"

The quality of Jesus' conversation with Mary is indicative of the respect in which he holds her intellect. When she finishes sharing the vision with the other disciples, Andrew responds like an angry child, with a what-makes-you-so-special attitude. He says that he doesn't believe her. Peter, his nose also out of joint, loses his former conciliatory attitude and sides with Andrew. "Did he really speak with a woman without our knowledge and not openly? Are we to turn around and all listen to her? Did he prefer her to us?"

Mary breaks down in tears at the thought that Andrew and Peter have accused her of making up the whole vision. Levi settles the matter by telling Peter to calm down, that he's always been a hothead, and now he's attacking Mary like she's one of their enemies. He continues, "But if the Savior made her worthy, who are you to reject her? Surely the Savior knows her very well. That's why he loved her more than us."

The Magdalen's story is set in a cross-tide of religious change. The wave of the Goddess era had crested and was going out. The wave of the jealous male Creator God was coming in. Goddess temples had not yet been stamped out in the first century C.E., but were anathema both to the Jews and the Christians who followed, since unification under a Creator God necessitated the continuous repression of Goddess worship, which proved to be tenacious and difficult to uproot. Active temples to the goddess Asherah still existed within the Holy Land at the time of Jesus, and when they finally shut down, the Goddess was still not vanquished. People loved her too much. She just shape-shifted into the Virgin Mary.

Mary Magdalene is usually spoken of as a prostitute although there is no specific biblical reference to this. If she was, it is crucial to realize that the role of a prostitute was entirely different in biblical times than it is today. In the days of the temples to the Goddess, not only the high priestess but every woman from every social strata apparently took a turn as a temple prostitute before she was married. Women who had served for any amount of time in that role were in great demand as brides. The Roman emperor Justinian's wife, Theodora, for example, was a revered temple prostitute before their marriage.

During sacred sex, the temple prostitute was believed to become the Goddess herself. Her male partner represented the god Tammuz, another name for Inanna's Dumuzi. The God and Goddess resident within the priestess and her consort enacted the Hieros Gamos, Greek for "Sacred Marriage." The sexual union of God and Goddess ensured the fertility of the land. It also brought inner balance, blessing, and an intense spiritual connection to the Divine to both partners.

Some sources make the theoretical suggestion that the Magdalen may have been a high priestess in the temple of Asherah in the town of Magdala a few miles from Nazareth. Rather than just taking a turn in the temple, the high priestess would most likely have had a lifelong vocation. These resident sacred prostitutes were well-educated women, meticulously trained both as priestesses and healers. They enjoyed extremely high social status and were revered for the compassion they dispensed in behalf of the Great Mother. Many were noted prophetesses as well. The Hebrew word *zonah*, in fact, means both "prophetess" and "prostitute."

Mary Magdalene was probably the same Mary of the New Testament parable of the alabaster jar. One night Jesus was having dinner with a Pharisee named Simon, and a woman from the town who "lived a sinful life" came to the house. She fell at Jesus' feet and washed them with her tears, drying them with her luxuriant hair. Kissing his feet, she anointed them with costly perfumed ointment from an alabaster jar.

This was an unusual act, performed with forethought by a woman who obviously had the means to buy the costly ointment referred to as nard, or spikenard. This ritual was common in the days of the Goddess temples, an anointing of the King, or Bridegroom, in preparation for the Hieros Gamos. In the Song of Songs, the Scripture that celebrates the Sacred Marriage, spikenard is also mentioned. Simon the Pharisee snickered at the anointing, allowing that if Jesus were any kind of seer he would have known what kind of sinner was defiling him with her touch.

The Magdalen was also the woman out of whom Jesus cast seven devils, reminiscent of the seven gates through which the goddess Inanna had to pass on her way to the Underworld and ultimate redemption. The relationship of Jesus to Mary extends the lesson of Inanna on the Art of Lovemaking that we discussed in the last chapter. At times when the disciples were afraid, unable to listen to Jesus' fears, she was there with the kind of deep love that can receive and hold pain. As the *galatur* and the *kurgarra* did for Erishkegal, the Magdalen mirrored Jesus' experience and formed a crucible in which his soul was held.

After the Passover meal, just before the vigil in the garden of Gethsemane where Jesus spent a sleepless night coming to terms with the fact that it was his destiny to be betrayed and crucified, he spoke to Peter about how he would die and the flock would be scattered. Peter swore that he would never forsake him. But Jesus knew better. He predicted, "I tell you that before the cock crows tonight, you will say three times that you do not know me." Peter insisted that he would die before denying Jesus, and all the male disciples agreed with him, but by the end of the night—fearing for their lives—they all turned their backs on him and hid.

Just before the fateful hour of betrayal, Jesus took three of the disciples to Gethsemane and asked them to keep watch with him while he prayed, for "the sorrow in my heart is so great that it almost crushes me. Stay here and keep watch with me."

Jesus wept and begged God to take the cup of suffering from him if possible, but ended his prayer with submission. Walking over to the three frightened disciples who were supposed to be keeping vigil, he found them asleep, unable to form a loving container for his sorrow for even a single hour. He retreated to the garden to pray again, and once more the frightened disciples fell asleep. Jesus aroused them with the announcement that the hour of his betrayal had come, as Judas strode into Gethsemane and greeted him with the fateful kiss of death.

Jesus loved Mary, at least in part, because she knew how to hold the torch of constant relational love. She could receive him fully, witness the fear and doubt that made him human. At the crucifixion, when the disciples fled for their lives, Mary waited at the foot of the cross. At the tomb she kept vigil, waiting until the Sabbath was over so that she could anoint Jesus' body, which had been claimed by Joseph of Arimathea, wrapped in a shroud and laid in a tomb until the Sabbath day was over and the women could anoint it properly, according to Jewish custom.

Very early on Sunday morning the Magdalen, along with another Mary, and according to one of the Gospels, Salome and Joanna as well, brought herbs to prepare the body, concerned about how they would roll the heavy stone away from the tomb. But an angel had already done it. It announced that Jesus was no longer within. He had risen. In a slightly different account of the resurrection told in the Gospel of Matthew, Jesus appeared to Mary Magdalene and Mary the mother of James, who fell in the dust to touch his feet.

He blessed them with peace and told them to bring word to the disciples that they would see him in Galilee. In the Gospels of both Mark and John, Jesus appeared to Mary Magdalene alone, who then spread the word that he had risen.

The love that Mary Magdalene and the other women had for Jesus did not have to be developed through listening to spiritual teachings or through the repetition of specific practices. It was innate and relational. They were there for him during his life. He valued them, often visiting his women disciples in New Testament accounts. Even after his return from death, they were the ones he visited first. In a rabidly misogynist society, his respect and care for women was a powerful teaching. Unfortunately, it went unlearned.

The story of Mary Magdalene told up to this point came from the New Testament, from the Gospel of Philip and the Gospel of Mary in the Nag Hammadi Library, and from a historical look at the Goddess religion in Jesus' time. Now we can fill in the blanks from a woman's point of view, creating a redeemed mythology of the Magdalen from research into an ancient heresy embellished by my fertile and willing imagination.

JESUS AND MARY MAGDALENE: A HERETICAL LOVE STORY

An ancient heresy, which even the Albigensian Crusades could not wipe out, holds that Jesus and Mary Magdalene were married. Although unproved, the theory has left its footprints in the places where the Catholic Church could not wipe it out: European folk tales, art, and literature.

Margaret Starbird, a Catholic theologian with an academic

background in medieval studies, linguistics, and Scripture first set out to disprove the heresy and later became one of its most vocal proponents. In the preface to her book *The Woman with the Alabaster Jar*, Starbird writes, "For years I had a vague feeling that something was radically wrong with my world, that for too long the feminine in our culture had been scorned and devalued. But it was not until 1985 that I encountered documented evidence of a devastating fracture of the Christian story."

That evidence was presented in the shocking and highly controversial international best-seller, *Holy Blood, Holy Grail*, by Michael Baigent, Richard Leigh, and Henry Lincoln. The central tenet of *Holy Blood, Holy Grail* is that the Holy Grail was actually the womb of Mary Magdalene which held Jesus' blood and, through their daughter, Sarah, gave rise to the royal Merovingian bloodline, which came to run in the veins of French nobility. The Merovingian dynasty, most active between 476–750 C.E., were great supporters of the Divine Feminine and of the Virgin Mary, who the Catholic Church declared Theotokos, or the Mother of God, in 431 C.E. in Ephesus, once the home of the greatest temple to the goddess Artemis.

During the time of the Merovingian dynasty, an enormous proliferation of statues and paintings of Black Madonnas—which may have represented either Mary Magdalene or her daughter Sarah—appeared throughout Europe. By medieval times, the cult of the Black Virgin was firmly entrenched along with tales of King Arthur's court and the troubadours. With the advent of the Albigensian Crusades, the heretical Christians were wiped out, men and women alike. The blood lust continued in the form of witch burnings that spanned the next five hundred years. The wisdom of women, from dream interpretation to midwifery, was forced underground upon penalty of death.

It is unlikely that the true relationship between Jesus and Mary Magdalene will ever be known, unless more ancient texts are unearthed. Until that time, we can only indulge in speculation. But even speculation can lead to new insights, psychologically and spiritually. Margaret Starbird amassed a great deal of circumstantial evidence and biblical references that led her to conclude that the marriage of Jesus and Mary Magdalene was a reality, and that it must have been kept secret.

Mary Magdalene was the sister of Martha and Lazarus, who were Benjamites. The tribe of Benjamin was powerful, with land rights to the entire environs of Jerusalem. A dynastic marriage between Mary and Jesus—from the equally powerful lineage of King David, from whom the Messiah was expected to arise—would have been a source of great hope and excitement for the oppressed Jewish people. The Zealots, in particular, may have taken enough hope from such a union to start an uprising against Roman occupation. If there had been such a marriage, and a child from that marriage by the name of Sarah, they would surely have been hunted down and killed after Jesus' crucifixion unless their secret remained closely guarded.

Just as women have rewritten the myths of Eve and Lilith, creating part of a new Scripture for women, I have rewritten the life story of Mary Magdalene, drawing on all the sources we have shared: the canonical and apocryphal Gospels, the cultural milieu of the times, and the research of Starbird, Baigent and his colleagues, as well as many others. My story honors both Jesus' love for and understanding of women and the role of Mary as full partner in his divine ministry. Here is how I see the role of the feminine in Christianity, brought to light through Mary's life.

JESUS AND MARY:
PARTNERS IN THE HIEROS GAMOS

Yehoshuah, a young Jewish boy who would eventually be called Jesus by the Greeks, was very sensitive. Prone to ecstatic dreams and flights of mystical communion, he was wise beyond his years. His trances and powers frightened the simple people of his village. Schooled neither in rabbinic theology nor *halacha*, the Jewish laws of moral and ethical conduct, he knew more than the scholars who debated fine points in the synagogue. His Hebrew was flawless, even though Aramaic and Arabic were the only languages he had ever learned.

Aramaic was the common tongue of Judaea, where Yehoshuah was born and spent all his life, save for the years when his parents took him to Alexandria to escape a murderous edict of the Roman emperor Herod, whereby all the male Jewish children under the age of two were to be killed. Yehoshuah's mother, Miriam, liked to tell the story of how her twelve-year-old son disappeared into a crowd and was found preaching in the temple, astonishing the learned men with his wisdom. He was a strange child, prone to sitting by himself and singing ancient holy verses in a voice more melodious than the soughing of the desert winds through the boughs of the cedar trees. Verses from the Song of Songs often flowed from his sweet lips. He would close his black eyes, the silky lashes long against his dusky cheeks. With the delicacy of a reed pipe, his voice floated through the village, "Set me as a seal upon your heart, as a seal upon your arm; for love is strong as death . . . many waters cannot quench love, neither can floods drown it."

The village children loved him, and gathered while he sang. Sometimes the girls would accompany him with tambourines or frame drums, dancing. He spoke to them of love. How the birds of the air find their mates, and from their love bear young, feeding them with joy. He spoke to them of respect for life, for God is in everything and everyone. And he spoke of the pure heartedness of women, how their heart wisdom enriches the mind knowledge of men. At the end of their "play" times he waved a hand in the air, and honey cakes would appear. Yehoshuah insisted that some of the cakes be offered back to Mother Earth for her small creatures to enjoy. And these littlest creatures loved him, too. The centipedes and scorpions, snakes and beetles, mice and rabbits would rise up and salute as he walked past. But in spite of all these things, Yehoshuah was lonely.

There were few with whom he could share the visions of Divine Light that graced him with the wisdom of compassion and forgiveness. And his heart was heavy with the suffering he saw all around him: poverty, illness, war, oppression, the thoughtless ways that people judged one another, holding them out of their hearts. The plight of women seemed especially heavy, for although they were the givers of life, they were treated like possessions. Their wisdom was heeded only in the healing arts, for they had the knowledge of herbs and understood the pull of the moon and the changing medicine of the seasons.

When Yehoshuah became a man at the age of thirteen, he left the tiny village where his home was. "My disciples are awaiting me," he told his anxious family. "I will preach the wisdom of Baruch Ha Shem, the Blessed Holy Name, to the people, in words they can understand. I will teach the truth of the Holy Torah, that through compassion and forgiveness the world is made whole. That through love alone can Baruch Ha Shem be reunited with His Shekhina, His exiled Bride, and the fragments of Holy Light regathered into unity."

Yehoshuah had heard of a mystical band of Jews living in the area of the Dead Sea, a barren landscape of sun-bleached cliffs riddled with caves. He sought them out for their wisdom, in preparation for his mission. Through austerities these Essenes sought God, eating only locusts and wild honey, lost in the sweetness of prayer, song, and meditation. But the community was one of men alone, and Yehoshuah knew that without the proper joining of men and women, the rift in the fabric of the Godhead could not be repaired.

After four years, he left the gentle enclave of the Essenes, enriched by their love and knowledge of the healing arts. From his quiet cave by the sea of salt, he set out on the back of a surefooted donkey to find the Mount of Olives. He had heard of a temple to the goddess Asherah there. It was nigh unto sunset several days later as he ascended the Temple Mount, surprisingly lush with olive trees and cypress. The fragrance of sage and jasmine and the medicine power of herbs reached out for him like the gentle arms of a mother. The alabaster dome of the temple reflected the pink and violet rays of the setting sun, a rainbow of light shimmering in the stark landscape of the arid Judaean hills.

Waiting for him at the end of an intricate mosaic footpath that led to the arched wooden gates of the entrance was an old woman, her beautiful face delicately lined. A fine, white woolen robe was drawn close about her thin shoulders, tied with a green sash woven from flax and dyed with sacred herbs. Her sandals were golden, and a great wealth of white hair hung down to her knees, surrounding her like a halo. The fragrance that arose from the woman was astonishing, the Breath of Life itself, Yehoshuah thought. Her name was Esther, a Hebrew derivation of Asherah, and she was the high priestess of the temple. Esther placed her hands together over her heart and greeted Jesus with the traditional salutation "Peace be with you."

"May peace be also with you," he intoned, the ancient response of the desert peoples, both Arab and Jew.

"We have been waiting for you," Esther smiled, "for seven times seven generations, ever since the worship of Asherah fell into disrespect among our people. Since then the wars have increased and men have turned against men. The voices of women keening over the dead bodies of husbands and sons ride the winds. Their tears water the desert and thorn bushes spring up, a fetid growth that poisons the children and hardens their hearts. It is time, once again, for the spring of renewal, for the song of the turtledove to be heard in the land. It is time for the feminine in the hearts of men to awaken, and for the love between men and women to reawaken God."

Yehoshuah felt a chill run through him and raise the hairs at the nape of his neck. He had experienced this scene before in dreams and visions, as he knew that Esther had. Just as he had in those reveries, he smiled at Esther and held out a barren olive branch that he had picked up on the path. The branch sprang suddenly into bloom as her hand touched it. Silence, thick and ancient, full and formless, came over them. Time seemed to stop as the world shimmied slightly on its axis. Esther's power flowed into him, opening Yehoshuah to an inner world of wonder in which he directly experienced the interrelationship of all things—from the electrons of an atom to the stars of the solar systems, to the power of love that shapes light into matter.

Yehoshuah was welcomed home to the temple, where his coming had been eagerly awaited and foretold in ancient prophecies. Days were spent in the simple prayers of ordinary life—plowing, sowing, reaping, shepherding the animals. Dusk brought mystery and initiation into ancient rites and rituals, instruction in the sacred arts of healing, which went beyond even the skilled teachings of the Essenes, and the balance between men and women. For thirteen years Jesus dwelled as the only male acolyte in the temple of Asherah.

When Yehoshuah was thirty, the hundred-ten-year-old priestess Esther took her final journey to the Spirit World. Her successor had been picked out twenty years before, when a young mother had dreamed that the beloved daughter she was about to birth was meant to be dedicated to the Goddess. The mother and her husband, both worshippers of Asherah, carried their tiny daughter, Miriam, from the remote village of Magdala, which means "watchtower" in Hebrew. "She is to be a guardian of life, a tower of strength, the Bride of the most sacred Bridegroom," they explained.

Esther had seen the coming of the child in a vision, in the sacred pool of the temple. And so little Miriam grew up wise and loving in the service of Asherah. Miriam was a small-boned, dark-skinned girl with delicate features and hair as black as night. The luminous green eyes that peered out from beneath her long, luxuriant lashes danced with warmth and understanding. Growing up in the temple, she had loved Yehoshuah as a brother. For years he had indulged her and the other little girls in games of hide-and-seek in the olive grove. But as she grew into womanhood, another kind of love blossomed.

Miriam would dream of being in Yehoshuah's arms, and in her dreams they would kiss and then talk long into the night, wrapped in the arms of a greater Mystery. Oddly, in these reveries she was the comforter, the source of wisdom and solace even though he was ten years her senior. When she saw Yehoshuah during the day, she had developed the habit of casting her eyes to the ground and rushing past, intent on hiding the telltale blush that crept into her cheeks at the sight of him.

Only in the months before Esther's death, as Miriam received the final initiations testing her readiness for the role of high priestess, did she realize that she and Yehoshuah were to enact the role of God and Goddess together in the rite of the Sacred Marriage. They were destined partners, soul mates in a cosmic drama. Her last months with Esther were remarkable, as the old woman passed on her wisdom in a series of rituals that often lasted for the entire night.

During these months Miriam matured visibly. Her step became sure and steady, her voice filled with both gentleness and the authority born of true wisdom. Even her face changed. The vestiges of girlhood left behind, her beauty matured into that most rare of types—the kind of features that not only empathetically mirror the essence of others but then manage to transform any interaction into one of hope and understanding. By the time that Esther had passed into the Spirit World, Miriam was ready for the final initiation to take place.

The ancient ritual of the Hieros Gamos, through which every high priestess had stepped fully into her power for thousands of years, took place on the full-moon of the month of Tammuz. The month was named in honor of Dumuzi, the consort of the Goddess known in other cultures as Ishtar or Inanna. On the evening of the Sacred Marriage, Miriam was bathed in herbs from the ancient temple gardens, anointed with precious spikenard ointment, dressed in a simple shift of white silk, and left to her prayers. As the moon rose over the perfumed cloister, the Holy of Holies in the center of the temple, she knelt to pray. "May this ancient act of Sacred Marriage, the holiest sacrament, repair the rift between God and Goddess. May the universe be made whole, and love restored to every human heart in our joining."

Yehoshuah, also dressed in a simple white silk shift, entered the walled garden and knelt before Miriam. Both were nearly breathless, shaking with anticipation of a ritual they had only dreamed of. Yehoshuah reached out, palms up, and took Miriam's small hands in his. A bolt of electricity ran through them as, looking into one another's eyes, they prayed.

Together the Bride and Bridegroom poured seven crucibles of perfumed olive oil into an alabaster bowl. Each crucible represented a note of the scale that, when the notes come together, sing the universe into being. As Miriam and Yehoshuah sang each note, their voices rose through the still desert air, answered by a chorus of wild creatures. Wolves and owls, jackals and locusts sang creation back to them. When the bowl was filled, Miriam gently lifted Yehoshuah's shift over his head and placed it on a pile of olive twigs and sage. Yehoshuah, in turn, lifted off Miriam's shift. He kindled the twigs, and the vestments that had covered them ignited with a burst of light and sweetness, symbolic of the purity of their uncovered bodies.

They turned to one another, male and female, a perfect embodiment of the mysterious energy of Baruch Ha Shem and the Shekhina. As in the first moment of creation, they saw one another's bodies as completely pure and were without shame. The moonlight accentuated Miriam's round breasts and belly, casting shadows that pooled in the silky black triangle of her womanhood. Yehoshuah's manhood already trembled with life, swelling with the fullness of his love for his Bride. Dipping their fingers into the bowl of perfumed oil they had consecrated together, each anointed the other in all their secret, holy places until the boundaries separating them disappeared, and flesh, once again, vibrated as primal energy.

Miriam's lips whispered praises of God as she ran them over Yehoshuah's face, his neck, and his lithe brown body, hardened by physical labor in the desert sun. Yehoshuah's lips whispered praises of the Goddess as he kissed her delicate ears, the rose-petal tips of her breasts, the lips of her womanhood that are the portals of life. In the total joining of their hearts, minds, intentions, and bodies, the stars seemed to dip closer to earth. The light of the moon washed over them, and the choirs of angels wept with joy that the rift in the Godhead was, for that moment, closed. All over the earth there was an instant when every heart was opened to love, when every creature realized its divinity, and the notes of creation were again in perfect harmony.

Miriam brought her small hand up to the face of her beloved, brushing the wet strands of hair from his eyes. "Tomorrow you must leave the temple," she whispered. "The time of your mission is upon us. For a moment the world was made whole through our love. Now you will teach people how to find their way back to that moment, so that what was given by grace can take root as a change of heart and mind. The years of your ministry will be trying and short, my beloved, but I will always be there with you, by your side. Every pain is made bearable through love and understanding."

The two lovers were quiet, resting in both the joy and the sadness of Yehoshuah's mission. The trees above them swayed gently in the warm breeze, breaking the moonlight into tender shafts that played over their naked, oiled bodies. Yehoshuah gathered Miriam's small form into his arms and loved her once again, the music of their joining spreading throughout creation. Still inside her, he nuzzled her hair and sang to her from the Song of Songs, the ancient Scripture of the Sacred Marriage. "Behold, you are beautiful, my love; behold you are beautiful, my beloved, truly lovely. Our couch is green; the beams of our house are cedar, our rafters are pine."

The Holy Couple, sated and complete in each other's arms, reclined together on their grassy bed and codreamed the details of Yehoshuah's ministry. When they awakened, the rosy fingers of dawn painting the horizon, Miriam brought out the jar of precious spikenard ointment once again. She spoke to Yehoshuah the ancient words of the Song of Songs, "O you who dwell in the gardens, my companions are listening for your voice; let me hear it," and then she began to weep with sadness that Yehoshuah's mission, his speaking of the Holy Word, must end in his death.

Leaning over her beloved, Miriam washed his feet with her tears. "The feet are symbolic of understanding, my precious love. May your understanding always be guided by love. May the dark clouds of confusion and sadness that hide the heart's true light and wisdom be kept at bay. May love guide your every thought and act." With that, she dried Yehoshuah's feet with her hair and sealed the blessing by anointing them with the precious spikenard ointment.

"When next I anoint you, beloved, you will know that the time of your travail is upon you. For now I anoint you for life, but then I will anoint you in preparation for death." And although she knew that love is stronger than death, and that they would be forever joined, nonetheless Miriam of Magdala cried for the parting of the flesh that it is the way of this world.

And so, as Jesus moved through the three years of his ministry, Miriam walked with him. When the male disciples proved unable to be present to their master's pain, Miriam was there. When wisdom was required, she helped provide it, interpreting dreams and signs. As the writer of the Gospel of Philip noted, Yehoshuah kissed her, the most beloved disciple, often and on the lips. To those who had the sight to see, Miriam was the sun. She was the completion of Yehoshuah and the fulfillment of all commandments to bring the Divine Bride together again with the Divine Bridegroom.

Did they have children? I think so. We are their children. And it is up to us to take the perfection of their love, that cast out war and hatred for the moment of their joining, and make it a reality in the healing of this world.

RITUAL AND PRAYER

Gathering in Spiritual Community

W e have journeyed together to identify Sarah's circle, the relational, intuitive connection that is a woman's innate spiritual path. Through reading other women's stories, I hope that you have had an experience of self-in-relation, knowing yourself better through their struggles and breakthroughs, their joys and their longings. Contrasting the feminine circular path to Jacob's ladder, the rational step-by-step path of men, we've looked at some of the biopsychological gender differences that predispose men and women to find God in our own ways. In the process we've dealt with some of the anger that women have voiced about the patriarchy.

The pain of being a round spiritual peg pushed into a square religious hole is all too real. But we'll never find our authentic spiritual Selves until we let go of residual anger and rejoice that we can and do have a path of our own. Celebrating that path in community, where we can grow through sharing experience, praying, and creating ritual pertinent to the details of women's lives, is a way that we can make Sarah's circle an explicit force.

When I was at Bryn Mawr College it was an all-women's school. Discussions in class were lively and uninhibited. We felt safe, free to toss out hunches, to let our intuition surface in discussion. In the few classes that I took at Haverford, our brother school, the atmosphere was distinctly different. More competitive and rational, it tended to squelch intuition. Being right seemed more important than taking risks and expanding the conversation. It was hard to find my voice in those classes, and I always ended up taking a backseat, literally and figuratively.

Many women have left organized religion because they felt similarly constrained by religions developed for male sensibilities. Others have found nurture there but still seek the company of women to deepen their spiritual journey. My own experience demonstrates that religious dropouts, even spiritual-minded ones, face special challenges in forming an intimate relationship with the Divine. It is easy to love God in general, but not in any particular way. It is easy to dig a hundred shallow wells, combining a little of this and a little of that practice, and end up exhausted and thirsty. It is easy to say we have faith, but without a community of worship or a spiritual practice that we can share with at least a few others, that faith may be more theoretical than real.

Women learn best with and through one another. Had Jan Maier not called to tell me about her snake walk miracle, the mythic synchronicities of that day might have eluded conscious recognition. In hearing her story, I was guided to look more deeply within myself. This is the woman's way. As a result of our conversation, I saw the small shoots of change beginning to push their way up in my life. Only then could I water them. Inspired by the way that women help one another to become more conscious and to change as a result, I wrote this poem.

SISTER SNAKE

How did it escape me that we were walking in Eden
plucking ripe apples on the equinox
one foot in darkness, the other in light
strolling down a country road in the Days of Awe?

How did I fail to faint with wonder
when our sister the snake waited for us
halfway across the road, stubborn in her staying power
seeking the safety of the grass only when we'd passed?

When will I learn that life is like a dream
full of strange and curious wisdom, wild as the wind
and just as liable to slip through our fingers
when attention wanders from the precious present?

When will I remember that no one sees it all?
We need one another to make the dream real,
to rise up in joy and in power, rubbing
against one another until we shed our skins.

WOMEN'S SPIRITUAL GROUPS

Like the pilgrimage to India, sharing in Jan's miracle helped renew my faith. Faith can be magnified by spending at least part of the time that we have set aside for God worshipping, praying, celebrating, and creating ritual in a community of like-minded women. In this chapter we will take a look at some of the ways in which women worship and create ritual together, how we rub against each another to aid in the shedding of skins that have served their purpose. Sometimes the stated purpose of a gathering may be to pray and honor God. Sometimes the purpose may be to honor a time of year, a death or a birth, or some special achievement. Sometimes we come together to heal one another, the community we live in, or even the world.

Beth Lawrence is a champion of prayer and women's worship. In almost every location where we have held a *Gathering of Women* retreat, Beth has made sure that a "pocket of prayer" forms. Women living close by exchange addresses and phone numbers and network to form small spiritual groups. Loyalists and returnees may also have a regular place of worship, but for dropouts these women's groups are "church."

We often get letters from women in these prayer pockets, telling us how their lives have changed. Some have been empowered to leave bad marriages. Others believe that they have found their life-purpose work. They talk about the seemingly mundane kinds of things that take up so much attention, but are the heart of the women's relational path. They have been able to let go of their adult children, managed to get along better with a difficult boss or spouse, learned to take time for themselves, started an exercise program, dealt with an addiction. Physical cures and profound psychospiritual healing in spite of continuing sickness are common themes of the letters. Some groups meet weekly, others monthly and on special occasions.

The organization of these groups varies, but there are three basic principles that we suggest. First, leadership rotates. Every woman has the opportunity to be the facilitator, the priestess, choosing the prayers, readings, and theme of the meeting. Second, every woman has the opportunity to speak and pray from her heart, uninterrupted. Third, general conversation waits until the group is over. Otherwise it is easy for this precious time of prayer and worship to turn into a coffee klatch. I will share a format that has worked well for many women, but each group will ideally find its own format and develop its own personal flavor.

Spirituality groups that have sprouted out of *Gathering of Women* retreats, or other meetings where many of the women don't initially know one another, may start with twenty or more women and then undergo a natural period of pruning until perhaps as few as six or eight or as many as twelve to fifteen remain as the core group. In our experience, once the groups stabilize, they stay together for years. Many of the women become intimate friends and anchors for one another outside the group.

Even when a group is relatively large, sitting in a circle ensures that all the women can see one another's faces. Rather than sitting in rows facing a facilitator, which carries a subtle message of being ministered to by an authority, sitting in a circle is participatory. It honors the God within every woman who is personally accessible to us without the need for priestly intervention.

Just as God is in the center of the circle of our lives, an altar representing the Divine can be placed at the center of the circle. Candles, sacred objects, pictures, stones, or anything spiritually important to each participant are placed on the altar and collected again when the meeting is over. A spirituality group that met at my house for years used to construct our altar on the floor. We liked a lot of candles. But after my curious Persian cat wandered through the altar one day, exiting with his bushy tail aflame like a torch, we moved the altar to a low table. Let cat lovers be forewarned.

When the sacred space is ready, the leader of the day signals the women to hold hands and leads the group in an opening prayer. Hands are dropped and the leader may then have a poem, a short reading, a brief meditation, a song, chant, or other activity that focuses the intention of the group on a particular spiritual topic. After this five-minute introduction, the leader hands a sacred object to the woman on her left that is the group's "talking stick." Holding the stick means that it is your turn to speak and that no one will interrupt you.

Proceeding around the circle in a sunwise direction, each woman has the opportunity to pray out loud with personal relevance to her life, addressing God in her own way. For example, "Mother-Father God, Mary and the saints, thank you for being with me this week. Thank you for the strength I needed when my son, Jason, called to say that he and Cheryl are getting divorced. Please comfort and guide them, and if it is for their highest good, help them find the love they once had for one another. I'm worried about my granddaughter, Anna. Please protect her and help her know she's loved. And I pray for the highest good of my other children, Sean and Timothy, and for my husband, Ben. I give thanks for the good friends in our lives, for our health, and for the many blessings. I have a special prayer today for the people of Bosnia, and all those who are oppressed, homeless, and suffering. May they have what they need. May peace, tolerance, and respect come into the hearts of all people worldwide. Day by day may I feel closer to you, God, and see You within everyone and everything. Amen." The talking stick is passed to the woman on her left until everyone has prayed.

Depending on the size of the group and the agreed-upon time for the gathering, the agenda may vary after the prayers are completed. There may be a period of group discussion about the theme of the day, a ritual like those described later in the chapter, a meditation, or singing. The facilitator ends the group promptly at the appointed time with a closing prayer. If refreshments have been provided, this is the time to have them. Beth Lawrence belonged to a spiritual group for years that met at 6:00 A.M. and then adjourned to a restaurant for breakfast before going to work. It is almost a cliché to speak of empowering women, but that is exactly what prayer and spirituality groups do. As women find our own authentic ways to worship, some are also joining together to help their communities. Woman to woman, as the next story illustrates, we can help to change the world.

ALTARS IN THE STREET

Melody Ermachild Chavis is a small woman with bright eyes and a quick smile. A private investigator who works on trials and appeals for death row inmates, she is a community activist, committed Buddhist, and author of *Altars in the Street: A Neighborhood Fights to Survive.* In the early 1980s she and her mate bought an old house in a quiet, interracial neighborhood in Berkeley, California. Whites, African Americans, Mexicans, Vietnamese, and Ethiopians shared the neighborhood. She and her husband lovingly restored the turn-of-the-century Victorian house they had bought and filled the yard with flower and vegetable gardens.

Melody raised her family in the warm old house on Alma Street, her oldest sons almost in high school when they moved there, and her daughter just eight. Racial tensions were definitely present in Berkeley, but so was camaraderie and understanding. Her children grew up experiencing both in a neighborhood where people knew one another and looked out for one another across the generations. Block parties, concerned groups of neighbors, porch and fence conversations made the neighborhood rich with stories and caring. But slowly the fabric of the community began to weaken, as if a cancer were spreading. Crack houses sprouted up, despite every attempt to stop them. Drive-by shootings and burglaries became a nightly occurrence, shattering the peace of the old neighborhood and planting seeds of fear in every heart.

At about this time Reverend Clara Mills, an African American woman, became the pastor of the South Berkeley Community Church. Free lunches for the hungry and HIV testing were among the programs that her church offered to the community. The block committee organizing against drugs outgrew the pizza place where they had been meeting. They sought the safety of Reverend Clara's church, where they became a group that would ultimately bring God more fully into expression through caring. Lounging on the corner by the church, the drug dealers targeted the helpless, the down-and-out, offering to sell crack to the poor who had just received a free lunch.

Chavis asked Reverend Clara what she thought about people getting a free lunch and then buying drugs. While she didn't like it, the reverend thought that at least they would eat. Otherwise, they would still buy the drugs and they wouldn't eat. She said, "It would be easier for me to minister to a congregation where I never saw people who were sick and poor and despised. But these are the people Jesus talked about. We must find something better for these young men to do. . . . I know it's hard to resist or recover if drugs are on every corner. But we are suffering mainly from poverty of the spirit. The only real answer lies with God."

Reverend Clara was studying for a doctorate in theology. Chavis was a Buddhist who felt strongly that people healed through their connection in community, no matter what their religion, and the two became strong friends and allies. The antidrug group met frequently at the church, hatching every kind of plan to rid the neighborhood of drugs, from suing the slum lords to burning down the crack houses to putting up fences to speaking to the kids involved. But the disease of drugs spread. Houses burned and gun blasts fragmented the quiet of the night. Children died.

Chavis started a community garden project where the young men could get good, well-paid summer jobs and learn respect for the earth. She spent time with the children and with the parents. They were her friends and food for her soul. She kept active by day with her work and in the neighborhood, but by night she frequently had to jump out of bed and seek refuge on the floor as the windows were shot out and bullets whizzed over her head. In time she became a combat victim. Melody developed post-traumatic stress disorder and became anxious, irritable, and depressed much of the time.

One day, sitting in Reverend Clara's study, the two women decided to have a peace march in the neighborhood that would honor all those who had been killed in the name of drugs. It took only a few minutes on the phone to the police department to determine the number killed in their small police beat, the few blocks surrounding Chavis's home on Alma Street and the church. Sixteen people, fifteen men and one woman, had been murdered in five short years. "We can't expect young men to protect life if we don't honor theirs," said Reverend Clara.

The two women called the press, the politicians, and the other clergy. Most of the clergy, all males, did not return the calls, did not want to work with a woman minister. Reverend Clara and Chavis were undeterred. They sent a leaflet out to the community stating the intention of the march: to honor those who died, to end the killings and the violence. They listed the victims' names and the dates of their deaths. Chavis arranged for an African American neighborhood band to provide music. She got the kids together and they made a poster for each victim and banners for the march. Only twenty-five people showed up, and one other clergyperson, Zen Buddhist abbot Mel Weitsman. Reverend Clara asked the people to wear the posters they'd made for each victim around their necks.

The small group walked the neighborhood, referring to a map that Chavis had prepared, with a star for the place where each person to be honored had been murdered. They hung the signs at each site—on trees or telephone poles. The children left bouquets of wildflowers at these impromptu altars in the street. "The majority of the killings were clustered near drug-dealing 'hot spots,' and those were mostly near where alcohol was sold. Reverend Clara said it was the first time she had ever led prayers at liquor stores."

At each altar Reverend Clara would lead a prayer like, "Thank you God . . . for the life of Joseph Wilson, and we lift up our prayers also for the soul of whoever has taken his life."

Reverend Clara's own son, Frankie, was one of the young men who had been killed. That she could pray not only for the victims but also for their murderers was a sign of divine forgiveness. Forgiveness is a bold choice, but a necessity if violence is ever to end. Although their march was small, the impact was large. The press ran articles about it. Neighborhood residents stopped at the altars and read the posters.

The local newspaper published a letter from a mother who had read about the march. "The story about people going around the neighborhood honoring the young men and women who were murdered made me realize that I had never visited the site where my son was found. He died of a drug overdose at a housing project three years ago. He was found out in the street, without his shoes on, dead. I would drive by and look the other way. My pain was too great to stop and look around. However, as a result of this article I called a friend and she and I went there. We met several women who showed us a mural on a building there with the names of people who have been killed. But my son's name wasn't on it. Now it will be added, and my friend and I are purchasing a bench for the courtyard there."

Reverend Clara commented that we have to imagine something before it can happen. It is up to each of us to imagine a world of peace, caring, respect, and love. Then, together, we can take action. Whether against the chemicals that cause breast cancer, the television violence that pollutes the minds and hearts of our children, or a political system that rewards the rich and penalizes the poor, women working together can make a difference. Through our actions, our prayers, our rituals, and our friendships the feminine principles of relationality can bring healing to our world.

Altars in the Street is an important book because it shows that our prayers and actions can make a difference even if the situation doesn't immediately seem to improve. Even if the drug dealers don't move out and we do, as Melody's family reluctantly did, positive things happen when we intend the good. The mother whose son was killed at a housing project was healed through their community "altars in the street" ritual. People that Melody Chavis and Reverend Clara will never know about may have been healed directly or indirectly through others who were touched. Healing and prayer are remarkable that way. Their effects are nonlinear and nonlocal. People at a great distance, and those with seemingly different problems, can be healed through the power of our loving intention.

Melody Chavis's and Reverend Clara's lives are both living prayers of service. Because they have cultivated an intimate relationship with the Divine, put their spiritual journeys in the center of their lives, they are like beacons of good shining out into a dark world. Beth and I have witnessed women's prayers groups creating miracles of healing, inspiration, and love. Some people have absolute faith that their prayers make a difference. Others are more skeptical; they want proof. When women get together to pray, sharing the ways in which prayer has made a difference, faith grows. And if there is not yet enough faith in your heart to pray, perhaps the scientific evidence on the distant effects of prayer and intention will help to light the fire in your heart.

THE SCIENCE OF RITUAL, INTENTION, AND PRAYER

There is a strong sense of intention in creating sacred ritual. The participant knows the purpose of the activity and focuses on coming into clear and harmonious relationship with that purpose. Partaking of the Eucharist carries the intention to become one with the body and blood, the heart and soul, of the Christ. Reciting sacred mantras and intending to become one with the deity of that mantra in Buddhist or Hindu practice is likewise a form of communion. Lighting the Sabbath candles is an intention to celebrate God and life, to honor the commandment to rest deeply, heal, and be restored. Smoking the *chanupa*, the sacred pipe, is meant to mend the Sacred Hoop, balance male and female powers, and send prayers for the good of all to the Creator.

Intention unleashes power, harnesses the wellspring of imagination. We can sense that power in our bodies perhaps as a little electric feeling, the telltale sign of goose bumps and hair raising, the generation of heat, or a sense of peace and Divine Presence. Breathing is nearly suspended, quiet, and expectant, and the body shifts gears into a different rhythm. Whether you call that rhythm prayer, trance, attention, meditation, or, as my former mentor Herbert Benson, M.D. does, the relaxation response, it is tangibly different from our normal state of mind and body. Scientific research points to this "sacred" state of mind as being indispensable to the positive effect of prayer.

One of the first people to articulate the importance of intentionality was Dr. Marilyn J. Schlitz, director of research at the Institute for Noetic Sciences in Sausalito, California. Two kinds of distant intentionality experiments have been performed. One type measures the electrodermal response (similar to a lie detector test) of subjects when "intenders" in a distant location imagine them either relaxing or becoming more tense. The other relies on the fact that the majority of people around the world, from different cultures, report that they can tell when another person is staring at them. The skin prickles. The hair at the nape of the neck rises. When Schlitz or other scientists who are open to these effects conduct the experiments, they get positive results. Skeptics, in contrast, whose hope is to find no result of imagining one another at a distance, generally find what they are looking for—nothing.

One such skeptic, Dr. Richard Wiseman, a researcher at Cambridge University, was unable to replicate one of Dr. Schlitz's studies that reported physiological changes in one person when another person, in a distant room, was staring at their image on a television monitor. Dr. Schlitz traveled to Wiseman's laboratory in Cambridge and both of them conducted the same experiment, using identical methods and equipment. She tested half the subjects; he tested the other half. She got statistically significant effects; he got random outcomes. Both investigators were fascinated by the results, which suggest that the mind-set of the experimenter affects the outcome. Each had a different intention. In both cases their intention influenced the results.

In the field of parapsychological research the so-called experimenter effect is well known. You tend to get what you expect. So if you don't believe in distant prayer or thought communication at a distance, you are unlikely to find positive results. These kinds of data led physician and prayer expert Larry Dossey to write that "science embodies the belief that dispassion is the ideal attitude for the experimenter. Experimenters in prayer have often observed, however, that a sense of holiness often correlates with a positive outcome of the study. Healers agree; they generally believe that a sense of sacredness and reverence is required if distant, prayer-based healing is to succeed. The emotionally sterile conditions of many laboratories and hospitals create inhospitable conditions for many intercessors." I would add that the emotionally sterile conditions of many churches and synagogues do the same thing, but that ritual stirs the soul and opens the heart, creating the conditions under which prayer is most likely to have positive effects.

What is the difference between prayer and distant intentionality? The latter, for example, might be an attempt to send someone feelings of calm or excitation, an activity that results in significant physiological effects in Dr. Schlitz's studies. Is this different from praying that a person feel peace, or energy? Dossey writes, " 'Intercessory' comes from the Latin root *inter*, 'between,' and *cedere*, meaning 'to go.' Intercessory prayer is often called 'distant' prayer, because the individual being prayed for is often remote from the person who is praying." In intercessory prayer as we usually understand it, one is asking for divine intervention, while in distant intentionality one is focusing the power of one's own mind and will. But perhaps the two are, in fact, the same thing.

Dossey points out that studies in distant intentionality often involve prayer, even if the title of the article doesn't make a distinction. In one study seven different people were asked to focus on making yeast cells in a test tube grow faster. The results were statistically significant in terms of mental intention affecting the growth of the yeast. But when the results were looked at more closely, only three of the seven "intenders" got positive results. These were so dramatic that they carried the experiment as a whole, the statistical p-value for these three indicating that the odds of getting such a result by chance were less than 14 in 100,000. The three effective intenders consisted of two spiritual healers and a physician who used prayer in his practice. The four who were ineffective, getting only chance results, were students with no particular interest in prayer or healing. So even though this experiment was supposed to test intention, in fact it tested prayer.

One of the most central elements in the efficacy of prayer, as measured scientifically, is love. "Love, empathy, compassion, and a sense of connectedness, oneness and unity" correlate with better results. These are precisely the feelings that effective women's rituals create. A woman named Rosie, at one of our retreats, had lost a child several months before. Her apparently healthy baby died of SIDS, sudden infant death syndrome, in the night. Her sadness sparked enormous empathy in the group, and a ritual spontaneously organized itself. Rosie was asked to lie down in the center of the circle, and the women laid hands on her. We prayed and sang to her. Dozens of hands moved underneath her body, and we lifted Rosie to the light, to rebirth while we imagined out loud the rebirth of her baby to the Spirit World. Profound emotion accompanied the ritual. Two months later I had a card from Rosie. After the ritual, she reported, she could at last sleep through the night again and feel some short periods of peace. Pictures of her baby had started to bring feelings of warmth and joy for the gift of his brief presence in her life, rather than overwhelming sadness and grief. She was healing.

Dossey believes that love and empathy form a bridge between the pray-er and the object of his or her prayers. Perhaps whenever we think of someone with love, we are, in fact, engaging in positive prayer. And perhaps when we think of someone with anger, we are in effect sending a curse. A Lakota medicine man I know is concerned with the lack of regard people have for the dark side and what he perceives as the very obvious effects of negative prayer. Dossey shares this concern, and the interested reader will be chastened by the data he has collected on negative prayer in his seminal book, *Be Careful What You Pray For.*

The fact that prayer can create both positive and negative results is well documented. More than a hundred fifty scientific studies on prayer are reviewed by Dossey in *Healing Words: The Power of Prayer and the Practice of Medicine.* A variety of other studies that touch on faith and attendance at church or synagogue services are cited by Georgetown University School of Medicine physician Dale Matthews in *The Faith Factor.* Prayer and faith are both implicated in longevity, protection from illnesses as diverse as depression, coronary artery disease, and cirrhosis of the liver, and in recovery from illness.

While prayerful people are likelier to have healthier lifestyles than those who lack faith, even when smoking, drinking, and diet are accounted for, those with faith live longer and healthier lives. In particular, community is important to health. In one study of people who had suffered heart attacks, two variables predicted whether or not they would have a second within six months: they were religious faith and belonging to a group that met regularly. While even a bowling league would do, imagine the power of meeting to pray with others.

My experience of prayer in the synagogue of my youth was impersonal and regimented. The intimacy required to create the flow of love so important to the power of prayer was lacking. The freedom to focus specifically and spontaneously on people's needs is critical to walking Sarah's circle. Women's prayer circles can meet these spiritual needs, creating a living community of faith and service. They can be the churches of dropouts, and supplement the spiritual lives of loyalists and returnees who may need a more intimate, feminine way to pray than what is provided in standard services.

Catie Geneva Cannon writes of a prayer ritual that her mother, a direct descendant of African slaves, used to lead in her home, after she would tell a story. This story-prayer ritual calls upon a faith that knows the nearness of God, and the heart's desire to share that faith by listening to the prayers of loved ones, witnessing together the goodness of God. "Believing that a direct personal relationship with God exists, my mother always concludes her stories with a long prayer of intercession, praise, and thanksgiving. Kneeling beside the couch, she prays for the needs of both the immediate and the extended family. She celebrates God's goodness, majesty and mercy. She frequently enunciates thanks for the gifts of the earth and for all the blessings received. After a period of silence, my mother then provides time for every family member to bear witness to the immediate power of Jesus as 'heart fixer and mind regulator.' "

When I was very little, I knelt by the side of my bed and said my prayers. "Now I lay me down to sleep, I pray the Lord my soul to keep. If I should die before I wake, I pray the Lord my soul to take. God bless Mommy and Daddy, Poppy and Grandma Libby, Grandma Sarah and Grandpa Sam, my brother, Alan . . ." and everyone else I could think of. The prayers were made ever so sweet by my mother's presence. She was there to hear me, to share in the magic of the moment. Even though she didn't think much of God, I felt her solidly there in the still, quiet place of the heart. My prayers were not the same when our bedtime ritual stopped. I wonder how many other mothers have performed this simple ritual with their children, unaware of its power.

THE FOUR TYPES OF WOMEN'S RITUAL

My friend Janet and I often joke about opening a store called Rituals for All Occasions. So many women are intrigued by ritual, sensing its power to focus intention and build community, yet they don't know where to start. We are conditioned to think that one needs training to conduct religious ritual. Because of this, some women are afraid to just take the plunge and do it. But in the spontaneous and participatory spirit of women's spirituality, every woman is a priestess. And if you find the courage to organize a ritual, the other women involved will instinctively add to it. The final form will be a community effort. Our "ritual store" would be a way to empower women to do what comes naturally.

We fantasize that you would enter a sacred realm just by coming through the door. The art, colors, flowers, wonderfully draped fabrics covering tables filled with beautiful, holy objects, the flickering candles, uplifting music, and delicate natural scents would immediately relax you, especially since our intention would be for the healing of all those who entered. We would listen to your needs, your hopes, and intentions, and then help you plan the type of sacred ritual most suitable to the orientation of the participants. For the neophyte not yet accustomed to creating ritual, we would provide a selection of music, costumes, scents, dances, and sacred objects. We might also have a section in our shop for therapeutic touch and spiritual healing and a listening booth where the talker could unburden her heart while the listener simply accepted her with great respect and love. We would not charge for these services, but accept donations instead. I don't think that we will ever open such a store, but perhaps someone else will. It's fun to imagine.

The kinds of rituals that women are most likely to organize, and which may involve only women or alternatively the entire community, fall into three main categories:

- those marking earth cycles, seasons, and holidays (holy days);
- those marking passages like birth, menarche, leaving home, menopause, and death;
- healing rituals for individual, community, national, or planetary circumstances such as trauma, illness, famine, war, replacing hurt or anger with forgiveness, righting past wrongs, divorce, infertility, abortion, miscarriage, stillbirth, or any untoward event.

The first two categories of ritual have been traditional parts of women's daily lives. We gather the clan for seasonal holidays and birthdays, make wedding and baby showers, plan parties for children leaving home and for other people leaving a community or joining one. We organize periods of mourning, feeding and comforting the bereaved. But these days, many women look for the deeper spiritual significance in these time-honored rituals.

A generation ago, rituals for life passages like menopause didn't exist. As Gail Sheehy pointed out, the "change of life" was a hidden passage. So was menarche. More women are hungry now to mark these watershed times. A generation ago divorce was rare. Now it is common and women seek the company of other women to heal and harvest the meaning from the relationship that has ended. A generation ago same-sex relationships between women were hidden. Now many women seek to bless and sanctify these unions openly, with a community ritual that blesses and acknowledges the union.

The increasing number of religious dropouts has helped create a greater interest in ritual. Catholic dropouts, for example, are often moved to tears when Beth and I invite all the women at our *Gathering of Women* retreats to light the Sabbath candles on Friday night. An altar covered with glowing lights, casting its magic in a darkened room, reminds them of the Mystery that may once have nurtured them in the Catholic Church. They realize that they miss ritual and can reclaim it in the company of other women.

Dropouts, returnees, and loyalists alike are realizing that they don't need the intercession of priests, ministers, and rabbis to make the journey to God. They can and do function as priestesses both within their own families and within groups of women specially convened to celebrate meaningful passages. Women also function innately as healers. Whether it is kissing the cut of a child, making a casserole for a sick friend, or sitting by a deathbed, our relational nature wants to comfort. While women have always been healers, special healing rituals like the one planned by Melody Chavis and Reverend Clara are springing up in communities across the country. The best way to learn about ritual is to attend one. The second best way is to hear stories about them. Another way to learn about ritual is through reading. Malidoma Somé's book *The Healing Wisdom of Africa: Finding Life Purpose through Nature, Ritual, and Community* is filled with cogent advice and practical approaches.

Taking a look at all three types of ritual, we will listen to the stories of women who have created and participated in these deep expressions of relationality.

EARTH CYCLES, SEASONS, AND HOLIDAYS

Most of us grew up celebrating seasonal holidays. There were Easter and Passover in the spring, Christmas and Hanukkah in the winter, and lots of other holidays in between. As children, most of us didn't know that Halloween was a celebration of All Souls' Day, an honoring of the dead taken very seriously in Europe. Some of us came from families where the holidays were religious celebrations. For others, they were cultural. Santa Claus and the Easter Bunny, presents and egg hunts, a time to visit with cousins and distant family members may have seemed more important than Jesus. Dreidels and menorahs, gifts and Hanukkah gelt may have seemed more real than an ancient miracle when one day's supply of oil burned for eight to keep the eternal light burning in the Holy of Holies of a reclaimed temple. But these holidays trace their roots to earlier times in which religious differences meld into one spiritual root.

The seasonal influence on our bodies, on the plants and animals, was once the most obvious focal point for a holy day. The trajectory of the sun in the sky and the procession of heavenly bodies was intimately related to survival. Rituals were performed to help the crops grow, to bring rain, to ensure a good harvest. But over the millennia these basic feminine rites of fertility were labeled pagan and stamped out. They never disappeared, they just transformed into Jewish and Christian religious holidays. And like it or not, if you celebrate Christmas or Hanukkah, Easter or Passover, you are a born-again pagan.

The Jewish High Holy Days of Rosh Hashanah and Yom Kippur, the Jewish New Year and the Day of Atonement, occur near the fall equinox when the hours of light and darkness are equal. One might wonder why they don't occur on the spring equinox instead, the obvious moment of renewal. But perhaps the Jewish New Year is in September, as the darkness of fall and winter begin, because the new day starts at sunset rather than at sunrise in our tradition. If this is so for the new day, why not the new year? As Jews we go first into the darkness and are then reborn into light.

Easter and Passover are both vernal equinox celebrations, the resurrection of the earth in the spring. In the days of the Goddess temples the Hieros Gamos would have been reenacted at this time. For Jews Passover marks the exodus from Egypt when we were slaves of the Pharaoh, building the pyramids. In Hebrew the word Egypt is Mitzrayim, which means the "narrow place." On this day we celebrate not only the physical freedom of our ancestors from the cruelty of slavery but also our individual journey to freedom by coming through the constricted places in our lives and personalities. Ideally, we have been working toward freedom since the High Holy Days in the fall when we took a careful inventory of ourselves, gave and received forgiveness, and made a heartfelt intention to be better people. Now the changes that have been occurring underground in the darkness are ready to break through the ground into the light. At Passover we also commemorate the journey to freedom by dedicating ourselves to help all people who are not yet free the world over.

Easter is likewise a celebration of rebirth. Christ arises from the tomb like a phoenix from its ashes. With God all things are possible, whether it is the splitting of the Red Sea or the resurrection of Christ two thousand years ago. And whether we view the resurrection as a literal or metaphoric reality, at Easter the Christ consciousness arises in our own hearts as an impulse toward greater freedom, compassion, consciousness, and responsibility. We hope that the blinders will fall away from our eyes and we will see that all women and men are sisters and brothers, that peace is possible only through forgiveness and respect.

Winter solstice occurs at Christmas and Hanukkah, both festivals of light. The solstice is the darkest day of the year, and therefore marks the return of the light. Even though ancient manuscripts suggest that Jesus was born in the spring, his birthday is celebrated at winter solstice, symbolic of a new light being born into the darkness of the world. At Hanukkah we celebrate the miracle that a crucible of oil, sufficient for only one day, burned for eight days in the Holy Temple of Jerusalem that had been desecrated by the Greek king Antiochus and was won back by an intrepid group of young men, the Maccabees. The profaned temple was rededicated, and the holy light burned on until a new supply of oil could be brought in. For some American Indian tribes, winter solstice marks the New Year.

The summer solstice is the only one of the four posts on the sun return that has no major Judeo-Christian religious celebrations associated with it. The longest day of the year, it comes in late June when the earth is beginning to bear fruit and flowers and the life force is at its peak. In some American Indian tribes, the sun dance is held at about this time. Participants endure four days of fasting from both food and water, while dancing and praying continuously in the hot sun, as an offering to the healing of the people and the earth. In some tribes the dancers also pierce their bodies with wooden skewers and attach the skewers by thongs to the sacred sun-dance tree, pulling against their tethers until the flesh breaks. Since we truly own nothing but our bodies, this ritual is carried out as a deep and reverential prayer for community healing. It is a form of self-sacrifice. Much the way Jesus was crucified as an offering for others, the sun dancers likewise offer their bodies so that other people will not have to suffer.

For several years in the late 1980s and early 1990s I belonged to a women's group composed entirely of religious dropouts. Rather than choosing to celebrate holidays that were Jewish or Christian, and were family-oriented times, we sought to find our feminine roots in the solstices and equinoxes. We put the word out to friends, and anywhere from twenty-five to seventy-five people would show up at my home for a celebration and potluck supper that were communally planned and carried out.

All of the rituals began with a circle, or sometimes two concentric circles, in which we all held hands and prayed. People who had written prose or poetry, or brought selections suitable for the day, then read to the group. Priestesses all, we tried to connect with the energy and the meaning of each season. In sharing our readings and writings, many different perspectives emerged, each like the facet of a jewel. Next there was singing and drumming. Most people love singing. For churchgoers it's often the best part of the service. We chose simple songs that people knew or that they could easily learn. The Shaker song "Simple Gifts," the soulful spirituals "Amazing Grace" and "Rock My Soul," and prayers set to music like the prayer of St. Francis beginning with the line, "Lord, make me an instrument of Thy peace," were some of our favorites. Hindu, Buddhist, Jewish, and Native American chants rounded out the repertoire.

Some of the chants were accompanied by drumming and rattling, and when the singing stopped the rhythm instruments continued. With drumming the energy rises to a crescendo after a time, and you can actually feel the energy change in the room. Almost every indigenous culture uses drumming as a way to enter an altered state and to focus energy and intention for prayer. The drums call the spirits and alert them to the fact that the community has gathered in a good way, to restore balance and harmony to the world.

When we got to the point in our rituals where the rhythm had gathered us into a coherent laser beam of prayerful intention, individuals prayed out loud. Nothing is more moving than hearing the heartfelt prayers of friends and strangers that spontaneously arise from the heart. The prayers often alerted us to the needs of a particular individual. Sometimes a sick person would agree to lie down in the center of the circle and there would be a laying on of hands. They would be blessed out loud or sung to.

After the prayer circle we might add a ritual specific to the time of the year. At the fall equinox there might be a burning ritual. We wrote down those things that were holding us back on a slip of paper, burned them in the fireplace, and buried the ashes outside. On winter solstice there was a candle lighting ceremony in honor of rekindling the Inner Light. At the spring equinox there might be a reenactment of coming out from the tomb, the narrow place, by passing through an arch of hands. At the end of the arch, the two people on either side would whisper a blessing in each ear of the person who had just come down the symbolic birth canal. At the summer solstice there might be a give-away where small gifts or found objects were exchanged to celebrate life's abundance.

Perhaps the most important aspect of our rituals is the feeling of intimacy, love, and safety in which people can pray out loud. When other people witness our prayers, creating a loving space into which to speak them, they join their intention with ours. While there are as yet no "dose-response" studies of prayer—that is, experiments that address the question of whether positive effects increase with the number of people praying—it is obvious that the heartfelt intention of someone praying is supported and intensified by the loving presence of others.

RITUALS MARKING LIFE-CYCLE PASSAGES

When I was pregnant with my first child during graduate school I had no overt interest in women's rituals. Yet the baby shower that a group of women friends gave me was just that. When I opened the first gift, a pair of yellow hand-crocheted booties, commenting that they would keep the baby warm and cozy, the woman who had made them responded with a little blessing. "May your child always feel warm and safe, loved and cared for." Many of the other women followed her lead. A secular ritual had found unexpected spiritual depth.

While women have always created baby showers and weddings, graduation parties for children, birthday parties and moving-away celebrations, the hunger for spirituality has made these more sacred occasions for a growing number of women. I have been to numerous fiftieth, sixtieth, and seventieth birthday parties where midlife women have designed a stunning assortment of rituals, acknowledging and blessing the life of the woman making her passage into the wisdom years. Almost all of the birthday rituals involved women sitting in a circle, each taking her turn to speak. In addition to saying whatever was in their hearts, they may have read to the honored woman or involved the rest of the group in a ritual.

At the fiftieth birthday party of a friend, which we held in my living room, one woman read a beautiful piece to her about Mary, the Divine Mother. I just happened to have a bottle of holy water from Lourdes, sacred to Mary, which I had excavated from the depths of a catch-all drawer that morning. I had no idea how, why, or if we would need it, but I felt compelled to find the holy water and have it handy. As soon as our friend spoke of Mary and her blessings, I knew why the water was there. I gave the little glass vial to her and she blessed and anointed the birthday woman, who then blessed each of us with a drop of water on our foreheads.

While birthday parties were common life-cycle rituals as children, menarche and menopause rituals were unheard of. Now there is a rapidly growing movement to celebrate both in a spiritually meaningful way. I went to my first menopause ritual in the late 1980s before this passage was getting popular among baby boomers. I have been to several others since. Some women refer to menopause rituals as "croning," but others, myself included, feel that croning occurs years later, in one's midsixties as we enter the elder years. Menopause generally occurs in the late forties to mid-fifties on average, when we are in the fullness of midlife.

I love these rituals because older women often attend, speaking to the menopausal woman and sharing their experience of the years between menopause and the elder wisdom years. At one gathering an eighty-four-year-old remarked, "So many of you have spoken of being in a time of transition. When you get to be my age you realize that you're always in transition. Nothing ever stays the same, so you might as well get used to it."

An elegant white-haired woman in her seventies with bright eyes and an easy smile brought down the house by speaking of the love affairs she'd had in her forties, both of how they had benefited her and how they had caused her marriage to dissolve. It is easy to see an elder and forget they were, and often are, very sexual beings. She reminded us that deep sexual urges often awaken near menopause as we begin to feel our oats, and that we'd better think carefully about how to channel them.

A lively woman in a wheelchair, due to a broken hip, spoke about publishing her first book of poetry at seventy-two, and two novels after that. She reminded us that the elder years are fruitful and that we are never "over the hill." A sixty-five-year-old spoke of still feeling like a girl inside and repeatedly feeling shocked at her own reflection in the mirror. "But you're only as old as you feel," she said, laughing, "and I'm about twenty-five. I think there's a core in every one of us that never changes in spite of all the passages we go through. I expect that's the Self, the Godself, I mean. And I'm sure I'll take that with me when I die and leave my body behind, no matter what age it is."

At one menopause ritual I attended, an arbor of beautiful flowers had been constructed and a crown of daisies made. After we had introduced ourselves and the elders had spoken, twenty or so participants formed two rows holding hands, the opening to the arbor between us. The elders stood behind the arbor and the menopausal woman walked between us, through the arbor and into the arms of the elders, who then welcomed her with hugs and the daisy crown. When she was crowned, we formed a circle again and everyone gave her a little gift, often a found object like a stone or other small but meaningful keepsake that we told a story about, suitable for her passage into the early wisdom years.

HEALING RITUALS

While celebrations and initiations into a new stage of life are common occasions on which a community of women may gather in a sacred way, some of the most moving rituals involve the passages we mourn. E. M. Broner's description of sitting shivah for a lost love, where friends gathered on the day that the woman's longtime lover married a younger woman, is typical of how we walk Sarah's circle, helping one another to heal and move on. Similarly, the ritual in which we used the myth of Inanna to help Susan heal from her divorce arose from the authentic concern we had for her well-being.

While healing rituals may involve women with whom we have intimate friendships, at times they may occur even in a group of relative strangers. During our women's retreats, when the presence of other women praying and sharing has created an atmosphere of safety and sacred space, spirit seems to loosen old wounds from the unconscious. When women are willing to give voice to the wounds, moving rituals of healing may organize around them, as Shelly's story illustrates.

Shelly sat in a circle of thirty women who had prayed and meditated together for two days, largely in silence. It was Sunday morning, three hours before our departure from this place of respite. The flat disc of the North Dakota sun had just risen over an icy landscape, the trees covered with tiny crystals that shone like stars in the rosy light. It was time for anyone who wanted to speak about the weekend to offer her thoughts and feelings to the group. Thin fingers of light fell across Shelly's face, a latticework created by Venetian blinds partially drawn to keep the full glare of daylight from intruding as the morning ripened. She rearranged herself tailor-style on the meditation pillow and began to speak out of the deep silence we had shared.

"It's been a hard weekend for me, but a healing one." She hesitated, lowering her head and rolling the hem of her navy blue sweatshirt between her fingers. Looking up with an apologetic smile she gazed around the circle. "I had an abortion twenty-three years ago, and until this moment I've never told a single person." Her slender hands moved up to her eyes, and she covered them for a moment. Nothing stirred but dust particles caught dancing in a beam of sunshine. I was reminded of how Jewish women cover their eyes after lighting the Sabbath candles, so that our first act after saying the blessings will be seeing the holy light of renewal.

Shelly dropped her hands into her lap and looked around the circle again, testing the effect of her words. It was silent enough to hear a pin drop. She continued, "I was young, a freshman in college, barely eighteen years old. Ever the overachiever, I got pregnant the first time I had sex. I never even told the boy. He was Catholic and he would have felt compelled to marry me and have the child. Isn't that ironic?" A wistful smile played over her full lips and a tear slid down her cheek. "Premarital sex was an okay sin, but birth control was over the line. I never thought I'd get pregnant, had just had my period, in fact. But it happened. I wanted to go to medical school, not marry a boy I didn't love and have a child I wasn't ready to mother. I was scared and ashamed, so I arranged for an abortion and went through it all without ever telling a soul. I'm still ashamed, and I worry about the soul of that child. This weekend I sensed her near me and I named her Leah, after my grandmother. I asked her to forgive me."

Tissues arrived in Shelly's lap, passed hand to hand around the circle. She was silent as she mopped away the tears. Blue eyes cast down again, she continued in a tear-roughened voice. "Leah asked for the blessing of this group on both of us."

She reached into the pocket of her well-worn jeans, produced a perfect heart-shaped stone about two inches across, and looked up again, holding the precious icon between thumb and forefinger. "I went for a walk yesterday afternoon down by the lake, in spite of the ice and cold. I just needed to move, to think, to feel the wind on my face. Leah told me to look down." She gazed at us plaintively. "I really did hear her."

There were nods and murmurs of assent from around the group. "This stone was right in front of me, sitting on top of a patch of ice. She wanted me to pass it around so that each of you could put your blessing into it. She wants to be remembered."

I had been in many women's circles where objects were passed around for blessing, and this was usually a silent process. But when Shelly passed the stone to her left, the woman offered her blessing out loud, cradling the heart stone in both hands and offering it up to the sky. "May your hearts be at peace, Leah and Shelly. May you celebrate reunion here and in the time to come, brought together by a love that is stronger than death."

The quiet weeping in the room escalated into a chorus of sobs, punctuated by the blowing of noses. The woman who had said the blessing kissed the stone and passed it to the woman on her left. She, too, held the stone up to the light and uttered a blessing, kissing the heart when she was done. And so the stone passed sunwise around the circle of twenty-six women, returning to Shelly wet with tears and filled with love.

Emboldened by Shelly's story, another woman spoke of her own abortion. A third began to weep loudly. She was forty-two years old, childless, single, and unexpectedly pregnant. This, she thought, would be the last possibility to have a child. But she didn't know how she could raise one alone, making enough money to support both of them. She had come to the retreat to pray about whether or not to have an abortion. The two women who had shared their experience offered to sit with her when the retreat was over, creating the kind of compassionate vessel into which she could speak and perhaps find clarity.

Not all healing rituals need to be serious. Laughter can often do the trick, and a sure sign of healing is when we can laugh at something that once caused pain. At one of our women's retreats we created an improvisational theater piece meant to heal the trauma of the biblical story of Adam and Eve and how it has been used for millennia to justify the second-class status of women. Fortunately, one of the women happened to be a theater director, and in two hours a small group of us had planned and rehearsed a skit to present at our women's liturgy the next morning. The plot was simple and elegant. I got to play Satan, which in Hebrew means "the accuser," the one who makes us look at ourselves deeply. Rather than an evil spirit, Satan is more like a depth psychologist who prods us into self-examination.

As Satan the Accuser my job was to put the characters in the story of Adam and Eve on trial for all the problems they have caused both for women and men throughout history. The cast of characters on trial included Adam, Eve, the snake, and God. A bluebird who watched the whole sorry drama go down from her perch in the Tree of Knowledge of Good and Evil got to be a kind of Greek chorus and independent counsel rolled into one. She would snatch up certain lines and either agree with them or refute them.

At a women's retreat in a rural setting, costume choice is limited, but Adam in particular was seized with a paroxysm of creative abandon. She arrived in a pair of khaki pants with the zipper undone, and a large banana hanging out, covered demurely with a lush green leaf. Eve wore a bedsheet tied over one shoulder, and the remnants of a wreath hung over her head, decorated with fruits. Her hair was bedecked with flowers. The bluebird must have been up half the night coloring, cutting, and gluing a perfect bird beak. The serpent was sleek and wily in a filmy silk jacket over leotards. And I, Satan the Accuser, was chic and understated in basic black. The skit was hilarious and many of us were quite literally peeing in our pants, one of the hazards of hilarity for midlife and older women. When we had finished with the gales of laughter, there were sighs of relief. A story that had been a religious millstone for some of the women had been cut down to size, allowing them to surface from a sea of ancient religious repression.

While patriarchal religions also make use of ritual, they are pre-scribed events. Baptism, circumcision, first communion, confirma-tion, bar mitzvah, marriage, last rites, and other sacraments are beautiful and meaningful steps on the ladder to God. While nour-ishing for women as well as for men, I believe that they are simply not enough for women. Too many passages are left out and there is little room for spontaneity and laughter. In Sarah's circle we grow through the intimate experiences of self-in-relation that can occur in rituals where there is an authentic-give-and-take from the heart, rather than a one-size-fits-all template. Ritual is precious because it provides common ground on which we can meet one another in a community of peers where every woman is a priestess.

DAILY LIFE

Doing and Being

We have come full circle, discussing the intrinsic relationality, intuition, and spontaneity that define Sarah's circle. We have seen how participatory women's worship can reflect a path of our own, relevant to the relationships and concerns of daily life. In this chapter we will take a look at work as part of our spiritual lives. Ideally every task, every action, reflects our relationship to the God within. Our life becomes our message and our legacy to loved ones and to the world.

When, as an adolescent, I was told by our rabbi that women were innately spiritual, that we didn't need the same kind of prayers and practices that men do, I didn't know whether to believe him. More inclined to think that I was getting a dismissive pat on the head rather than authentic spiritual guidance, I put his comment in a mental file and left it there. Now I know that he was correct. For women, the journey of walking Sarah's circle is more a matter of who we are rather than of what we do. It is a path of being rather than of doing. Yet doing is a big part of modern life. But if in the completion of our tasks we forget how to be, we will lose our way, caught in the complexities of a world where there are few role models for powerful women who are committed to spiritual ideals.

Contemporary women have grown up in the crosscurrent of two colliding times. The generations before us resided in an old-time woman's world defined by home and family. The current generations have been brought up with a work ethic. Making it in what was previously a man's world has been both an exhilarating process and one of frustration. The glass ceiling still exists. The old-boy network is considerably more entrenched than the old-girl network.

In the process of equalizing the playing field at work, many women have suppressed their innate relationality in favor of developing their male aspects of rationality and goal orientation. We all need these male skills. But if they are out of balance with the feminine, which appreciates the interconnectedness of life and the complex web of relationships in the universe, we cannot serve a spiritual ideal. In this age of rapid technological expansion, the earth and all her children must be protected. If quick profits continue to take precedence over the long-term interests of the earth, quality of life is sure to decline precipitously and soon. As women, one of our most important roles is that of the guardian who, like the she-bear, is willing to rise up on her hind legs and protect what is precious.

In rapidly changing times it is easy to become disoriented. This has happened before, throughout human history, and it is sure to happen again. Vast empires like ancient Rome rose and fell. Truly great cultures like those of the Native Americans flourished for thousands of years and were all but wiped out in a brief flash of time. When a culture is in trouble, a symbol of the feminine will often appear to give guidance and restore balance. Listening to the feminine principle of guidance is crucial if the culture is to re-create itself. Just as appearances of the Blessed Mother are increasing in frequency worldwide, other symbols of the Divine Mother have appeared to more ancient cultures. The Oglala Lakota story of White Buffalo Calf Woman is a reminder of how we need to balance our male and female aspects, being and doing, to keep the fabric of life whole.

WHITE BUFFALO CALF WOMAN

White Buffalo Calf Woman came to the Oglala hundreds of years ago. She brought them the gift of the sacred pipe and seven rituals based on it, all of which help to remind people how to live in harmony, how to be a part of nature and community. The pipe restores a person to their essential self, guides, and heals. One day, two young Indian braves were out hunting when they came upon a beautiful young woman, as resplendent as the sun, dressed in white buckskin and carrying a bundle on her back. One had impure thoughts about her and was immediately enveloped in a white mist and reduced to a pile of bones. The other, who was properly respectful, received instructions. He was told to go to the village and tell the elders to prepare a medicine lodge and gather all the people.

When the lodge had been readied and the community brought together, White Buffalo Calf Woman appeared. She entered the lodge in a sunwise direction and handed the medicine bundle she was carrying to the chief. In it was the *chanupa*, the sacred pipe. In smoking the pipe, she explained, all people would remember that the entire universe was their relation. She took the pipe from the bundle, along with a round stone that she placed upon the earth. Offering the stem of the pipe to the sky she said, "With this sacred pipe you will walk upon the earth; for the earth is your grand-mother and mother and she is sacred."

The smoke from the pipe would carry their prayers to the Above Beings, and it was to be used in a ritual way to promote prayer and healing and the telling of truth. When the pipe was smoked, only the truth could flow from the people's hearts through their words. Their actions would be pure and they would remember the Great Spirit in everything. The wooden stem of the pipe represented the male aspect of creation. The red stone bowl represented the femi-nine, the womb of creation. The twelve feathers that hung from it represented the spotted eagle and the winged creatures. She touched the pipe to a round stone that represented Mother Earth, and said, "With this pipe you will be bound to all your relatives: your grandfather and father, your grandmother and mother."

Seven circles were inscribed on the round stone that represented seven rituals that would help the people remember the correct bal-ance of life. She taught them the first one that day, a ritual called the ghost-keeping ceremony for honoring the dead so that their souls would be released to Wakan Tanka, the Great Mystery. She told the people that the other six rituals would be revealed at a later time and that she herself would reappear in four different ages, and at the end time.

After instructing women in their sacred duties, and similarly in-structing the men, she spent a long time with the children, re-minding them that the purpose of life is to serve Spirit and to live in a good way, remembering that everything in the universe is our relation. White Buffalo Calf Woman then left the lodge, and a short distance away she sat down and turned into a red-and-brown buf-falo calf. The calf walked a little way, sat down, and transformed into a white buffalo calf. The white buffalo walked a bit farther, sat down, and arose as a black buffalo who walked on, turned to salute the four directions, and then disappeared over a hill.

The other rituals White Buffalo Calf Woman gave the Oglala are the purification and prayer ceremony of the sweat lodge or *inipi*, the vision quest or *hanbleceya*, the sun dance, the *hunka* ritual—or making of relatives—the girl's puberty ritual, and the throwing of the ball. In this latter ritual a young girl throws a ball painted to represent the universe to people standing in the four directions. The one who catches the ball similarly offers it to the four directions, the earth and sky, and then throws it back to the girl. "The ball is symbolic of knowledge, and people's attempt to catch it represents the struggle of people submerged in ignorance to free themselves."

In 1994 a white buffalo calf was born in Wisconsin and has changed color three times. The elders of many tribes believe that this is White Buffalo Calf Woman, returning in the end time when Earth will purify herself. My hope is that we can throw the ball of knowledge to one another and heal the earth, averting a purification. The healing required in ourselves, our families, our neighborhoods, our governments, and our nations is urgent. It requires a reclamation of the feminine knowledge that we are all relations, coming into balance with the masculine power of expansionism and growth. Only in balance can all the people and creatures of the earth grow together as relations.

BALANCING MALE AND FEMALE ASPECTS IN THE WORKPLACE

The ball of knowledge is easy to throw, but, without a spiritual orientation, it may be hard to catch. The basis of that spiritual orientation is our relationship to self, to the Inner Light that guides us in finding the balance between inner male and female, doing and being. At a business meeting where I was a speaker, a woman in her early forties stood up and told the story of how she had recently defected from her position as a vice president of a large multinational corporation. With tears in her eyes she spoke of how she felt creatively and interpersonally strangled by the linear thinking and hierarchical decision making of which she had become a part. Some of the corporate policies were short-sighted. Immediate profits took precedence over how the world would eventually be affected by corporate policy. Over a period of months she became convinced that she would simply die if she stayed there.

Women of her age tend to speak that way. They don't say things like, "Well, I think I'd be happier or more fulfilled in some other setting." Instead, dissatisfaction often takes on life-and-death proportions. I've wondered why that is. Is death of the body a metaphor for death of the spirit, the sense that something invaluable is dying inside us? Or do we realize that when the voice of our inner divinity, our inner authority, speaks to us the only healthy choice is to act on it? When the gap between our inner knowing and outer actions becomes too wide, the body cannot bridge the chasm.

As women mature we become more aware of the inner voice. With the help of one another we find the authentic power to speak it in the world. Intuitively, women can feel themselves losing vitality and health when the stress of being smaller than their vision, or out of right relationship with the larger whole, comes into focus.

The vice presidential "defector" voiced the sentiments of many other women who, surveys have shown, tend to leave the corporate sector in great numbers when they hit their early forties transition, a time when we take stock of our lives. What really matters? Knowing this, how then shall we live in a way that reconciles our outer lives with our innermost yearnings? This is the process of coming to authenticity that we discussed in Chapter Six as part of Inanna's journey. Taken to the Underworld, where we have to give up the outer trappings of ego and power, we claim the blessings of Truth and the Art of Lovemaking with the help of our friends.

The "defector's" language was potent and familiar. It wasn't that she felt drawn to a particular new career. She was called to the feminine, to the soul. She was committed to a vision of bringing healing and hope, connectedness and meaning to the workplace and the world. She had tried to do that where she was, but her efforts bore no apparent fruit. Knowing that her workplace was toxic for her, she took the plunge into the great unknown and quit before she found a new job. Although she was anxious about what the future would bring, she had the faith that she would find a position in which her talents could be used in a way that the Buddhists call "right livelihood." She felt compelled to find a position where she would be working for the common good.

I felt the same way when I chose to leave medical academia in 1988, a decision that left many colleagues stunned. Why would a successful person do such a thing? Look at all the people who would love to work at Harvard. Who would pay attention to me as plain old Joan Borysenko, divested of the cloak of power that Harvard had so graciously draped over me? I had asked that question myself, and it had delayed my exit by several years. Squeezed through the wringer of ten years of graduate education, I had valuable things to offer the world, a hard-won understanding of mind-body medicine. And while men undergoing career changes think similar thoughts, women have additional challenges. We are often pioneers in fields where women are recent additions and are afraid to leave because it may injure the chance of other women coming into positions of influence.

Like most fields in academic medicine, the fledgling mind-body arena was male dominated. Some friends worried that without the relational influence of women thinkers and clinicians, mind-body medicine might get reduced to a set of formulas. Think this. Do that. Adjust your chi with these herbs, that diet, or some acupuncture. Approach your aches and pains with the right attitude and they will diminish or even vanish. Without regard for a person's emotions and all the levels of healing, of what it requires to reestablish right relationship in our lives, they were concerned that the fix-it approach suggested by many men was too limited.

"Take two meditations and call me in the morning," these friends pointed out, is not much different from taking two aspirin. The relational approach of women was important to this field. I had spent years developing it. Who was I to throw it all out? Added to these concerns was plain old gut-wrenching fear. Perhaps I would not be able to make a living if I went out on my own. Yet I had feelings very similar to the woman who left her position as a corporate vice president. My body was sending the message that the Harvard work environment was physically and emotionally toxic. Afraid to stay and too cowardly to leave, I felt stuck between a rock and a hard place. It took a head-on collision to clear my head and point the way out the door.

I shared this experience with the other women, validating the story of the former corporate vice president. The group polarized around our stories. They began to bristle with nervous energy. Voices rose as several women shared stories similar to ours. Others reacted with anger as if by leaving corporate America and the "power" hierarchy, my sister defector was volunteering to be chained to the bedpost. It was as if by her act of conscience she was single-handedly forfeiting all the ground that women had so arduously gained.

"If we leave corporations and academia," several women voiced, "how will the system ever change?" There's the rub, of course. But there's some feminine narcissism in that comment as well. Companies like Ben & Jerry's ice cream are socially concerned, non-hierarchical, and a model for businesses whose policies inspire not only their workers but the general public. Ben and Jerry, of course, are men.

The conversation reminded me of the one women often have about religious institutions. Unless we hang in and try to change them, how will the feminine aspect ever rise into balance with the masculine? How will the ladder, built as it is to deliver one person at a time higher and higher, ever learn to coexist with a participatory circle in which everyone evolves in a way consistent not only with their own efforts but with group contribution? It is not that corporations are uninterested in this question. Japanese quality circles made their way into the corporate sector in the 1980s, T groups in the 1960s. Even I get called on to consult for organizations from time to time, usually when the CEO or other high-level executive has had a heart attack and the dry, academic notion of stress has come home to roost like a looming vulture, waiting to pick off the powerful.

Shortly after the heated debate, there was a panel discussion. One of the other panelists was an environmentalist who had lived in and studied indigenous cultures around the world. Inspired by her wisdom, I commented about the dubious value of homogenizing culture so that wherever we go in the United States the malls and fast-food places are essentially the same. The loss of local and regional differences, of small shops and restaurants, is a little bit like the extinction of species. We need the diversity. Feeling my oats, I launched into the importance of preserving indigenous cultures and offered the thought that their rituals—which bind together earth and sky, plants, animals, and humans—might actually be an important aspect of what keeps the world functional. "Perhaps," I mused, "they are more important to Western culture than we dare to think. Perhaps their connection to the sacred actually keeps the world going around."

BEING TRUE TO OURSELVES
IN A MAN'S WORLD

At the end of the panel discussion, we all filed out the door. An elegantly coifed fifty-something woman in a blue St. John's knit suit came over, smiling conspiratorially. She was also a Jewish woman and we spent a minute bonding as "members of the tribe." She leaned up against a wall and seemed confident that I would see the light as soon as she pointed out the fallacies in my thinking. "I think you went way overboard about indigenous people and lost a lot of your credibility. Really, Joan, who cares about a few extinct tribes? What possible difference could it make? After all, as you well know, wisdom never dies. We just incorporate it and it enriches subsequent cultures."

"You're a Jew." I smiled and tried to break the ice with a joke. "Have you heard this one? What are the nine words that describe every Jewish holiday?" She looked at me warily. I replied, "They tried to kill us. We won. Let's eat."

"That's a good one." She relaxed a little.

"Maybe it's funny because of the relief we feel that we're still here after millennia of persecution and genocide. But now there are so few Jews left, and so many of us are secular. Doesn't the prospect of the final elimination of our tribe bother you—the fact that we may soon be extinct? Or do you think that's okay because somehow our wisdom will be incorporated and go on?"

"It'll never happen," she announced, evading the issue, "they'll never kill us all off." And that argument put to bed, she launched into a supportive tirade for the homogenization of culture. Malls create jobs. There is comfort in going anywhere in the world and finding a McDonald's. And furthermore, McDonald's in Russia or Paris is different from the one in Dubuque. They have local color.

"What about the local cows," I mused, thinking of the grazing economy that has destroyed the environments of indigenous cultures worldwide. "What about the cutting of the rain forests—the lungs of the planet for pastureland? Can we justify the destruction of animals and plants with medicinal value that we will surely need as more and more deadly viruses are released from their delicate niches in the ancient ecosystem to find new habitats in animals and humans that have no resistance to them? What about the fact that the grazing land created from the ravaged carcass of the rain forest lasts only three to five years before it turns to dust and blows away, leaving a sterile desert?"

I left these questions unvoiced because the woman probably could not hear them. She had obviously pigeonholed me as a "crunchy granola" from Boulder, a leftover from the sixties. I thought sadly, "The lady doth protest too much." But having once been in her mind-set myself, I recognized that her vehemence was, in part, an attempt to deny her own pain and to silence what her inner Self was telling her.

Women have had to work very hard to achieve entry into the predominantly male worlds of business, academia, and medicine. And there has been a price. Some of us have lost our connection to our own feminine natures and to God. In some settings we have lost our right to dress as we choose, wearing the same dark-colored, funereal suits as our male peers. Others have lost their health and even their sanity. My friend physician Christiane Northrup speaks of how we have struggled to become "junior males," forgetting what it is to be women. All this loss is in the name of gender equality.

Jungian analyst Judith Duerk wrote in *A Circle of Stones:*

Woman's Journey to Herself of how women defend themselves against the tyranny of working in a man's world, justify staying in it even when their bodies are urging them to quit. "The fears a woman may have before leaving the competitive mode may rage for a long time and make her defend dogmatically the activities that a deeper part of her already dimly senses are harming her. As she struggles toward new choice, she may not know where to turn for support. A woman speaks of her experience with illness: 'Part of what kept me in the professional world for so long was fear of what my women friends would say if I quit. They were all successful in their fields and disapproved copping out for any reason. When they were sick they were worse than any male boss in expecting themselves to overcome [it] . . . [They were] like drill sergeants . . . even with their children.' "

When the nagging sense that we are harming ourselves with our work persists, no matter how service oriented or interesting that work may be, an inner wisdom prompts us to defect or die. When I was slow in listening to this inner wisdom, although life felt seriously out of balance, a head-on collision made the situation painfully obvious. Jung might have called this event a synchronicity. The outer world was manifesting the inner struggle of coming to terms with myself. The inside and outside worlds met head-on. Not until faced with the seriousness of the situation for my psychological, spiritual, and physical health did I finally find the courage to leave.

There is a societal notion that leaving any situation is bad unless you know where you are going. This is the male aspect of goal orientation. We can't ascend the ladder until we know the steps. The male model dictates that we should be moving toward something rather than fleeing the past. But the idea that the future is always visible from the place where we stand is unrealistic. Sometimes we have to walk on for a while until a new horizon comes into view.

In the work world, where seminars speak of setting goals and objectives and then working relentlessly to obtain them, the apparently aimless exercise of walking without direction seems addled and unwise. Yet this is often an important theme of women's work and career stories. When we are walking Sarah's circle, there is no final destination. The process, the journey itself, is one of staying in alignment with what our own inner guidance is telling us. If we quit listening, we begin to feel anxious and inauthentic. The important relationship to our own spiritual Self, and our relationship to God, suffers.

"Where would you have me go, what would you have me do, what would you have me to say, and to whom?" A friend of mine who is a religious dropout repeats these words, which she found in *A Course in Miracles*, every day on her way to work. She knows that there is no separation between the sacred and the secular world. Another friend of mine, a liberal Jewish woman, is likewise concerned that her work life be spiritually guided and motivated by a desire for the highest good of all involved. The concept of *tikkun olam*, the healing of the world, directs her actions. Her rabbi might be surprised that she routinely speaks to her spirit guides about what to do at the office. They "zap" her, she says, referring to an odd sensation of electricity she feels at the crown of her head, if anything she says strays from the path of healing relationship.

I remember a film in which a Mafia don went to church. He prayed to God, confessed his sins, and then went out to deal drugs, run a numbers racket, and kill anyone who got in his way. If we are really walking Sarah's circle, we cannot behave in such a grossly fraudulent way. Even a minor lack of congruence between our spiritual beliefs and behavior is uncomfortable. Our inner body tells our outer one that we are off beam. We leave a job because of the sense that it is killing us, or because the corporate policies are killing the earth. We don't know yet where we are called to go. We leave anyway because some inner voice tells us that if we do not, there will be hell to pay. Then we wander for a while in the strange place called "don't know." Don't know where I am going. Don't know what is coming next. Don't know who I am anymore. This is courage, not confusion; it is wisdom, not folly. It creates the space for something new to be born.

Much as women are changing religion not by fighting it but by defecting from it, we are doing the same for business. The fastest-growing sector in the economy is women-owned small businesses. I own one of those businesses, Mind-Body Health Sciences, Inc. The only two full-time employees are my fabulous friend and business manager, Judy Dawson, and me. But we have many part-time employees and collaborators who work with us in women's retreats, courses in mind-body medicine, and spiritual getaways around the world. This community of friends and colleagues is what brings joy and growth to the work.

In the end, the value of our work is less about what we do and more a matter of who we are. Technique can help a therapist, for example, but not nearly as much as her presence as a human being, the wisdom and love she embodies. Women's spirituality is about that presence as we walk through daily life, at work and at home, seeking the place of the heart from which healing and joy naturally flow. As we come to the constricted places in our lives, the inner resources of humor and friendship, breathing and mindfulness can help establish a balance through which we get into the groove, the flow, and our lives become a spiritual expression of being that enriches whatever it is that we may be doing.

TAKING CARE OF OURSELVES

One of the hardest things about being a woman in a busy world is that we tend to put ourselves last on the to-do list. Caught up in a culture of doers, we become what many writers, male and female, have labeled human doings, instead of human beings. While both genders can fall into the doing trap, women have a harder time getting out. As Carol Gilligan has written, the central tension in a woman's life revolves around relationality. We are natural healers, intent upon reestablishing right relationship in the world. The big question becomes, "How can I get what I need without being selfish to others?" As long as we think that spending time on ourselves is selfish, the vicious jaws of the doing trap will stay locked around our ankles.

My husband, Kurt, laughs good-naturedly when I get trapped by a frenzied state of doing. I look like a cartoon of the thousand-armed goddess, simultaneously dusting, sorting piles, writing checks, answering mail, cooking, feeding the dogs, and cleaning the kitchen counters. The White Tornado will stop for nothing. Even when offered a hug, my body is liable to be as stiff as that of a pointer restrained on a leash when she has caught an interesting scent. I am everywhere but here. I am stunningly efficient, but not present.

When we come down from a frenzy and everything is finished in record time, we tend to be burned out, our blood pressure may be high, we are as lifeless as a wheat field in a drought and as irritable as a colicky baby. As an expert on stress, I understand full well that this kind of extremist guerrilla doing is a disservice to mind and body, but it is a discipline to be otherwise. For women on a mission, coming into a balance of right and left hemispheres, being and doing, doesn't come naturally.

One of my favorite women writers is Elizabeth Berg, whose stories often reflect that tension between being and doing, being true to ourselves when there is so much we want to do for others. I often use an excerpt from one of her insightful and engaging books, *The Pull of the Moon*, as the basis for sharing our stories at women's retreats. The book has a fascinating premise. A midlife woman by the name of Nan goes into a store where she finds a beautiful turquoise leather journal, an item to which she would not usually be attracted, and which at forty dollars seems far too expensive. Yet it seems to hold within it the promise of something dear and incalculably precious. She realizes that she could buy it and run away from home. And that is exactly what she does.

Nan takes a week-long road trip and records her inner and outer journey in two places: daily letters home to her husband, Martin, and entries in her journal. The striking difference between the two kinds of memoir is, in itself, a study in how differently we talk to men and women, including ourselves. In her first journal entry Nan writes of setting out on her trip. "I think I will not use a map. And I think I would like to stop at a house now and then and ask any woman I find there, how are you doing? No, but really. How are you doing?"

Along the way she does meet other women, immersing herself briefly in the stream of their lives, but in the main the trip is a swim in her own depths, a midlife retrospection and pause to chart a course for the second half of life.

She writes in her journal, "And now, in my own stillness, I hear something. 'Where have you been?' my inside body whispers to my outside one. Its sense of outrage is present, but dulled by the grief of abandonment. 'I had ideas. There were things to do. Where did you go?' What can I answer? Oh, I had some errands to run. I had a few things to do. I needed to get married and have a child and go underground for twenty-five years, be pleasantly suffocated. I meant to come back. But the bread crumbs got blown away."

When I read this excerpt to women, there is a soft chorus of aaahs, women's way of saying aaah-men. "That is true," we sigh in unison. "I know what she is talking about. The grief of self-abandonment is an unwanted visitor in my bed as well."

"What then," I ask the women, "are the bread crumbs that got blown away? What is it that connects you to the place inside where you feel rooted and at home with yourself, in a true state of being? When is it that you feel most authentic and present to your own true nature?"

Women sit in threes for this contemplation. One woman speaks—tells a part of her story for ten minutes or so—allowing memories and reflections to surface while a second woman listens with silent and rapt attention. She may mirror the speaker's story in her face or posture, but her job is to bear silent witness in a way that invites the speaker more deeply into herself. There is no interruption to the flow except for the occasional silences of the speaker, whirling like eddies in a river, swallowing the thread of conversation for a moment and spitting it back out again with sudden energy. The third woman sits with her eyes closed, listening, a kind of container for the other two. Each woman gets the opportunity to be speaker, listener, and container.

The discussion that results from listening to Nan's story and sharing our own often revolves around the fact that our authentic, spiritual selves emerge most strongly when we take time out to be, rather than when we discipline ourselves to do. This emergence of the authentic self during the being state includes not only work issues but also spiritual disciplines. When meditation and yoga are done with an attitude of "Better hurry up and do this so I can get enlightened and help everybody else," they can work against us.

I was curled up in bed with a book, in the early morning. And I was feeling guilty. It was a murder mystery, not even a book with redeeming social or spiritual value. Those double-D cup frontal lobes were working overtime, spurring me on to be good, to get out of bed and do something worthwhile. I could be cleaning the kitchen, preparing a lecture, meditating, calling a friend or colleague who had asked for some input. Shaking off the urge to rise and shine, I snuggled into the warmth of the old down comforter. I pulled our miniature schnauzer Squeezirat close and stroked his white beard and fuzzy tummy.

When I got up at 11:00 A.M., the murderer safely behind bars, my mind was unusually clear and empty. I pulled on my slippers, got a cup of coffee, and thought about how many things there are to enjoy, to love. I went out on the front deck, facing east over the prairie, feeling graced. The boards were warm beneath my feet. Without thinking about it, without trying to be holy, I sang the Jewish morning prayer to the bluebirds and sparrows. I did familiar chi gong exercises in a way that felt new to my body, knit it into the warm sun and the cool breeze, the mountains and the prairies. These activities came not from the mind, from the need to be good and spiritual, but from the heart. I did them not because they were righteous but because I could not resist them. Entrained by some deeper rhythm, I was called into being.

THE SYNERGY OF DOING AND BEING

Physician Larry Dossey calls being a form of prayer. By staying in bed to read, I entered a state of grace by allowing myself to rest, to empty, to follow the animal urge of the body to burrow beneath the comforter. The intention to be was, most likely, an unconscious form of prayer. But we can enter the state of being consciously as well, even while doing. This results in a flow state, when ideas and insights seem to come from a clear space, beyond our ordinary knowledge and perceptions. Touching genius, the synergy between being and doing is spirituality in action. It is a state of grace that erases the boundaries that separate us and restores us to wholeness, to holiness. Being feels like a homecoming, a sense of everything being right with the world. A natural high, this state is a connection with our own true nature, the Inner Light or spiritual Self.

The discipline of conscious being has a great deal to do with the breath. Right now (simply because I am thinking about it) I am centered in my breathing, feeling its gentle rise and fall as my tummy expands and presses against the edge of the computer desk with each inbreath. I can feel my lower back expanding as well, pressing into the firm yet comfortable chair, and am aware of the way that my feet rest on the floor. I sigh a little as the breath goes out, and relax into the chair. My hands and arms stay soft and supple in the process of writing and I can hear the soft tinkling of wind chimes outside the window, the rhythmic click of the computer keyboard.

If physical tension begins to build up in this state of conscious, synergistic being/doing, I am likely to notice it and get up to stretch, or rotate the shoulders. I am aware that the work is sacred, creative, that it is a privilege to be a writer. When our work is grounded in being, it is soulful and inspired by something beyond ourselves. In *Writing Down the Bones*, Zen practitioner Natalie Goldberg speaks of the preparation for writing as a kind of meditation, a being, a connection to the deeper reaches of self.

She writes, "Walk with an animal walk and take in everything around you as prey. Use your senses as an animal does. Watch a cat when he sees something moving in the room. He is perfectly still, and at the same time, his every sense is alive, watching, listening, smelling. This is how you should be when you are in the streets. . . . Be still—some part of you, at least—and know where you are, no matter how busy you are."

The process of shifting from doing to being has been described in many ways: the cultivation of mindfulness, the practice of the present moment, bringing the mind home, meditation, the fruit of gratitude, yoga. I remember my first attempt to cultivate being. I was in my midtwenties studying the weekly lessons of Paramahansa Yogananda's Self-Realization Fellowship. The lesson stressed the fact that breathing was the cornerstone of awareness. I was walking down the street in Boston's infamous "combat zone," the red-light district where Tufts Medical School, where I worked, was located. I was counting my steps, synchronizing my breath with the rhythm of walking, but had not yet expanded my awareness beyond the breath to what was around me.

I was trying so hard that my face was obviously scrunched up as if I had been sucking on a pickle. A "lady of the night" walked over to inquire as to whether anything was wrong. I was so startled, and so touched, that I instantly shifted into a state of gratitude. While still aware of my breath, I was simultaneously aware of body, surroundings, and the sweetness of this stranger—a person whom I might otherwise have judged negatively but who, in that moment, revealed the deeper essence of her own being.

In the spirit of teaching whatever it is you need to learn, I spent about a decade as a hatha yoga teacher. This is one of the easiest ways of moving into being, since each posture requires an attention to breathing and the physical sensations of the stretch. Every out-breath is an opportunity to let go into the flow of sensation and allow the body to relax a little bit more into the posture. Chi gong creates a similar experience of being. Even though I enjoy both of these body meditations immensely, I find myself doing them less and less these days. I am called more to walking and nature, the state of mindfulness informed by years of focused attention to breath and body movement.

When we feel stressed and isolated, out of synch with ourselves, the people around us, and the natural cues from the environment, it is hard to be. The spiritual core, the sun of wisdom and compassion that is always shining within our heart, gets obscured by our own dark thoughts. Healing, spirituality, is a state of coming back to harmony, synchronizing, coming into right relation with the multitude of forces around and within us. Many people, men and women alike, unconsciously seek time in nature for this reason.

BEING IN THE NATURAL WORLD

The corporate defector we met at the beginning of the chapter had a conscious recognition of the importance of nature. Rather than seeing it as a resource to be exploited for raw materials, she recognized it as precious in itself. One of the reasons she left her company was that she could no longer participate in the degradation of the natural world. Like indigenous people, who are of the earth, she spoke of how everything is interconnected, a part of what Native Americans call the Sacred Hoop. In the feminine worldview, we are called upon to take responsibility for our part in the Hoop. Unlike the expansionist vision where human beings are preeminent, with dominion over the earth, in the emergent feminine vision we are simply a part of things, no more or less important than a tree, or a dog, or a river.

Sometimes I long for the old times in the Americas, where, contrary to unfounded scientific opinion, the indigenous peoples did not die young from disease. In fact, disease was so rare among the Plains Indians that there weren't even words to describe it. People routinely lived into their eighties and nineties. Many were a hundred or more. They worked for an average of only about five hours a day, and lived in harmony with an Earth that was their Mother, their Grandmother.

My friend Rima has a mindful relationship to nature like that of the old, indigenous peoples. She works hard to maintain nature in its pristine state both in her own backyard and in the larger world. People love to visit Rima's mountaintop retreat because her home is a sanctuary not only for wildlife but also for people. Visiting this place of clouds and trees, grasses and wildflowers, coyotes, mountain lions, deer, rabbits, and birds is an invitation to being that is hard to resist. It is quiet there, both outside and inside. You can hear the wind and the sound of your own breathing.

Shortly after moving to our little mountain town, I paid Rima a visit in her home, made from stones gathered from the surrounding meadows, and heated only by the sun and a small woodstove. Her beautiful jewel of a home is at ground level and feels like a natural extension of the earth. Unlike my home, which is set high over the land, Rima's place seems like part of the earth itself. The wildlife must think so as well. The first thing I noticed on that early spring day was the enormous number of birds, and their music. Enchanted, I made my way through the meadow, encountering a pair of rabbits grazing.

Arriving at Rima's door, gentle lessons in being a part of nature began. She pointed out a small trail that led from her driveway. She suggested that I walk back that way, rather than over the meadow, so as not to disturb the wild plants and the homes of rabbits and voles. It was so clear how my usual get-there-quick approach not only inhibited mindfulness of the natural world but was also sometimes destructive of it. When I walk the hills now, the plants seem alive, with identities like those of people. Like many residents of the mountain, I know hundreds of plants personally, stopping by to check on their progress at different times of the year. Stepping around them, careful to leave as little human trace as possible, I leave them to weave their spell of beingness for the next passerby.

White Buffalo Calf Woman reminded the Lakota that the earth is our Mother, our Grandmother. It is our closest, most primal source of nourishment. It is the womb in which we spend all our days. We can rest our heads upon her breast, hear her heartbeat, celebrate her bounty. It is an act of soul to seek refuge there, and to protect this beautiful earth, our home, for future generations.

SURRENDERING WITH HUMOR

It is hard to feel mindful, to maintain a state of being in a world where happiness is gauged by material success. We have too little time in a natural world that is disappearing in the wake of what we call progress, where time is money, and the stress of too much e-mail may be clogging our arteries as well as our hard drives. Every year the government invents new forms to fill out. Catalogue companies reproduce like rabbits and send hundreds of pounds of slick advertising our way every year. When my guard is down, and I'm feeling stressed, I am likely to take refuge in the offerings of L.L. Bean. If I'm too busy to go on a camping trip to recharge my batteries, at least I can buy a new camp stove or a brightly colored anorak. It arrives and sits in the closet. I am still too busy. The beast roars louder. Simplify.

"Sell the children," I think. That would simplify life. I am still paying tuition, still worrying about them. "Marry someone rich. Maybe you should have listened to your mother, an ophthalmologist might have done nicely," the inner cynic continues. I read the homely, wise prose about simplifying life in women's magazines. Tidy the house, shop less, make time for friends, unplug the phone and fax and go off-line for a while. I do these things, I think, with a small glow of satisfaction. But they are not enough. The older I get, the louder the beast roars. "I mean really simplify."

I consider this. I am not a high-maintenance woman. I don't

crave a lot of stuff or spend a lot of money on much of anything but books. Basically, I like money because I can give it away to people who need it more. We have considered selling everything and moving to a small cabin somewhere. But in the absence of a loving community of friends and family, that kind of simplicity loses its appeal. The cost would be too high, although some people have made such moves quite successfully.

Perhaps the most neglected and simplest form of simplicity lies in surrender. We live in a busy world that shows no signs of slowing down. As all the polls indicate, women are even busier than men. Those who work outside the home have a second full-time job inside the home. Unless we win the lottery, that's unlikely to change. If I unplug my phone and fax machine too often I'll lose business. If I let the house get too dirty, we'll get cholera. I believe that learning to accept what is, with some sense of humor, is a crucial ingredient in the spirituality of being.

Generally an easygoing person, I do tend to lose my balance when it comes to housecleaning. Miss Spiritual turns into the Gestapo. All the males in my life have been less tidy than I. My husband, Kurt, adorable as he is, is like a blender on legs. Rooms turn into vortices of destruction in his wake, even though he tries his level best to keep things organized. So what is a woman to do? Clean up and feel resentful or live in an undeclared state of emergency? While you may not view this as a spiritual matter, it is. It affects one's state of being, thoughts, actions, and relationships.

Having author and PBS star Loretta LaRoche as my friend and humor guru has helped me find a more spiritual way to live. I surrender to the fact that as many times as the house gets cleaned, it will inevitably degenerate into chaos once again. Perpetual battles with tidiness are a joke. Whether or not we choose to get the jokes in our life is a personal choice. When we see our neuroses as amusing, they become a source of nurture rather than distress.

I once cofacilitated a weekend women's retreat with Loretta and physician and chi gong teacher Martha Howard. Judging from the laughter and knowing nods in the group as Loretta spoke, I discovered that mine was not the only household where, when the toilet paper roll runs out, I am apparently the only one with enough mechanical expertise to replace it. If the toilet paper runs out when someone else is using it, the new roll is installed perilously at the edge of the sink. Over the years I had added the mantra, "Oh, me, poor me, I am the only one who changes the toilet paper (and paper towel) rolls," to my internal list of martyred grievances.

Loretta gave us a great stress-busting idea. If your husband, lover, roommate, child, co-worker, or whoever can't master the art of putting a new roll of toilet paper in the dispenser, don't follow the normal modus operandi of doing it yourself while steaming about the fact that it would never get done without you. Instead, get a strong piece of twine and hang a new roll of toilet paper around your neck, hiding any remaining rolls. When the members of your household or business complain about being out of toilet paper, all you have to do is say, "Oh, really. Well, I've got mine."

Humor is a form of graceful surrender, a realization that life is never going to be perfect in just the ways we think it should be. I have never actually worn toilet paper as a pendant, but the very thought helps me realize that there is a joke here, and I am it. It is not worth wasting energy in resentment over such small stuff. Either we have to tell people to shape up in a way that makes an impression, wear our toilet paper rolls proudly, put new rolls on the edge of the sink ourselves, or continue to put it in the dispenser with a sense of humor. Life is too short to lose our peace of mind to a roll of toilet paper.

PEACE OF MIND IS THE JOURNEY
AND THE DESTINATION

Perhaps the best indication of whether we are walking Sarah's circle is peace of mind. In the ladder model of men, heaven is a promise of things to come, as is a close relationship to God. In the circular model, heaven is now, and God is already and always was here. We find the Divine in the light of our own intuition, by growing into an authentic sense of self, by seeing God in other people and in the natural world, and by doing what comes naturally, bringing out the best potential in others by mirroring the goodness inside of them. When we are doing this, the peace of mind that is our birthright shines through.

We have used the metaphor of the spiritual Self as a sun that shines within the heart. That peaceful sun, whose rays are wisdom and compassion, is always shining. But when clouds of self-doubt and fear, judgment, and unforgiveness cloud our inner horizon, we cannot see the sun's true light. If you, like many women, still harbor resentment at the ways in which religion has devalued women, that old anger surely clouds the Light within. Although anger is a first step to taking our power back, it has to be let go of in order for us to continue the relational journey and to find peace.

We have discussed how old anger, which lives on as continual resentment, can block the development of faith and stand in the way of the religious tolerance that is key to the feminine path. If we are angry at a patriarchal God, it may be hard to respect the faith of a woman who loves, and is deeply nurtured by God the Father. If we insist that our own way of naming God is the only way, then we will fall out of the relational path that most clearly sustains us. The feminine path requires living the advice of Miriam Therese Winter, knowing that the household of God is big enough for all.

We have discussed faith as an integral part of Sarah's circle. For women, faith is less a matter of belief in dogma than a personal experience that parts the clouds of self-doubt and enables a healing into our peaceful, wise spiritual Self. My pilgrimage to India not only reaffirmed my faith in God but was also a profound teaching in how God speaks to us through other people, through relationship. When I became trapped by the insistent desire to categorize my experience, to know whether Sai Baba was really a divine incarnation, I lost peace of mind. It took the wisdom of a stranger, the Indian reflexologist, to remind me of what I had forgotten. God can be known only through the fruits of the divine relationship in our lives. I would have to live along into a relationship with Sai Baba, rather than putting him on some kind of unreachable pedestal. If I were to ask him for guidance, would my life be enriched by that guidance?

Step by step, day by day, walking Sarah's circle develops an open mind and an open heart. The woman's spiritual journey calls us to trust the moment-to-moment unfolding of our lives. It is a radical call to complete trust even though the future is unsure. No plan is perfect. At any time we may have to abandon ship and jump into the unknown. There is no pot of gold at the end of the rainbow; the journey itself is our destination.

The stories of our lives, and the ways in which we develop trust and live our faith, are an integral part of the feminine path to God. I am forever grateful for the years I spent as a therapist because of all the stories I heard. Everyone suffers. Buddha's First Noble Truth stated just that, to live is to suffer. The ways in which we turn that suffering into growth and learn to experience joy in an imperfect world are the stuff of mutual inspiration. Mythic stories like that of Eve and Lilith can similarly help us understand our personal stories. They provide a framework for the way in which women grow. As we reclaim the true meaning of these precious stories, freeing them from the negative interpretations of the misogynist cultures in which they were first told, they can give us a template for the journey to our deepest selves, to the indwelling God.

When our Eve nature, our innocent acceptance of our limitations, is challenged by the inner Lilith to move beyond the comfortable walls of the garden, we grow. Drawing closer to the Inner Light, we listen to the guidance that leads us into new experience, an expanded world of relationship. Just as Eve and Lilith needed each other's company on the journey, so do we need the company of other women. When Lilith came to Jan on our snake walk, the relationship between us was integral to the experience. Her awakening and healing from fear became an anchor for my own continued healing and the growth of my faith that God is always with us, working mysteriously through other people and through synchronicities.

Because the feminine path to God has not been clearly articulated, role models for the journey are few. As you read the stories of women like yourself, and thought about women you know, perhaps you identified living role models, as my friend Janet Quinn is for me. Perhaps the ancient story of Mary Magdalene provided another role model, albeit of more mythic proportions although she once walked the earth as we do.

Perhaps there are so few role models because the feminine journey is egalitarian. It is based on honesty rather than perfection. Our culture expects role models to be perfect, which no one is. Paragons of perfection are placed on pedestals, from which they usually fall with considerable ruckus. But the model for the feminine path can never occupy such a lofty and remote place. Our failings and vulnerabilities, and the honest way that we work with these realities of life, are what women look for in a role model. The women we admire most are simply other human beings, dealing with their hopes and fears with integrity and openheartedness.

Whether you are a loyalist, a returnee, or a religious dropout, I hope that you have found ways to deepen your spiritual life in our time together. Communities of worship containing both men and women are rich and varied. You may belong to one that works well for you. But in addition to worshipping in a church or synagogue, you may want to add a women's spiritual circle to your life. If you are a religious dropout, such circles have the benefit of providing an anchor, a home in which to deepen faith through relational connection and sharing prayers.

The most basic message of Sarah's circle is simple. Our lives are our paths. Every form of relationship is a relationship to God. We don't have to do great things in the world, to go on a hero's journey, in order to realize our potential and find our place in the household of God. We don't have to repent of who we are to find God. We have only to love as deeply as we can, using every part of our embodied selves to be present. In our mindfulness, in our attention, we mirror the creation back to the Creator. When we do that we feel grateful. And in our gratitude our safety and peace of mind are secured.

When we have learned to trust ourselves and to have faith in God, even amid the sufferings and unfairness of the world, we become a healing and revealing presence to those around us. They know themselves more fully because of who we are. Our presence is like the sun that causes plants to reach upward for the light. Through other people's relationship to our authentic spiritual Selves, we ourselves are mutually mirrored and revealed, deepened and expanded. In this intimate place of being, the heart's true home, we reach the culmination of the journey through one another.

THE HEALING OF
THE WORLD

And Strangers Shall Be as Friends

W hen we walk Sarah's circle, bringing out the peace and wisdom of the Inner Light within each other, the world around us moves into greater harmony. Like the pendulum of a powerful clock, we entrain other pendulums in our rhythm. Strangers become friends, and our inner peace is mirrored back in the world around us.

Many women are also working outwardly for world peace and healing within their communities. Some of them are nationally known like Marion Wright Edelman of the Save the Children Foundation and the late Mother Teresa. Others work behind the scenes, counseling heads of state. Women the world over are saddened, grief stricken, and frustrated by the continuing holocausts, ethnic cleansings, and violence born of intolerance and competition for scarcer and scarcer resources. These things will change not only by the important work, the doings of women concerned with the world as a web of relationships, but also by the subtle power of our being, our spiritual presence as we walk on a path of our own, creating a world of greater understanding and tolerance.

In 1997 a window in time opened between a business trip to Crete and a conference at which I was scheduled to speak in New York City. My husband and I used the four precious days to fly to Israel and explore the ancient city of Jerusalem and the ruins of Masada near the Dead Sea. I had been drawn to Israel for most of my childhood, had watched the movie *Exodus* over and over as a teenager. There was adventure and romance in fighting for freedom. There was meaning in the tired, the weary, the survivors of not just one brutal Holocaust but thousands, coming home again. This seemed a bigger, more mythic life than the privileged and stultifying boredom of suburbia.

My friends went to Israel with their Jewish youth groups. But I, who was consumed with longing, did not go. I could not go because of the certainty that if I did, I would never return. I would make aliyah, emigrate. Somehow I knew that my destiny lay here in the United States, so I buried the longing for Eretz Yisroel, the Land of Israel. But like a shadow, it had always been with me, dodging in and out of sight.

When I first started spending the summers at a Zionist camp at the age of eight, the state of Israel was only six years old. We were both war babies. Every summer we sang Hebrew songs in celebration of freedom. We glowed with pride that our people had taken a barren desert and made it bloom. Instead of playing capture the flag, we played capture the oil from the Arabs, who, without thinking, we embraced as "the enemy." We raised money to plant trees in the Israeli desert. There was a vicarious thrill in relating to the strength of the sabras (native-born Israeli Jews) and others who had fought for the land. But we experienced both a deeper meaning of a safe homeland, and a chilling terror, the morning we awakened to find a swastika painted over the yellow Jewish Star that was the central motif of our camp's sign.

At nine or ten years old I knew nothing about the Holocaust, but some of the other girls did. We huddled together as those in the know told us about concentration camps, dead family members, friends and relatives who were Holocaust survivors, and a demon called Adolph Hitler. One girl earnestly assured us that Hitler had committed suicide and no longer posed a threat. Another was just as sure that the death was faked. The Nazis were gathering forces in Argentina, she whispered earnestly, preparing to take over the United States and kill all the Jews and blacks. I slept with a large rock in my hand for weeks, ready to fight for our lives.

Although my brother had been chased home from school by Irish Catholic boys who taunted him for being a Christ killer, I was a relative neophyte to discrimination in general and anti-Semitism in particular. It never occurred to me that when my bunk spontaneously changed a game of capture the flag into capture the oil from the Arabs, we were participating in another face of anti-Semitism. In my lack of understanding, I failed to recognize the plight of Arabs dispossessed from their homeland when the state of Israel was established. So many languished in squalid camps while their dreams festered into nightmares. My Hebrew name is Yehudah, which derives from the word *Judaea*, the ancient name for the land of the goddess Asherah and her consort Tammuz, the land of Elohim for the Jews, the sacred world of Muhammad, and finally of the rabbi Jesus and the Christian religion that sprang from his teachings.

Even though I had not thought of myself as a religious Jew for thirty-five years, when I stepped off the plane in Tel Aviv my whole body shuddered with recognition. The desert sands whispered the ancient litany of belonging, "You are Yehudah, daughter of Fegeleh (my mother's Yiddish name), daughter of Sarah. Your foremothers were Sarah and Miriam, Rebekah, Leah, Deborah, and Rachel. Miriam of Magdala and Miriam the mother of Yehoshuah were your sisters. Their blood flows in your veins. The patriarch Abraham sired Yitzhak, the Jewish name of your father. Abraham sired Ishmael by Sarah's Egyptian serving maid, the concubine Hagar, as well. And Ishmael became the patriarch of the Islamic faith, surely also your relatives. You have come home, daughter."

Kurt and I entered the Old City of Jerusalem late in the day, when long shadows were beginning to fall over the ancient ruins and colorful modern bazaars. Here was the cradle of the three religions of the Book: Judaism, Christianity, and Islam. And here was a living tribute not to the fact that we are all relations but that we are historically enemies. A guide approached us in the street. Would we like to tour the city? What religion were we? I wondered whether the guide was Arab, Jew, or Christian and what he thought about tourists of other religions. It felt incomprehensibly sad that this sacred place had been a killing ground for thousands of years.

I looked up at him and smiled. "We're Native Americans," I said, choosing neutral territory. My husband, with his obsidian eyes and long braids, looked the part. Though I, with blue eyes and reddish brown hair did not, the guide probably didn't know or care anyway. He just wanted to do his job and support his family, maybe bring us to a cousin's or uncle's shop and sell us a few souvenirs.

As we toured the four quarters of the city, we were equally mesmerized by the Jewish and Christian sites, while feeling excluded from the Islamic sites, many of which were off-limits to nonbelievers, or infidels. The Dome of the Rock, housed in an Islamic mosque on the Mount of Olives, is reputedly the site where Abraham bound his son Isaac for sacrifice and where Muhammad ascended to heaven. Jesus, too, is supposed to have ascended from the Mount of Olives, and it is here that the Moshiach, the Messiah of the Jews, is prophesied to come.

We trudged from site to site, from the tomb of Mary to the room where the Last Supper was held, to the Western Wall—the only remaining part of the sacred Second Temple of Israel. The Wailing Wall, as it is usually called by Gentiles, is the holiest place in the world for Jews. I longed to go and pray there. But that was for another day.

Most of the next morning was spent in a bank getting local currency since ATM cards didn't work in Israel. An Arab woman was in line ahead of me. We kept smiling at each other. She was dressed in a typical black chador, her head modestly covered. I was dressed in colorful Western street clothes, quite immodest by her standards. We didn't speak each other's language, but we shared a deeper language. We were women. There was an easy bond between us that seemed to reach across cultures and religions. I could imagine sitting down to tea with her and discussing our lives, laughing with the careless ease of women speaking of friends and families. And yet, historically and politically, we were supposed to be enemies.

"If the world were run by women," I thought, "there would be far fewer enemies." At that unexpressed thought, this stranger looked deeply into my eyes and smiled so radiantly that I thought she must have read my mind. Our wombs were in silent communication. They told the stories left out of religious Scripture and history books. They reached across the chasm between cultures to murmur the tales of women who were doing their best to bring love and healing to their families, to their communities. For thousands of years we Middle Eastern women had been trying to make sense out of violence, bandaging the wounds of sons and husbands. "We could pray together, this Arab woman and I," I thought. "We could work together for peace."

From the bank we proceeded directly to the Jewish Quarter of the Old City, where we passed by guards and through metal detectors to reach the Western Wall. It is split into two sections. Men on the left and women on the right. I took my place against the ancient stones, reached out to touch them and to feel the many stories they had witnessed. They were cool and comforting even in the midday heat.

My wallet was filled with prayers that friends, Jew and Gentile alike, had given me to place in the cracks between the stones. These days you can even fax prayers to Israel, and volunteers will place them in the holy crevices of the wall. I took out the small scraps of white and yellow paper, made rich by the prayers for peace and healing scratched onto them. It was a minor struggle to find unoccupied niches in a wall sprouting paper slips of grief, gratitude, hope, and remembrance.

The prayers installed, I looked around, trying to get some sense of protocol. But there wasn't any. Some women read from prayer books. Others davened, rhythmically praying and swaying back and forth, their heads brushing the hoary stones. Some leaned against the wall and sang. And most of us wept. Something about the place melts away the veneer of complacency that coats the rawness of our souls. The deep well of pain over the inhumanity rampant in the world overflows. There is wailing here, after all.

The suffering that millions of people had experienced in Jerusalem for thousands of years shook my bones with a chill. The destruction of two temples, the waves of oppression by Romans, Babylonians, Philistines, Christians, Arabs, and Jews seemed simultaneously present. But I also sensed the holiness, the hope of healing that radiated from this place. The ongoing prayers of Jews, Christians, and Muslims, which reach beyond differences to the realization that all people are related, seemed somehow to comfort me.

Jerusalem is said by some to be the center of the planet, the heart of the world. It is a city that speaks to your soul. This city of gold, its alabaster stones glinting in the desert sun, readily spawns apocalyptic fantasies of death and resurrection. It is easy to believe that you can hear the ancient heartbeat of God beneath the cobblestones. Time to heal. Time to heal. Time to heal. If we do not, it is also easy to imagine that the next world war may break out here. The Middle East is a powder keg, and we don't need ancient prophecies to understand that it is connected by a short fuse to the economic and political interests of all the world's superpowers.

I was depressed at the thought of war, tears of anguish staining the stones of the wall. I began to pray the Native American way, as we do in the sweat lodge. *Mitakuye oyasin,* "all my relations," was the prayer of my heart. May we all be whole. May there be harmony within and among people. May the prophecy of the nineteenth-century Lakota warrior, Crazy Horse, come true. May people of all four colors—red, black, white, and yellow—from all the directions of the earth come together under the Great Tree of Peace.

Praying gave way to a moment of silence. As if on cue, the old woman next to me began to chant a solemn prayer. I couldn't understand the Hebrew, but it seemed to speak of the solidarity of people of good heart. Her soft, shaky voice was soon joined by the reedy tones of a small girl, perhaps six or seven years old, standing on the other side of me. The song of the two strangers touched the tender place of hope inside. I thought we were attended by the ghosts of an unbroken chain of women praying, singing, grieving, teaching, and birthing all through the history of Jerusalem, a history written almost exclusively through the eyes of the men.

Another ancient prophecy came to mind. "This is the time of the women." Sweet Medicine, a Lakota holy man and prophet with the stature of Jesus to his people, had spoken of how the Sacred Hoop would be broken. Hundreds of years ago, he entrusted the four sacred arrows of his people to the women to bury until the time of renewal. For it was the women, he was sure, who would lead the way to the mending of the circle, the healing of the world.

For many years the masculine aspect of autonomy, expansion, and conquest has predominated in Western society. There has not been a balance with the feminine aspect of healing and interdependence. The circle of life, the Sacred Hoop, has been broken. Many of the indigenous peoples of the world have been eradicated. Many species of plants and animals are extinct or endangered. Wars, famine, and holocausts continue. But the feminine spirit is on the rise. Women are becoming progressively more socially active, and many men are cultivating their feminine aspect.

Vickie Downey, a Tewa Indian from the Tesuque Pueblo in New Mexico, says, "It's the time of the feminine. With a woman it's what we feel. When I look around at different women I see sadness and a heaviness in themselves. What they're experiencing is what the earth is experiencing—her sadness and her heaviness because of the way that her children are living today. Women, they have that; the feeling is there in their hearts more so than the male people, 'cause the male is always doing things. The male also has to realize that he has a female part to him, and he has to start feeling that same feeling."

When men and women view one another as commodities, or even enemies, there can be no peace within families or among nations. Vickie Downey's simple description of how each person embodies both the male and the female principles within them is the start of tolerance. Tolerance is the seed of understanding. Understanding is the mother of empathy. And empathy is the universal expression of spirituality through which we are all related.

Kuan Yin is the Chinese bodhisattva of compassion, the One Who Hears the Cries of the World. She is said to be a dangerous goddess because she walks her own path, unencumbered by dogma, creeds, and rules. Like a she-bear, she is ferocious in the service of life, a fierce destroyer who battles fear and ignorance. She is also a source of solace, love, and protection. A collection of one hundred poems is associated with her worship. They are used for divination. You open the book and see where your finger lands, how the words of the poem relate to your life. Kuan Yin holds up a candle so that we can see the next step in our journey to God.

I consulted her prophetic poems to find an ending to our time together. She offered us poem number twenty-one. It is entitled "Together." Numerologically, twenty-one is the product of seven and three. It seems a fitting summary of the woman's journey to God. Seven is a number sacred to all the world's religions. There are seven branches on the Jewish tree of life. There are seven sacraments, seven chakras, and seven heavens. Siddhartha Gautama walked around the bodhi tree seven times before he sat down for his final meditation from which he awakened from illusion as a Buddha. There are seven directions: the four cardinal points, above, below, and within. Inanna had to pass through seven gates on the way to the death of her ego and her rebirth into Truth and the Art of Lovemaking. Mary Magdalene, too, was purged of seven devils before she became the spiritual partner of Jesus. Three is the face of Mystery itself. Whenever two or more of us are gathered in any Holy Name, that spirit of guidance is there with us.

Kuan Yin speaks to us across the ages,

The Ultimate and Heaven together make the yin-yang way,
And the melding of man and woman is joyously the same—
So the dragon shall coil and twist with the snake . . .
And together they shall come into the same dreaming Garden.

ENDNOTES

Preface

The inspiration, and part of the information about the bear, was provided by Terry Tempest Williams, *An Unspoken Hunger*. Vintage Books, New York, 1994, p. 53.

Introduction

The title of the introduction, The Household of God Is Big Enough for All, was taken from a phrase in the introduction of *Defecting in Place: Women Claiming Responsibility for Their Own Spiritual Lives*, Miriam Therese Winter, Adair Lummis, and Allison Stokes, Crossroad, New York, 1995.

The quotations from essays by Mary Daly and Elisabeth Schussler Fiorenza were taken from an article by Mary Helen Gillespie entitled "The New Feminine Spirituality," which appeared in the *Boston Sunday Herald*, Sunday People, on April 4, 1993.

The statistics about what proportion of the baby boom generation are religious loyalists, dropouts, or returnees can be found in the book by Wade Clark Roof, *A Generation of Seekers: The Spiritual Journeys of the Baby Boomers.* HarperSanFrancisco, 1994.

. . . feminist women are distinguishing between religion and spirituality. . . . Miriam Therese Winter, Adair Lummis, and Allison Stokes, *Defecting in Place: Women Claiming Responsibility for Their Own Spiritual Lives.* Crossroad, New York, 1995, p. 194.

The story by E. M. Broner of sitting shivah for a lost love can be found in *Four Centuries of Jewish Women's Spirituality: A Sourcebook,* edited and with introductions by Ellen M. Umansky and Dianne Ashton. Beacon Press, Boston, 1992, pp. 275–76.

How would you feel if "every time a professor says 'womankind' she means, of course, 'all humanity'?" This thought experiment was cited by Cullen Murphy in *The Word According to Eve: Women and the Bible in Ancient Times and Our Own.* Houghton Mifflin, Boston and New York, 1998, p. 8.

The self, myself, while wrestling with these issues was also—in my own writing, in my own praying, in my own loving—more and more encountering a strange and enormous God. . . . Sara Maitland, *A Big Enough God: A Feminist's Search for a Joyful Theology.* Riverhead Books, New York, 1995, pp. 4–5.

Only 151 of 1,400 people who are referred to by name in the Hebrew Bible . . . These and other fascinating facts about the gender gap in religion are referred to by Cullen Murphy in *The Word According to Eve: Women and the Bible in Ancient Times and Our Own.* Houghton Mifflin, Boston and New York, 1998.

This survey made me realize how little time I have devoted in the past year to my spiritual growth. . . . Miriam Therese Winter, Adair Lummis, and Allison Stokes, *Defecting in Place: Women Claiming Responsibility for Their Own Spiritual Lives.* Crossroad, New York, 1995, p. 173.

Chapter 1

If you are interested in reading more about Sai Baba, four books are particularly good to start with:

Brian Steel, *The Sathya Sai Baba Compendium*. Samuel Weiser, Inc., York Beach, ME, 1997. This is a thoroughly indexed compilation of facts, stories, and definitions of Sanskrit terms, plus an excellent bibliography.

Erlander Haraldsson, *Miracles Are My Visiting Cards: An Investigative Report on the Psychic Phenomena Associated with Sathya Sai Baba*. Century Paperbacks, London, 1987.

Phyllis Krystal, *Sai Baba: The Ultimate Experience*. Aura Books, Los Angeles, 1985. Reprinted by Samuel Weiser, Inc., York Beach, ME, 1994.

Howard Murphet, *Sai Baba: Man of Miracles*. Muller, London, 1971. Reprinted by Samuel Weiser, Inc., York Beach, ME, 1973.

Chapter 2

Such obstacles to women's freedom, they asserted . . . From Maureen Fitzgerald's Foreword to *The Woman's Bible*, Elizabeth Cady Stanton. Northeastern University Press, Boston, 1993, p. xii.

Details concerning the life of Elizabeth Cady Stanton came, in part, from the excellent article entitled "What Really Happened at Seneca Falls," by Louise Bernikow, published in *Ms. Magazine* as part of their hundred-fifty-year celebration issue of the first women's rights convention, which took place in Seneca Falls, NY, in 1848. *Ms. Magazine*, vol. 9, no. 1, pp. 66–67 July/August 1998.

. . . and referring to the writers as unattractive "old maids" or "mannish women, like hens that crow." Ibid.

He has made her, morally, an irresponsible being, as she can commit many crimes with impunity, provided they be done in the presence of her husband. . . . The Declaration of Sentiments, Ibid., pp. 67–68.

. . . fraudulently deprived of their most sacred rights. Ibid., p. 67.

The Bible teaches that woman brought sin and death into the world. . . . Elizabeth Cady Stanton, Introduction to *The Woman's Bible*. Northeastern University Press, Boston, 1993.

If you would enjoy reviewing the forbidden tales of the Bible, *The Harlot by the Side of the Road* is a great way to do that. Many of the horrific tales left out in Sunday school are featured, including the rape of Tamar by her brother Amnon. Their father, David, a religious hero reviled in *The Woman's Bible*, is a party to that terrible crime.

He was ruled entirely by his passions. . . . Ibid., p. 57.

A rediscovered language of sacred sisterhood can change the world. . . . Brenda Peterson, *Sister Stories: Taking the Journey Together.* Viking, New York, 1996, p. 93.

The version of the Twenty-third Psalm is a composite of the King James and Revised Standard versions, true to Margaret's memory of how the psalm was repeated in the church of her childhood.

Chapter 3

And he dreamed that there was a ladder set up on the earth. . . . Genesis 28:12, The Holy Bible, Revised Standard Version. Thomas Nelson, Nashville, 1972.

Leaving his home the man must set out on a path of individuation. . . . Daniel Levinson, *The Seasons of a Man's Life.* Ballantine Books, New York, 1978, p. 21.

The left half, or the left hemisphere of the brain, is the seat of logic. . . . Mona Lisa Schulz, M.D., Ph.D., *Awakening Intuition.* Harmony Books, New York, 1998, p. 57.

Mona Lisa Schulz's story about the neuroscientist driving in England can be found on p. 64 of *Awakening Intuition.*

The research on brain-laterality shifts during the menstrual cycle was performed by M. Altemus, B. Wexler, and N. Boulis, "Neuropsychological Correlates of Menstrual Mood Changes." *Psychosomatic Medicine* 51:329–36, 1989.

The study by David Skuse et al., from the Institute of Child Health in London, was published in the prestigious journal *Nature* on June 11, 1997. It was immediately picked up by all the major wire services and many popular magazines. The proposed gene was cited as a genetic basis for women's intuition and led to speculation that the gene may be inoperative in the maternal X chromosome inherited by boys because social competence and empathy might be disadvantageous in hunting and war. In other words, it's hard to kill if you can identify with the prey. The premise of Skuse, that boys need stricter social education, opened the Pandora's box of gender bickering. Skuse commented that he didn't think they had found the gene for criminal behavior, but the implication was that such behavior was much easier for males than for females because of genetic differences in empathy.

When a man sells his daughter as a slave, she shall not go out as the male slaves do. . . . Exodus, 21:7–11, The Holy Bible, Revised Standard Version. Thomas Nelson, Nashville, 1972.

You shall not wrong a stranger or oppress him, for you were strangers in the land of Egypt. . . . Exodus 22:21–27, Ibid.

In this love, you are understood as you are without mask or pretension. . . . John O'Donohue, *Anam Cara*. HarperCollins, New York, 1997, p. 14.

Chapter 4

Let us make man in our image, after our likeness. . . . Genesis 1:27. The Holy Bible, Revised Standard Version. Thomas Nelson, Nashville, 1972.

To my people, God is the Creator, our Grandfather, the Great Spirit, and we see him everywhere in all his creation. . . . In an essay by Wawokiya Win, In *The Divine Mosaic: Women's Images of the Sacred Other.* Yes International Publishers, St. Paul, 1994, pp. 205–208.

Nor did they understand that in worship they called 'primitive,' we were respecting and connecting to/with the unseen power that governs the universe. . . . Gloria Wade-Gayles, from the Introduction to *My Soul Is a Witness: African-American Women's Spirituality.* Beacon Press, Boston, 1995, p. 6.

. . . prostration of the priest, pouring of libations, invocations of saints and ancestors, African instruments, African American spiritual and gospel songs, and the Eucharist . . . Ibid., p. 244.

. . . the "extreme principle of God manifest in the image of Gongoro . . ." From the essay "God Dances," by Akiko Kobayashi, in *The Divine Mosaic: Women's Images of the Sacred Other.* Yes International Publishers, St. Paul, 1994, p. 68.

Even I, who live in modern times, feel like worshipping an old man whenever I see one praying silently in a temple or a graveyard because it reminds me of the great spirit of the space into which he will soon dissolve. Ibid., p. 69.

The Christian Spaniards felt that space-earth had been given to humanity by God and that humans had a right to claim it, to use it for their own good. . . . Jeanette Rodriguez, *Our Lady of Guadalupe: Faith and Empowerment among Mexican-American Women.* University of Texas Press, Austin, 1994, p. 7.

. . . the Mother of God, who is the God of Truth; the Mother of the Giver of Life; the Mother of the Creator; the Mother of the One who makes the sun and the earth; and the Mother of the One who is near. . . . From an essay by Jeanette Rodriguez, "God Is Always Pregnant," in *The Divine Mosaic: Women's Images of the Sacred Other.* Yes International Publishers, St. Paul, 1994, p. 116.

This fair lovely word 'mother' is so sweet and so kind. . . . Julian of Norwich, *Showings.* Paulist Press, New York, 1978, p. 299.

Female and male, called yin and yang in Tao, give joy to each other. . . . Dr. Lily Siou, in the essay "The Voice of God, The Mother of Life," in *The Divine Mosaic: Women's Images of the Sacred Other.* Yes International Publishers, St. Paul, 1994, pp. 149–50.

"O Birther! Father-Mother of the Cosmos . . ." The translation of the Lord's Prayer from the original Aramaic can be found in Neil Douglas-Klotz, *Prayers of the Cosmos: Meditations on the Aramaic Words of Jesus.* Harper & Row, San Francisco, 1990, p. 12.

Chapter 5

Human presence is a creative and turbulent sacrament, a visible sign of invisible grace. . . . John O'Donohue, *Anam Cara: A Book of Celtic Wisdom.* Cliff Street Books, New York, 1997, pp. xvi–xvii.

Our mothers told us that we should wait for the right man to come along. . . . Carmen Renee Berry and Tamara Traeder, *girlfriends*. Wildcat Canyon Press, Berkeley, 1995, p. 23.

Candles, music, flowers, and wine—these we all know are the stuff of romance, of sex and of love. . . . Riane Eisler, *Sacred Pleasure*. HarperSanFrancisco, 1995, p. 15.

Two women braided another's luxurious black hair; on the deck were languid sighs over head and foot massages. . . . Brenda Peterson, *Sister Stories: Taking the Journey Together.* Viking Press, New York, 1996, p. 193.

I remember the full moon like white pupils in the center of your wide irises. . . . Audre Lorde, in the story "Excerpt from Zami: A New Spelling of My Name," in *Touching Fire: Erotic Writings by Women*, edited by Louise Thornton, Jan Sturtevant, and Amber Coverdale Sumrall. Carroll & Graf Publishers, New York, 1989, pp. 147–48.

I thought about the words of Jesus when he said that not even Solomon, in all his wisdom, could equal the birds of the air. . . . Jalaja Bonheim, from "The Story of a Nun," in *Aphrodite's Daughters: Women's Sexual Stories and the Journey of the Soul.* A Fireside Book, Simon & Schuster, New York, 1997, p. 169.

O that you would kiss me with the / kisses of your mouth! . . . The Song of Solomon, 1:1–3. The Holy Bible, Revised Standard Version. Thomas Nelson, Nashville, 1972.

Awake, O north wind, / and come, O south wind! . . . The Song of Solomon, 4:16, Ibid.

I slept, but my heart was awake. / Hark! my beloved is knocking. . . . The Song of Solomon, 5:2–5, Ibid.

This love, Sister, is a love that endures. I have drunk from the cup of nectar. . . . *The Devotional Poems of Mirabai*, edited by A. J. Alston. Motilal Banarsidass, Delhi, India, 1980, p. 50.

I cannot nor do I wish to write. . . . Carol Lee Flinders, *Enduring Grace: Living Portraits of Seven Women Mystics*. HarperSanFrancisco, 1993, p. 44.

Listen to me, dear Playmate, I was pleasantly half-drunk with love; this is why I speak tenderly from the senses. . . . Mechtild of Magdeburg, *The*

Flowing Light of the Godhead, translated by Frank Tobin. Paulist Press, New York, 1998, pp. 109–110.

Ah, Lord, love me passionately, love me often, and love me long. . . . Ibid., p. 52.

When I shine, you shall glow. / When I flow, you shall become wet. . . . Ibid., p. 76.

You are like a new bride / Whose one and only lover has slipped away as she slept. . . . Ibid., p. 95.

A couple of years ago I was walking through the forest, by myself. . . . Inès's story, printed in *Aphrodite's Daughters: Women's Sexual Stories and the Journey of the Soul*, Jalaja Bonheim. A Fireside Book, Simon & Schuster, New York, 1997, p. 15.

Chapter 6

From the Great Above she opened her ears to the Great Below. . . . This excerpt is taken from *Inanna, Queen of Heaven and Earth: Her Stories and Hymns from Sumer*, Diane Wolkstein and Samuel Noah Kramer. Harper & Row, New York, 1983. Cited in Inanna's descent on the Twin Rivers Rising homepage, http://web2.airmail.net/apkallu7/inanna.html.

Then Erishkegal fastened upon Inanna the eye of death. . . . Ibid.

She fastened her gaze upon him: the gaze of death. . . . This translation was cited by Professor Richard Nirenberg in a lecture posted on the Internet, http:/www.albany.edu/projren/9697/teama/hades.html.

Chapter 7

Judith encouraged Carol to write her thesis on Elie Wiesel and the Holocaust even after the man who had been Carol's advisor dismissed the subject with "Why would you want to write about a depressing topic like that? . . ." In the preface to *Womanspirit Rising: A Feminist Reader in Religion*, edited by Carol P. Christ and Judith Plaskow. Harper & Row, New York, 1979, p. x.

And God and Adam were expectant and afraid of the day Eve and Lilith returned to the garden, bursting with possibilities, ready to rebuild it together. Carol P. Christ, in the essay "Spiritual Quest and Women's Experience." Ibid., p. 207.

"She said, 'I will not lie below,' and he said, 'I will not lie beneath you, but only on top. For you are fit only to be in the bottom position, while I am to be the superior one." From *The Story of Lilith: The Alphabet of Ben Sira*, question no. 5 (23a-b), translated by Norman Bronznick (with David Stern and Mark Jay Mirsky). http://ccat.sas.upenn.edu/~humm/Topics/Lilith/alphabet.html.

Lilith, she maintains, "is the shadowy side of our power, the power that has not yet been tamed and put to use in the service of our greatest personal gifts, whatever they may be. . . ." Lynn Gottlieb, *She Who Dwells Within: A Feminist Vision of a Renewed Judaism*. Harper San Francisco, 1995, p. 73.

No Essene takes a wife, because a wife is a selfish creature, excessively jealous and an adept in beguiling the morals of her husband and seducing him by her continued impostures. . . . John A. Phillips in *Eve: The History of an Idea*. Harper & Row, New York, 1984, p. 51.

And the companion of the Savior is Mary Magdalene. . . . James M. Robinson, ed., *The Nag Hammadi Library*, The Gospel of Philip. Harper & Row, San Francisco, 1988, p. 148.

Do not weep and do not grieve nor be irresolute, for his grace will be entirely with you and protect you. The Gospel of Mary, Ibid., p. 525.

. . . we know the Savior loved you more than the rest of women. . . . The Gospel of Mary, Ibid., p. 525.

The soul answered and said, 'What binds me has been slain, and what surrounds me has been overcome, and my desire has been ended and ignorance has died. The Gospel of Mary, Ibid., p. 526.

Did he really speak with a woman without our knowledge and not openly? Are we to turn around and all listen to her? Did he prefer her to us? The Gospel of Mary, Ibid., p. 526.

But if the Savior made her worthy, who are you to reject her? Surely the Savior knows her very well. That's why he loved her more than us. The Gospel of Mary, Ibid., p. 527.

For years I had a vague feeling that something was radically wrong with my world, that for too long the feminine in our culture had been scorned and devalued. . . . Margaret Starbird, *The Woman with the Alabaster Jar: Mary Magdalen and the Holy Grail.* Bear & Co. Publishing, Santa Fe, 1993, p. xix.

Set me as a seal upon your heart, as a seal upon your arm; for love is strong as death. . . . The Song of Solomon, 8:6–7, The Holy Bible, Revised Standard Version. Thomas Nelson, Inc., Nashville, 1972. (Please note, in some versions of the Holy Bible, the Song of Songs is referred to as the Song of Solomon.)

Behold, you are beautiful, my love; behold you are beautiful, my beloved, truly lovely. . . . The Song of Solomon, 1:15–17, Ibid.

Much of the information about sacred prostitutes in this chapter was taken from lectures and books by Barbara Walker, a historian to whom we owe a great debt for her many volumes on women's spirituality.

Chapter 8

It would be easier for me to minister to a congregation where I never saw people who were sick and poor and despised. . . . Melody Ermachild Chavis, *Altars in the Street: A Neighborhood Fights to Survive.* Bell Tower, New York, 1997, p. 62.

We can't expect young men to protect life if we don't honor theirs. Ibid., p. 152.

The majority of the killings were clustered near drug-dealing 'hot spots,' and those were mostly near where alcohol was sold. . . . Ibid., p. 154.

Thank you, God . . . for the life of Joseph Wilson, and we lift up our prayers also for the soul of whoever has taken his life. Ibid., p. 154.

The story about people going around the neighborhood honoring the young men and women who were murdered made me realize that I had never visited the site where my son was found. Ibid., p. 157.

On the inability of Wiseman to replicate Schlitz's results, please see "Observation Increases Skin Conductance in Subjects Unaware of When

They Are Being Observed," Marilyn J. Schlitz and Stephen LaBerge, *The Journal of Parapsychology,* 61:197–208, 1997.

Alternative Therapies in Health and Medicine is an excellent bimonthly journal edited by Larry Dossey, M.D., a physician, scientist, and researcher of prayer and what he calls nonlocal mind, the part of our attention that is connected to all other minds. Subscription information can be obtained from Alternative Therapies, P.O. Box 627, Holmes, PA 19043-9650, or through e-mail at alttherapy@aol.com.

Science embodies the belief that dispassion is the ideal attitude for the experimenter. Experimenters in prayer have often observed, however, that a sense of holiness often correlates with a positive outcome of the study. . . . *Alternative Therapies in Health and Medicine,* vol. 3, no. 6, November 1997, p. 113.

'Intercessory' comes from the Latin root *inter,* 'between,' and *cedere,* meaning 'to go.' Intercessory prayer is often called 'distant prayer', because the individual being prayed for is often remote from the person who is praying. Ibid., p. 11.

Love, empathy, compassion, and a sense of connectedness, oneness, and unity. . . . Ibid., p. 12.

Believing that a direct personal relationship with God exists, my mother always concludes her stories with a long prayer of intercession, praise, and thanksgiving. . . . Katie Geneva Cannon, in her essay "Surviving the Blight" in *My Soul Is a Witness: African-American Women's Spirituality,* edited by Gloria Wade-Gayles. Beacon Press, Boston, 1995, p. 25.

Chapter 9

With this sacred pipe you will walk upon the Earth; for the Earth is your Grandmother and Mother and she is sacred. William K. Powers, *Oglala Religion.* University of Nebraska Press, Lincoln/London, 1975, p. 82.

With this pipe you will be bound to all your relatives: your Grandfather and Father, your Grandmother and Mother. Ibid., p. 82.

The ball is symbolic of knowledge, and people's attempt to catch it represents the struggle of people submerged in ignorance to free themselves. Ibid., p. 103.

The fears a woman may have before leaving the competitive mode may rage for a long time. . . . Judith Duerk, *A Circle of Stones: Woman's Journey to Herself.* LuraMedia, San Diego, 1989, p. 40.

And now, in my stillness, I hear something. . . . Elizabeth Berg, *The Pull of the Moon.* Jove Books, New York, 1997, p. 175.

Walk with an animal walk and take in everything around you as prey. . . . Natalie Goldberg, *Writing Down the Bones: Freeing the Writer Within.* Shambhala, Boston and London, 1986, p. 83.

Chapter 10

The Ultimate and Heaven together make the yin-yang way, / And the melding of man and woman is joyously the same. . . . Poem twenty-one, "Together." Martin Palmer and Jay Ramsay with Man-Hokwok, *Kuan Yin: Myths and Prophecies of the Chinese Goddess of Compassion.* Thorsons, an imprint of HarperCollins, London, 1995, p. 141, reprinted with permission.

ACKNOWLEDGMENTS

My deepest gratitude goes to Amy Hertz, my spectacularly gifted editor at Riverhead Books. She was the midwife for both *A Woman's Journey to God* and *A Woman's Book of Life*. Thanks, Amy, for your persistence, and for your miraculous x-ray vision that sees the bones behind the words, allowing me to bring forth the best that I have. Thanks, too, to Jennifer Repo for her editorial assistance, and to Deborah K. Miller, who added precious details and clarity in copyediting the manuscript. My wonderful agent, Ned Leavitt, did me a great service in finding Amy and Riverhead Books.

Elizabeth Lawrence—priest, healer, and friend—and I have been cofacilitating women's spiritual retreats since the early 1990s. We have grown together and through the grace of the many hundreds of women who have attended our *Gathering of Women* retreats. Much of what I know about women's spirituality, ritual, and healing has come through our work together. Beth's reclaiming of the priesthood, not in spite of but because of her Catholic roots, has been an inspiration to many women. And her friendship is one of the special sweetnesses of life. We've been through the wringer together, and have lived to tell about it. Thank you, Beth, for your love and caring, your passion and purpose, and your get-down-and-boogie style of sacred dancing. We've had a lot of fun all over the world. May the dance play on.

Jan Maier, musician par excellence who has collaborated in many of our retreats, has given us the gift of finding our voices and weaving them together in beautiful harmonies. Through raising our voices in song, we have built communities of caring and worship. Thanks, Jan, for teaching us all that we don't have to mouth the words. And thanks for your patient collaboration on your story about our snake walk. Working on it with you was an experience of self-in-relation that enriched me as well as the book.

In the early years of our retreat work Anne Disarcina gave us the gift of humor and compassion, and Joan Drescher the gift of artistic expression. Many other women have come forward in our temporary retreat communities and shared poetry, dance, theater, music, writings, rituals, healings, calligraphy, and their good hearts. You are too many to mention, but you know who you are.

Janet Quinn and I have partnered in a number of silent women's retreats that grew out of her commitment to centering prayer and healing. Her deep wisdom, fabulous sense of humor, and presence at all the important passages—from weddings to breast biopsies—has made Janet the kind of friend that we would all love to have. Teaching with her in various settings such as conferences and courses in mind/body healing always amazes me, because I keep on learning from her. Thanks, Janet, for who you are.

Loretta LaRoche is my old friend and humor guru. I refer to her as Her Holiness, The Jolly Lama. She has kindly included me in a number of women's retreats she has organized, and taught me a lot about the reverence of irreverence. I don't think we've been reported to the religious police yet, Loretta, but if they do burn us at the stake, I'm sure we'll go out laughing.

Mona Lisa Schulz is another wise and funny sister, the kind of friend who is always there for you. I can schmooz about biology and psychology with her. She has taught me about intuition, women's bodies, and brains. M. L. has also modeled having the guts to speak out even when your gifts may be suspect in the eyes of "the establishment." Thanks, sweetheart.

Robin Casarjian is a close friend of many years from whom I have learned about forgiveness, compassion, and basic goodness. She helped me to learn how to love myself. Robin's healing work with prisoners, in the national Lionheart Prison Project for Emotional Literacy, and her unceasing efforts to make the world a better place for the despised and forgotten, are a model of spirituality in action. Thanks, Robin, for burning as a steady flame.

Chris Hibbard is another beacon of caring. Not only can we discuss science, psychology, spirituality, and healing but also the nitty-gritty of family. She and her husband, David, took us in when my family moved to Boulder. They adopted and cared for us. I am grateful for their love and collegiality.

Celia Thaxter Hubbard is an elder and precious friend, my BB or Best Buddy. I am a better person because of her, and a more informed one as well. She is like a one-woman research department. She'll call and ask, "Have you found such-and-such a book yet?" If not, she'll often send it to me. Her search for religion, and for a spirituality that goes beyond religious bounds, has been a continuing source of inspiration. Long into the night we discuss the historical Jesus, the ins and outs of Gnosticism. We emote over Rumi and adore the Dalai Lama. Celia is like a mother to me, and I love and understand my own mother, Lillian Rubenstein Zakon, may her soul rest in peace, more deeply because of her.

The number of women who have inspired this book is enormous. I cannot possibly mention them all, and long after this book is published I will keep remembering their contributions and wishing that I had listed them by name. Some of them include the Reverend Mary Manin Morrissey, spiritual leader of the Living Enrichment Center (LEC) in Wilsonville, Oregon. Mary invited me to participate with her in facilitating a women's spiritual retreat many years ago, where we bonded en route driving to the retreat center through a blizzard. She is one of the most inspired and inspiring speakers and writers I know, and her friendship is a blessing. Jean Houston is a mutual friend of ours whose books I enjoyed for years, but who became a friend through Mary when Jean and I were faculty in a wild and woolly ten-day program called "Birthing the Universal Human" that Mary sponsored at LEC. Jean reminded me that I am a goddess. Inanna, in fact.

I want to thank Rima Lurie, a friend and neighbor whose love of nature and commitment to the inner life are a wonder; Nancy Mason, another friend and neighbor whose enthusiasm for the West— for rock art and blue skies, red rocks and long hikes—reminds me that my busy life is a choice, just as her mindful life is crafted by choice; Terry Jordan, whose wisdom and resilience in living through the death of her daughter Emily from leukemia and the loss of her infant son inspired so many of us; Rachel Naomi Remen for her writing and healing work and her friendship when I was at the very bottom; Jan Shepherd for her friendship and commitment to writing; Andrea Cohen for volumes of research and fresh eyes to appreciate the wonder of it all; Victoria Christgau for her music and enthusiastic bringing of women back to our bodies and voices; Judith Gass and Sheelah Black for wild and mindful dancing, and ritual to open the heart; Jalaja Bonheim for the thoughtful interviews with women that reveal our sacred nature; Liza Ingrasci for her friendship and commitment to bringing healing into the world through the Hoffman Quadrinity Process; and a great big hug to my friend Naomi Judd, whose commitment to God, to her family and friends, and to the women of the world are the truest measure of her artistry.

And thanks to the foremothers of women's spirituality who helped to remind us that we have a path of our own and in whose footsteps we all follow. A few I know personally, most only through their writings. Many have been omitted from this brief list. Elisabeth Schussler Fiorenza, Carol P. Christ, Judith Plaskow, Rosemary Radford Ruether, Mary Daly, Marcia Falk, Ellen M. Umansky, Dianne Ashton, Carol Flinders, Karen Armstrong, Nelle Morton, Elaine Pagels, Miriam Therese Winter, Lynn Gottlieb, E. M. Broner, Kathleen Norris, Audre Lorde, and Carol Gilligan. And thanks to Mary Oliver, whom I have never met but whose poetry has been the most natural and profound of spiritual teachings.

A heartfelt thanks to all the women who have participated in the retreats. Your stories have healed me. Your honesty has astounded me. Your love and prayers have supported me. Your laughter has renewed me and your voices uplifted me. I have honored your confidentiality throughout this book, changing names, ages, and any identifying circumstances and locations, and creating composite stories that reflect similar experiences of many women. These vignettes are true to what you taught me and to the heart of women's wisdom, true because you informed them even if you did not personally live them. Thank you for becoming part of my life.

A special thanks to my incredible business manager and friend, Judy Dawson. Her bright mind, constant support, common sense, and endless good humor make all things possible. She is one of life's most evident blessings.

And finally, a gracious thanks to my husband, Kurt Kaltreider. Thank you for all the discussions, the laughs, and for your interest and commitment to indigenous cultures that has enriched my feminine perspective. Thanks for the fruit frappes, the vitamins, and the patience you have in living with a woman who is forever answering the call of an insistent muse. Thank you for your love.

INFORMATION ON
RETREATS AND PROGRAMS

To sponsor a *Gathering of Women* retreat in your area, please contact Mind-Body Health Sciences, Inc.:

> 393 Dixon Road
> Boulder, CO 80302
>
> 303 440-8460 phone
> 303 440-7580 fax
>
> or e-mail Judy Dawson at judydaw@aol.com

Information about existing programs can be found on the Web site, www.joanborysenko.com

- Elizabeth Lawrence can be reached to conduct retreats or LuMarian healing sessions or workshops through her Web site www.lumarian.com
- Janet Quinn can be reached to conduct retreats on many aspects of spirituality, healing, women's wisdom, centering prayer, and therapeutic touch through her Web site www.haelenworks.com or by phone at (303) 449–5790.
- Jan Maier can be reached to conduct workshops on singing and community building, or to lead church services, weave music at conferences or retreats by e-mail at jemsong@tiac.net.